Cape Flattery

Neah Bay

Sekiu

Clallam Bay

Pysht

Strait of Juan de Fuca

Joyce

Port Townsend

Sappho

Lake Crescent

PORT ANGELES

Sequim

Discovery Bay

Chimacum

Forks

Center

Port Ludlow

LaPush

Quilcene

Destruction Island

Brinnon

Duckabush

Queets

Eldon

Quinault

Hoodsport

Taholah

Moclips

Humptulips

Matlock

Shelton

Pacific Beach

Carlisle

Copalis

McCleary

Ocean Shores

Tumwater

Hoquiam

Grays Harbor

Aberdeen

Montesano

Elma

Westport

SEATTLE

W A S H I N G T O N   S T A T E

Port Angeles, Washington: A HISTORY

Volume I

by Paul J. Martin

researched by
Peggy Brady

OTHER BOOKS BY PENINSULA PUBLISHING, INC.

* **A History of the North Olympic Peninsula** . . . . Patricia Campbell
* **The Early Days . . . IN PHOTOGRAPHS** (7-booklet series) . . . . Paul J. Martin
and
Elbert Whattam
* **The Gold Key To Writing Your Life History** . . . . Leone Noble Western
* **Kids in the Kitchen** (aka **Kindergarten Cooks**) . . . . Nellie Edge
* **Kids Dish It Up . . . Sugar-Free** . . . . Cindy S. Wishik
* **Tales of the Menehune** . . . . Viola Rivenburgh
* **Totem Tales** (6-booklet series) . . . . Traci Wehrli

Printed in the United States of America
5   4   3   2

ISBN 0-918146-23-2 (Paper)
ISBN 0-918146-25-9 (Cloth)

Library of Congress No. 82-82187

Published by Peninsula Publishing, Inc.
P.O. Box 412, Port Angeles, WA 98362

LINCOLN STREET, circa 1914, just before construction of the planked thoroughfare was finished, and prior to installation of hands on the Clallam County Courthouse clock. Building on knoll at left was originally the old Catholic Church, used as a courthouse when this photo was taken, and the site of the Port Angeles Branch of the North Olympic Library System when this book went to press. The trestle spanned a gully which has since been filled. A stream ran down the gulch parallel to Lincoln Street. Near Third Street, the stream entered Peabody Creek behind what is now the library and the Senior Center. PHOTO SOURCE: Bert Kellogg

Table of Contents

Table of Contents, continued

Foreword

The three-year collaboration of Paul Martin and researcher Peggy Brady has produced a splendid history of this little town along the shores of the Strait of Juan de Fuca.

Port Angeles, Washington: A History — Volume One is not a "family" history, or genealogy textbook in any sense of the word. Instead, it represents what we think is an honest attempt to present within the covers of one book, the day-to-day, year-by-year evolution of a town. Reading it, we were impressed by the fact that it is not a "typical" history book, spelling out dates and names in a wearisome fashion, perhaps dotted occasionally with photos of early pioneers. The Martin-Brady book is a story. A good story, narrated well by two people who have done their homework.

A few things about Volume One of **Port Angeles, Washington: A History** are especially noteworthy. For one thing, it seems to be remarkably uncluttered. Footnotes at the back of the book — some of them quite lengthy — offer details essential to the story, yet are not distracting to the reader.

Many different time periods are covered, but always Martin and Brady have provided a sense of balance and perspective. The reader knows what is happening in Port Angeles at any given time — yet is made aware of events happening simultaneously elsewhere in the world.

It offers something for every reader. An historian seeking intricate details of people and events has only to scour the hundreds of footnotes. Yet, one with no interest in specifics will discover an enjoyable narrative about a courageous little town. And nearly 200 captioned photographs make it a visually attractive item. Finally, **Port Angeles, Washington: A History** is indexed, making it a valuable tool to all those interested in the history of this region.

We are certain the general reading public will enjoy this fine book.

Graham W. and Opal (McLaughlin) Ralston

Author's Dedication

To Ann, Patrick,
Maureen and Jackie

Chapter One: The Beginning — 1860
Migration, Discovery, Settlement

"Most of our history has been treated as if it were a function solely of white culture in spite of the fact that till well into the 19th Century, the Indians were one of the principal determinants of historical events."
—Bernard De Voto

Long, long before civilized man created his artificial boundary lines throughout North America, long before there was a Washington State or a place known as Port Angeles, there was the Indian.

From what remote place did he come? What ancient land spawned this mysterious creature whom early explorers found practicing strange customs and displaying even more peculiar dress? Early explorers attributed the Indians' ancestry to the Greeks, Phoenicians, African Mandingos, Chinese, Romans, Irish, Welsh, Tartars, Indian Hindus, Norse, Japanese — and even the Huns! It was said by some that Indians had descended from the Ten Lost Tribes of Israel; others said that Indians were the children of Babel, doomed forever to a primitive life as penance for their sins.

"Land Bridge" Brings the Indian

But most 20th Century anthropologists agree that the ancestors of today's Indians *walked into* this untouched New World from the great Siberian land mass. They migrated — some say, trickled — over a period of perhaps 10,000 - 20,000 years, following the aimless movements of big game herds, their main source of food.

The first group of hunters arrived in present-day Alaska by way of the so-called land bridge over the Bering Sea — a "bridge" as wide as 2,000 miles in places — which was exposed during the Ice Age. During this era, which began about one and one-half million years ago and is known as the Pleistocene, or Glacier Epoch, mammoth ice sheets locked up vast

THE BERING STRAIT "LAND BRIDGE" — all the area shown within the dotted lines -- as it probably appeared during the last Ice Age about 40,000 years ago. At that time, mammoth glaciers locked up huge amounts of the earth's water, exposing a wide expanse of land between Asia and North America. It was this "Bridge" which enabled early hunters to move inexorably southward, thus populating both continents in the Western Hemisphere.

amounts of the Earth's water supply, thus lowering the sea level and rendering the continents of Asia and North America virtually indistinguishable. (In fact, present-day Alaska and Siberia, taken together, probably represented the equivalent of a subcontinent at that time.)

This bridge existed for hundreds of thousands of years. In an age when boats, if available at all, were probably incapable of ocean crossings, man's passage into the New World had to occur at this land-accessible place of entry.[1]

Archaeological techniques such as radiocarbon dating definitely establish man's presence in North America 13,000 years ago. Actual crossings of the land bridge probably occurred much earlier, possibly as long ago as 40,000 years.

No precise time has as yet been pinpointed. What is known is that man, in the person of the Indian, has been here a long time: Irrefutable signs of human occupancy at least 9,000 - 10,000 years old have been found from the Bering Sea to the tip of South America, and from the Atlantic to the Pacific Oceans.

Man on the Olympic Peninsula

Conclusive evidence verifying that man resided on the North Olympic Peninsula 12,000 years ago was

MASTODONS, similar to the one pictured here, were forest dwellers which obtained food by browsing. They became extinct in North America near the close of the Pleistocene Epoch. PHOTO SOURCE: Clare and Emanuel Manis

SCATTERED AMONG THE BONES at the Manis dig, archaeologists found a whittled tool 10,000 years old, believed to be the oldest human made wooden object ever found in the Western Hemisphere — and possibly in the world. PHOTO SOURCE: Clare and Emanuel Manis

unearthed in 1977 by Emanuel Manis on his farm near the town of Sequim, Washington. There, a team of archaeologists, under the direction of Dr. Carl Gustafson of Washington State University, excavated the well-preserved bones of two Mastodons, one of which had the remnants of a bone spear tip *still imbedded in one of its ribs.* This discovery furnished the first confirmation that man lived in the Pacific Northwest as long as 12,000 years ago -- and the first positive evidence in all of North America that he hunted and butchered Mastodons.

The Indians likely diffused throughout North America in exactly the same way they originally migrated from Siberia: Bands of hunters trailed large, rambling herds of grass-eating mammals wherever they roamed. Most of the hunters followed game trails, one to another, generally southward, while others settled permanently in regions of plenty.

EARLY TRIBAL DISTRIBU- TION along North America's west coast. The relatively dense popula- tion of tribes in the Pacific Northwest was due primarily to the abun- dance of food available from the sea.

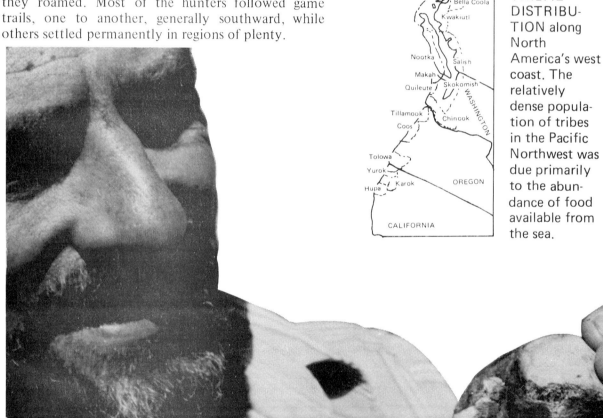

BONE POINT broken off in rib of Mastodon excavated on the farm of Clare and Emanuel Manis in Sequim, near Port Angeles, Washington in 1977. Dr. Carl E. Gustafson of Washington State University displays the first certain evidence in all of North America that man hunted and butchered Mastodons. PHOTO SOURCE: Clare and Emanuel Manis

TRADING COINS of early tribesmen on the North Olympic Peninsula. PHOTO SOURCE: Sibyl Morgan

One such region was the narrow strip of land west of the major mountain ranges running north to south along the Pacific Coast, from present-day Alaska to California. While other hunting bands foraged and gathered food as best they could throughout North America's deep virgin forests and parched, dusty plains, Indians who settled in the area now known as the Pacific Northwest were blessed with an abundance of food from the sea. Halibut and cod crowded the ocean's surf, shellfish lay for the taking, smelt could be netted and trapped with ease and salmon runs choked coastal rivers and inlets six or seven times each year.

Tribal Structure

Such readily available harvests greatly affected the cultures which arose and encouraged most Northwest Indians to learn methods of food preservation, thus enabling them to build up stores for consumption year-round. Food surpluses, in turn, led to large populations, numerous tribal settlements up and down the coast, and ultimately, to chiefdoms.

Transcending mere tribal organizations, chiefdoms consisted of two or more villages united under a single authority. This unique structure provided a large number of people with a monarch. With the chief as organizer and economist, the system featured more efficient use of natural resources and more

equitable distribution of goods. The structure which evolved served to preserve the land on which the Indian lived. Probably his only affront to nature was the habit of periodically burning certain grasslands and forests to modify the landscape according to taste. Though this may have changed the face of the land for a short time, most geographers and foresters believe that such scorching actually was conducive to development of the great Douglas Fir now so much a part of life in the Pacific Northwest.[2]

Throughout thousands upon thousands of years, the Indian left virtually no blight upon the gorgeous Northwest landscape — much to the delight of later white settlers. Hundreds of different Indian cultures flourished and died during that time, yet Indians scarcely harmed the land at all. Such remained for "civilized" 19th Century man to undertake.

Early Indian Legends

Early Oriental sailors, castaways and shipwreck victims carried by the inexorable Japanese Current probably were the Peninsula's first non-Indian visitors; a few cloudy Indian legends suggest such arrivals several centuries ago. Nevertheless, taking place long before caucasians made contact with the Indians, such rare episodes had little influence on the lifestyle of those encountered. Many of the unfortunate sailors were no doubt killed or enslaved by one of the coastal tribes.

It is unknown how many different tribes there were, or how many people lived, hunted, fought, reproduced and died along the bountiful Pacific coastline before the white man's appearance. There

MAKAH TRADING BEADS. Shown here are two strings of dark blue, glass trading beads of a type once used by Makah Indians, who live in the west end of Clallam County. The beads were obtained by Dr. Harold H. Butler, Port Angeles dentist, who occasionally traveled to Neah Bay in the early days of this century. PHOTO SOURCE: Mrs. Wilfred Bower

were no recordkeepers. The Indian knew of his own origins by legends handed down from father to son, generation to generation. Such tales reflected the Indian's total acceptance of his environment, coupled with a natural belief in some kind of Spirit or Supreme Being.

Some legends claimed the Indian originated in the sea. Tales of other tribes told how they had come from the ground. Some legends attributed creation to the sunrise; others, to the sunset.

Most Pacific Northwest tribes maintained they were created by the great spirit of Coyote: Their stories portray the Indian as having been formed by Coyote from different parts of a great Beaver named Wishpoosh which Coyote had killed.

On Washington's Olympic Peninsula, legend has it that the Indian was the offspring of a fallen star and a magnificent wild animal which roamed the woods.[3]

Point of origin aside, several facts present themselves: The Indians *were* here before anybody else —

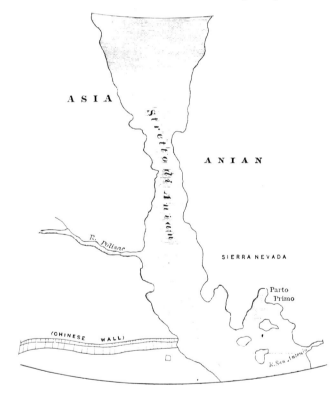

THE FABLED "STRAIT OF ANIAN" as conceived by Europeans in the 16th Century. This is the passageway that many thought was a short, convenient route from Europe to the Orient — a direct sea channel from Hudson Bay to the Pacific Ocean. Juan de Fuca (real name, Apostolos Valerianos) allegedly discovered the Strait at Latitude 47° 30" while sailing to the Pacific Northwest, and the body of water found at that latitude was named after him by an English sea captain, Charles William Barclay.

no evidence to the contrary has ever been found in North America; their family structures evolved into efficient tribal settlements; their lifestyle was, despite plentiful food in the forests and ocean, rigorous and demanding; they greatly feared what they believed to be harsh Spirits which lived in the Olympic Mountains; and, from an early explorer's standpoint, the Indians and their magnificent land lay yawning and exposed like a giant pearl longing to be "discovered."

White Man Cometh

Into this mysterious, primal world sailed white men in their giant canoes, tall white wings mounted on trees, catching the slightest breeze. And, whether they came from the south — Spaniards and English — or from the north — Russians — the visitors' colorless, sickly complexions and odd mannerisms puzzled the Indian. Each tribe on the Olympic Peninsula received them differently, for white men by their very presence aroused conflicting emotions in the Indian. He was fearful of the big ships, yet curious about these waxen faced creatures. Some openly hostile actions did occur from time to time but violence was infrequent.

The "Northwest Passage" and The Strait of Juan de Fuca

Eagerly seeking trade, European nations, especially Spain, began busily assigning ships to the Northwest region in the 16th Century, about 50 years after Columbus' famous 1492 voyage. They all coveted the gold, furs and other riches believed to be in abundance here — but just as important, they desperately sought a short, convenient route from Europe to the Orient. Known as the Northwest Passage, or by the more archaic name of the Strait of Anian (an ancient northwest kingdom), this waterway was thought to run from Hudson Bay to the Pacific Ocean. The prevalent notion that such a passage existed stimulated vast wishful thinking and false stories — leading in turn to many explorations.

For years, exaggerated tales were bandied about the courts of Europe by voyagers who proclaimed they had found the elusive inlet from the ocean. One story, though many doubt its credibility, took hold. Certainly from an historical viewpoint it was the most significant of all the narratives. It was told to an English merchant, Joseph Lok, by a grizzled old Greek navigator named Apostolos Valerianos, known as Juan de Fuca when he sailed under the Spanish flag. His somewhat feeble claim to have found an inlet at 47° Latitude (which he believed to be the Northwest Passage) in 1592, may or may not be

EARLY COIN. Perhaps a relic of an early trading venture or exploration of the Strait of Juan de Fuca, this 1711 Spanish-American coin was found on Agate Beach, west of Port Angeles, by Mr. Morley A. Ludlow in 1949. Representative of coins struck in Spanish-American mints before 1880, chief characteristic of which is the pillar in the center, the "Pillar dollar," or "piece of eight" as it was commonly known, was made famous in Robert Louis Stevenson's **Treasure Island.** This coin has markings on it indicating that it might have been used as a button at one time. There is no way of determining when it was left at Agate Beach. PHOTO SOURCE: Clallam County Museum

valid; most historians — with good reason — doubt that he ever saw the Northwest.

Nevertheless, de Fuca's story about finding the east-west channel (a tale published 27 years later by clergyman Samual Purchas in his book *Purchas: His Pilgrims),* kept the embers burning, and perhaps even stirred renewed interest among sailing nations. However, Spain, which had a strong foothold here and was the most likely country to undertake a full-scale search for the Passage, was entangled in severe civil strife and periodic wars that were to last for the next 150 years; she could not afford to finance any major explorations on these shores. Other European nations also felt the economic pinch and 170 years elapsed before Juan de Fuca's story could be further validated.

In a 1786-87 voyage, just a few years after the Revolutionary War ended, just as the Constitutional Convention was in process in Philadelphia, an Englishman, Captain Charles William Barclay,[4] sailed his *Imperial Eagle* into the waters at 47° Latitude. While there, he checked topographical landmarks described by the Greek navigator in 1592. Finding them to be reasonably accurate, he promptly — and permanently — bestowed Juan de Fuca's lilting name to the broad sea channel. In doing so, he ignored earlier mariners' challenges to the authenticity of de Fuca's claim. For example, during a 1776 journey to Cape Flattery at the tip of the Olympic Peninsula, quite near the inlet to Strait waters, the esteemed English Captain James Cook had haughtily portrayed the waterway as the "pretended Straits of Juan de Fuca." Cook said he never saw the entrance to the

Strait and sneered " . . . there (is not) the least probability that ever any such existed."[5]

More European Explorers

Barclay's christening of the Strait in 1787 coincided with a flurry of Spanish, English and Russian voyages to America's west coast, and the waterway named for Juan de Fuca was the scene of vigorous exploration for a period of 50 - 60 years.

Spain, seeking gold, furs and conquest — not necessarily in that order — had dispatched Juan Perez, Bruno Heceta and Juan Francisco de Bodega y Quadra up the coast in separate voyages just a few years before Barclay arrived. Heceta was, in fact, the first officer of a European nation to set foot on what later became Washington soil, when he debarked at what is now Destruction Island in 1775.

For their part, the Russians concocted several grandiose and expensive — plans for exploration, aimed at cornering the fur trade. Almost without exception, they failed miserably.

England, loftily disregarding its recent defeat at the hands of the upstart colonies — which now, of all things, were calling themselves the United States of America! — was busy on the west flank of the continent. Besides Cook's voyage in 1776 and Barclay's visit 10 years later, Captain John Meares explored part of the Strait in 1788 (naming Mount Olympus along the way). Meares was on his way north to Nootka Bay on what is now Vancouver Island to barter for furs.

Beginning in 1790, the famous Captain George Vancouver, a splendid navigator and meticulous recordkeeper, sailed up and down coastal waters and throughout Puget Sound for five years. He charted topography, named bays, inlets and landmarks (Puget Sound was named for his first officer, Peter Puget), and made favorable contact with the native inhabitants. Curiously, during his travels through the Strait of Juan de Fuca, he made no mention whatsoever of Port Angeles' harbor or its rather prominent sandspit.[6] Vancouver's charts were useful to seamen for decades after his voyage, and over 70 English names which he bestowed upon parts of the region stand today as enduring testimony to his perseverance.

Puerto de Nuestra Señora de Los Angelos

And the Spaniards? Ah, the tenacious Spaniards. Their journeys to the Northwest continued. In 1791, Don Francisco de Eliza sailed the *San Carlos* into the Strait of Juan de Fuca, saw a natural seawall jutting out several miles from the mainland and dropped anchor inside its deep, sheltered harbor. He declared it to be Spanish territory, then christened it "Puerto de Nuestra de Señora de Los Angelos," or Port of Our Lady of the Angels.

One year later another Spaniard, Alcala-Galiano, shortened the cumbersome name to Port Angeles, as it is called today.

Despite all this activity, Spain's influence on the Olympic Peninsula — indeed, throughout the Northwest and the entire continent — was diminishing rapidly. After establishing a "permanent" settlement on the coast at Neah Bay (Bahia de Nunez Gaona — later disbanded), and Manuel Quimper's voyage to Admiralty inlet in the early 1790s, Spain was forced to pull out. In 1800 she ceded all of her enormous claims throughout the New World to France, and her Pacific explorers began to fade into the shadows of history, victims of war, economic stress at home and their own inability to get along with the natives. Other than a few colorful Spanish names sprinkled up and down the coast, they left behind very little.

The Westward Movement Begins

For the next 50 years, the area that would be Port Angeles lay dormant, its only inhabitants the everpresent Indians, its only visitors fur trappers and an occasional British or Russian vessel gliding through the Strait. Residents of this isolated region were unaware of the restructuring of Europe by Napoleon Bonaparte, or of the enormous changes taking place in the United States of America. Unknown to them, Thomas Jefferson and others were molding the feisty young nation into a giant (it tripled in size with the Louisiana Purchase in 1803) and its people were being tempered by events like the War of 1812 and Texas' Alamo. The Peninsula's few residents were likely unaware how anxious the good citizens of the United States were to push westward in search of land . . . but they would find out soon enough!

Captains Meriwether Lewis and William Clark in 1804 took their overland expedition to the Pacific Ocean, thus giving the United States a strong claim to the Northwest. White settlers began pounding a rhythmic path toward the west coast. Their own federal government, via negotiations and a series of treaties with other nations and with the Indians, acquired much land throughout the west. However, the "Oregon Country" — all the land from the Columbia River northward to some undecided boundary line — still lay open to settlement by both England and the United States. Both claimed it.

England, plotting to retain the territory explored by Vancouver, signed a "joint occupancy" treaty with the United States in 1818, hoping to win the area by patiently waiting for everybody else to go away. The bustling, ambitious Yankees, however, had other plans.

Two major U.S. expeditions were dispatched to the Sound, and land-hungry Americans began settling throughout the territory, disdainful of any treaty formalities. By 1845, as Texas and Florida were being accepted as new states, the first non-trading, non-missionary party of Americans was just settling in Puget Sound. A scant five years later, the United States Census showed over 1,000 white inhabitants living north of the Columbia River![7]

Consequently, despite valid claims it had made on the Oregon Country through the years, England had to face the inevitable. In 1846, another treaty with the United States was signed, locking the northern boundary at 49° North Latitude and running the westernmost end of that boundary line down the center of the Strait of Juan de Fuca, like the divider strip on a modern interstate highway.

Port Angeles Encounters Civilization

With that vital matter resolved, settlement of the Northwest began in earnest, and Port Angeles awakened to the fast-approaching crunch of civilization. Its arrival was heralded by Captain Henry Kellett of the British Royal Navy, who gave Port Angeles' unique three-mile sandspit a name, "Ediz Hook" (from the Clallam Indian word 'Yennis' — meaning "good place"). The name first appeared on English sailing charts in 1847. With some frequency now, white trappers were paddling canoes into the Strait of Juan de Fuca and trudging into the forests to set their lines. Thousands of people were finding their way into Puget Sound country, many of them

THE BEAVER, a 101-foot-long London-built craft (1835), was the first steam powered vessel on the North Pacific Ocean. Owned for most of her life by the Hudson's Bay Company, the *Beaver* plied Puget Sound waters for over 50 years before sinking on rocks near the coast of Vancouver, B.C. in 1888. PHOTO SOURCE: Bert Kellogg

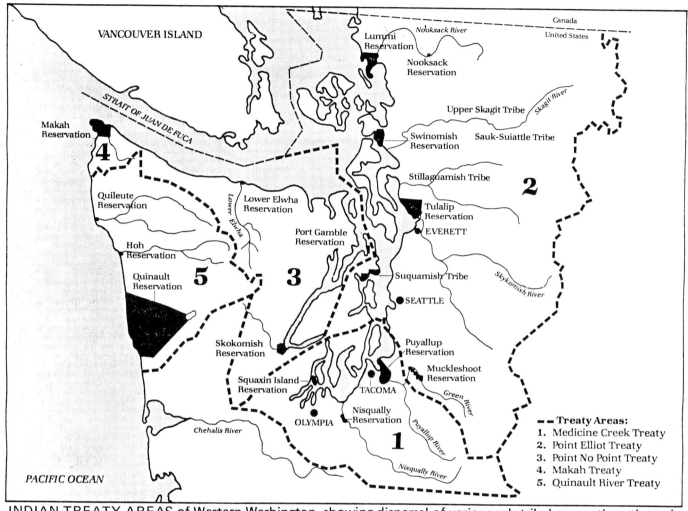

INDIAN TREATY AREAS of Western Washington, showing dispersal of various sub-tribal reservations throughout the area. PHOTO SOURCE: Point No Point Treaty Council

frustrated fortune seekers drifting north after California's 1849 gold rush. In 1852, a U.S. Coastal Survey first charted Port Angeles — naming it "False Dungeness," a slightly insulting reference to the existing area of Dungeness (now Sequim), 15 miles to the east. By then, Robert Fulton's invention, the wood-burning steam engine, was enabling Puget Sound boats to ease into almost any bay or inlet — a feat impossible for sailboats. The *Beaver*, a remarkable, durable sidewheeler owned by the Hudson's Bay Company, traversed the waters of Puget Sound for 52 long years, until 1888. More than any other technological achievement, steamboats such as the *Beaver* and *Eliza Anderson* (affectionately known as The "Old Anderson" during her 50 years of service), pried open Port Angeles' and the Peninsula's unwilling doors.

Finally — the ultimate label of the encroaching multitudes — Washington was officially declared a Territory of the United States in 1853. One year later, Clallam County was formed, having been named for the dominant Indian tribe of the area (the word — sometimes spelled Klallam — meaning strong people).

The Peninsula's Indians were disturbed by all this activity taking place in territory they knew to be rightfully theirs. White settlers scattered across the Olympic Peninsula, knowing they were outnumbered about 100 to 1, were scared. The whites, therefore, did what they always did best: They began negotiating treaties. And though words like "compromise" and "give-and-take" were frequently used during these parleys, white men, in the grand tradition of conquerors everywhere, took much and gave very, very little. Treaties negotiated here and elsewhere throughout the West, almost without exception, merely pacified the Indians, promised safety for white settlers — then put a hammerlock on as much of the land as whites could possibly grasp. It is estimated that in six treaties negotiated during 1854 and 1855 Indians in the Pacific Northwest gave up

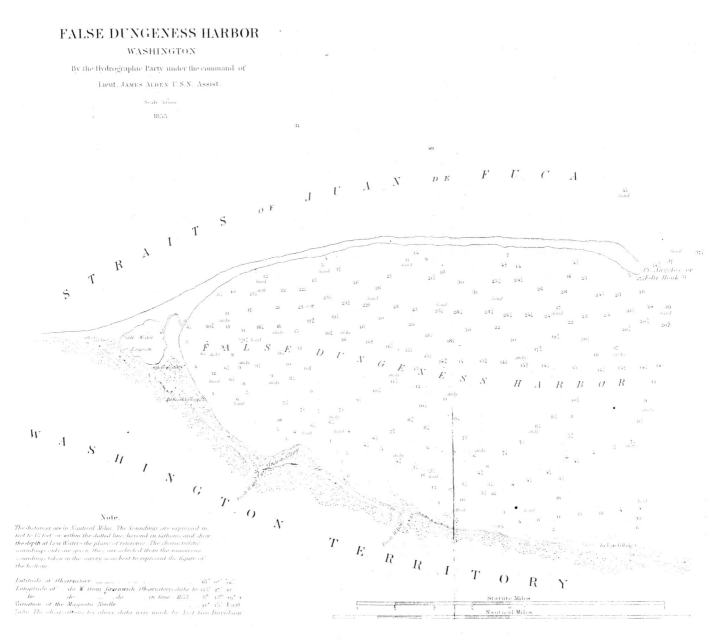

"FALSE DUNGENESS HARBOR," now Port Angeles, Washington, as shown in a U.S. Coastal Survey map done in 1853. PHOTO SOURCE: Merton Franklin

property rights to 64 million acres.

Washington Territorial Governor Isaac Stevens tended to take that stance one step farther. Feeling that it was the white man's duty to replace Indian culture with what he considered obviously superior white customs and civilization, he totally ignored the Indian's plea that traditions and religious mores were being violated by the treaties. The 1855 Point-No-Point Treaty, negotiated by Stevens and Klallam Chief Chetzemoka (also known as The Duke of York), claimed for the whites a tract of land totaling hundreds of thousands of acres — and magnanimously reserved for the tribe a total of 3,840 acres at the head of Hood Canal. It also prohibited Chetzemoka's tribesmen from trading with their neighbors on

Vancouver Island (a valued tradition dating back centuries), required them to accept certain medical vaccinations and prohibited the practice of slavery — which, while it may have been the "moral" thing to do, struck at the very heart of village hierarchy and tribal structure. Congress ratified the Point-No-Point treaty in 1859.[8]

Nevertheless, hostilities between white settlers and Indians — referred to locally as "Indian trouble" — were rare in Port Angeles. In fact, the entire Olympic Peninsula was relatively trouble-free, except for the 1887 beheading on Whidby Island of Colonel Isaac N. Ebey by Canadian Kake Indians, who mistakenly thought he was a "hyas tyee," or white chief. Some have speculated on the reasons for such a trouble-free existence; perhaps none is more plausible than writer Patricia Cambell's explanation. Port Angeles, located virtually at the "end" of the continental United States, was settled long after other western towns, and Indians here, theorizes Mrs. Campbell realized "the battle was weighted in favor of the whites."[9]

Whatever the reasons, white men came and settled, and the Indians bothered them little.

Port Angeles' First White Settler

There is considerable disagreement as to the identity of Port Angeles' first white settler. Some noted pioneers, among them Judge James Swan, who first traveled through the region in the late 1850s, stated emphatically that one Angus Johnson was the first to make his home at False Dungeness, in 1857. Others insist that Alexander Sampson, William Winsor and Rufus Holmes, the three principals in a fishing and trading venture calling itself the Winsor Company, had already staked a claim and settled the previous year. In any case, by the mid-1850s white people had selected the remote site as a permanent home and had planted the rudiments of civilization inside Ediz Hook. Just a few years later, the question of settlement became academic when the area was designated a United States Government Lighthouse and Military Reservation. Independent land development was effectively frozen at that time.

By all accounts, the first white settlement was indeed a humble one. Populated almost exclusively by bachelors (Alexander Sampson had a wife from whom he was long separated), the tiny group of settlers had few of the "luxuries" available to older Puget Sound communities.

Port Townsend, for example, 40 miles to the east, boasted a Customs House, several taverns, a Marine Hospital, and the important designation of Port of Entry for ships entering Puget Sound (meaning all ships had to stop at a Customs House to undergo cargo inspection, with foreign vessels required to pay import duties).

Settled in 1851 by Alfred Plummer and Charles Bachelder, Port Townsend seemed to have a much brighter future than Port Angeles, although the quality and availability of the eastern town's drinking water always was suspect (availability still is a concern).

Back in Port Angeles, others soon joined the bachelors living within the protective arm of Ediz Hook. In the latter part of 1857, Fred Roberts and Peter Riley[10] built the first frame house in Clallam County. In December of 1859, several men — William Taylor, Morris H. Frost (Customs Collector), Dr.

CAPTAIN ALEXANDER SAMPSON. Considered by some to be *the* first white settler at Ediz Hook, Captain Sampson's own papers at the University of Washington raise doubts about this matter. It now appears likely that Rufus Holmes and William Winsor established residence at Ediz Hook before Sampson. PHOTO SOURCE: Seattle *Times*

P. M. O'Brien (owner of the Port Townsend Marine Hospital), John White, Joseph Frazier, Major G. O. Haller[11] and A. W. Thorndyke (of Port Ludlow) — staked claims to portions of the choice beach front, and with the three founders of the Winsor Company formed a speculative firm called the Cherbourg Land Company. Created for the express purpose of laying out a townsite and selling lots, the investors chose to ignore that legally such land claims were to be secured for settlement only — not for speculation.

None of the men, therefore, actually owned the land. They considered this a mere technicality, however. All of them were investing money in it and some of them lived on it. So they proceeded to stake claims and moved onward with their plans. On paper, the Cherbourg Land Company appeared attractive and over the next few years had no trouble whatsoever luring other investors. Therein lay the firm's real importance, for one of these later investors was a headstrong, controversial gentleman named Victor Smith.

Chapter Two: 1860 — 1883

Victor Smith

". . .The (local) Judas Iscariot . . . probably caused more turmoil, dissension and hatred than any other figure in Pacific Northwest History."

—Ruby El Hult

Considering the fact that he is commonly referred to as the founder of Port Angeles, and was a prolific letter-writer who left a veritable mountain of records in his turbulent path, precious little has been published about Victor Smith and his activities while he was Collector of Customs in Puget Sound. Some of his more bizarre antics have been detailed, but there remains much more literary "flesh" on his old bones than has ever been exposed.

It is generally accepted that Smith, for personal gain, plotted to develop what is now Port Angeles, at the expense of Port Townsend. According to this theory, Smith hatched the plot alone and only *after* making the arduous journey west to assume a federal post in Port Townsend. But that version fails to acknowledge an uncommonly high number of coincidences — 13, to be exact — which point convincingly at a plot conceived by Smith and some men in Washington, D.C. to grab power, money and land on the Olympic Peninsula.

Smith, Salmon P. Chase and Cherbourg

For all his adult life, Victor Smith was, first and foremost, a promoter. In the post-Civil War, expansionist era in which he found himself, such promotional instincts would inevitably lead him westward.[1] During the 1850s, he had been a newspaperman, working for the Cincinnati (Ohio) **Commercial**. There he met Salmon P. Chase, former U.S. Senator, two-time Governor of Ohio and — later — frequent aspirant for the Presidency of the United States. Because of similar political beliefs shared by the two men (both were abolitionists), a lasting friendship formed. Chase would later become Abraham

SALMON P. CHASE, prominent statesman, Secretary of the Treasury under President Lincoln. Chase was a close friend of Port Angeles founder Victor Smith and was largely responsible for Smith's powerful role in Northwest history.

Lincoln's Secretary of the Treasury. In the latter part of 1860 and spring of 1861, as seven southern states commenced secession procedures from the Union, and while towns on the Olympic Peninsula were still in their formative stages, Victor Smith and Salmon P. Chase spent much time in Washington, D.C.

Chase was in the nation's capital because he had just won a Senate seat from Ohio; only a few months before, he had lost the Republican Party's presidential nomination to Abraham Lincoln. Smith accompanied his friend, performing some small jobs for his Party, all the while sniffing the promotional winds.[2] While doing so, he detected what appeared to be an extraordinary opportunity in the remote Pacific Northwest, where lay a strategically located, deep-water harbor. Just 17 miles due south from the important northern trading town of Victoria, British Columbia, Port Angeles was a bay with terrific potential, where a townsite company already was firmly established, claiming it controlled three and one-half miles of protected beach front.

The opportunity was real, for its likelihood as a port of significance was being trumpeted by none other than the illustrious Isaac Stevens, former Washington Territorial Governor and now a Congressional Delegate (the way a Territory was represented in the House of Representatives, before becoming a State). Stevens was not only a surveyor, politician, idea man and statesman, but a soldier as well. He expressed the belief that naval installations were essential throughout Puget Sound, and went so far as to portray Ediz Hook and environs as the likeliest spot to become another "Cherbourg of the Pacific," (a reference to the seaport town on the English Channel,

in Normandy, France, where a fortified naval station had been established by Louis XIV (1638-1715)).[3] Stevens thought so highly of the idea that in 1860 he sought Congressional money to study the area's military potential and confirm his beliefs about Ediz Hook's perfect location. His vivid description of the harbor as the "natural Cherbourg" was catchy and was quickly noted by prominent citizens in Port Townsend.[4] Thus, the name for the Cherbourg Land Company.

Hearing all this in Washington, D.C. in 1860, Victor Smith leaped at the prospect. He apparently bought the rights to a homestead near the Riley claim in "Cherbourg" – sight unseen – and a financial interest in the land company.[5] In light of these purchases, his subsequent activities were fascinating indeed.

In 1860, Salmon Chase sought the Republican nomination for the Presidency, eventually losing it to dark horse Abraham Lincoln. Some historians have interpreted this – and a later attempt to garner the nomination (in 1864) – to mean that Chase harbored anti-Lincoln sentiments. However, available correspondence suggests that the two men rather admired one another.[6] Shortly after his election as the 16th President of the United States, Lincoln asked the Ohioan to become his Secretary of the Treasury. Chase accepted the post just two days after Lincoln's inauguration (March 6, 1861), thus becoming the overseer of approximately 10,000 patronage jobs.

Federal Appointment (s)

Remembering his old friend from Cincinnati, the new Treasury Secretary, in May of 1861, appointed Victor Smith to a position (or positions, depending on one's interpretation of available records) within the Treasury Department. It appears that Smith originally was appointed simultaneously to two different jobs – confidential agent of the Government in Washington Territory, and Collector of Customs for the Puget Sound District. Smith, however, muddied the water by describing himself in correspondence as only a treasury agent, but one with broad powers. He wrote that he was a "Special Agent of the Treasury Department . . . instructed to inquire into and report upon all matters connected with Customs Houses and their location, Revenue Cutters, their stations and cruising ground, lighthouses, branch mints, marine hospitals, etc."[7]

Whatever the job or jobs, the appointment meant Smith was to be headquartered, by "coincidence," just where he wanted to be – in Port Townsend, Washington Territory – rather conveniently near his holdings in Port Angeles, also known as Old Dungeness, False Dungeness and Cherbourg.[8]

THE STEAMER *ELIZA ANDERSON*, one of the more famous boats ever to serve Puget Sound and the Strait of Juan de Fuca. Built in Portland, Oregon in 1857, the *"Old Anderson,"* as she was known, carried freight, passengers and mail between Olympia and Victoria for many years, often announcing arrivals and departures via her loud steam calliope. She carried Victor Smith and his family from Olympia to Port Townsend on their first trip to Puget Sound in 1861. Later, in 1898, she was abandoned and left to fall apart in Dutch Harbor, Alaska. PHOTO SOURCE: Bert Kellogg

Because of his purchases at Port Angeles, Smith had been making plans to move to Puget Sound even before a job was offered to him. He apparently divulged that information to somebody, for the story preceded him to Port Townsend. **The North-West**, a weekly newspaper in Port Townsend, reported it had learned "Mr. Smith intended coming hither . . before the Collectorship was tendered him."[9]

Smith Arrives in Puget Sound

Victor Smith's four years of tumultuous administration as a customs collector and treasury agent began when he and his family arrived in Port Townsend, Washington Territory, on July 30, 1861, aboard the steamer *Eliza Anderson.*[10] From that day until his death in 1865, virtually every public action in which the eccentric Smith participated, was characterized by bombast, bluster and bluff.

Victor Smith was no shrinking violet. Blunt, tactless and antagonistic, this "lean, sandy . . . dyspeptic-looking" man[11] had a genuine talent for alienating people. One historian, referring to Smith's eccentricities and unpopularity, graciously described him as being " . . . deft, to a notable degree, in the gentle art of making enemies."[12]

Smith had served for several years as railroad editor for the Cincinnati **Commercial**. The writing experience, combined with his aggressive personality, resulted in an abundance of lengthy, bizarre correspondence mailed to newspapers, public officials and friends all over the country — some of it written with the force of a meat cleaver! His obtuse, occasionally bad grammar, however, indicated Smith probably had an exaggerated opinion of his own fluency.

Nevertheless, he went about the task of aggrandizing his adopted hamlet of Port Angeles with a single-mindedness bordering on fanaticism. Unfortunately for the future of Port Townsend, he did it all to the detriment of that little community, and soon came to be known there as the local "Judas Iscariot (who) . . . probably caused more turmoil, dissension and hatred than any other figure in Pacific Northwest history."[13]

Smith and Port Townsend — Instant Animosity

Reports and letters written just after his arrival disclose Smith's obvious dislike for Port Townsend. On August 17, 1861, barely two weeks after he stepped ashore, he wrote an uncomplimentary report to his superiors in Washington, D.C., clearly aimed at discrediting the little town, and — already! — suggesting that the Port of Entry be relocated to a more "suitable harbor." In a word, the letter was blunt. He called Secretary Chase's attention to the fact that Port Townsend "was not convenient to . . . vessels destined for ports northeast of Whidby Island" and that the Customs House was in an "infelicitous location," with no fresh water within two miles. Though he stopped short of recommending any specific site, saying he was "not yet prepared" to do so, Smith made it clear there were such places along the Strait of Juan de Fuca.[14] This immediate denunciation of Port Townsend, it seems, is another "coincidence" which raises at least some question of intrigue in high circles, and certainly brings Smith's veracity into question.

Of course, the Customs Inspector loudly proclaimed that prior to his moving to Washington Territory, he had no pre-conceived notions about the location of the Port of Entry. Port Townsend residents thought they knew better, and soon began to say so. They charged Smith with ulterior motives in his attempts to transfer the Customs House. But the treasury man said he merely had looked at existing circumstances and a transfer seemed to be the best course of action. He was forced to deny these – and more damaging – charges many times during his tenure as Collector. If it were not for the seriousness of the matter, Smith's reactions might have been entertaining: They always featured an abundance of rhetoric, with an air of hand-wringing, injured innocence. On one occasion, he said, "If I availed of it (the opportunity to make money in a land speculation at Port Angeles) for my personal gain . . . let me be condemned and suffer a loss of official repute!"[15]

Well, pehaps it *was* only disgust with his surroundings that prompted his August 17th report to the Treasury Department. However, in light of the man's high ambitions and his financial interest in the Cherbourg Land Company, Smith's lightning-like attempt to malign Port Townsend seemed to have the aroma of a plot, possibly hatched months before in Washington, D.C., while he, Chase and others listened to the stories of Isaac Stevens.

Smith the Correspondent

Smith certainly exhibited a flair for the dramatic when, on October 5th, he officially tendered his resignation as a Treasury Department agent, effective September 30, 1861 (exactly two months after he disembarked from the "Old Anderson"). What better way, after all, to emphasize his desire to flee Port Townsend? In his letter of resignation, however, Smith expressed his desire to stay on as Customs Collector, telling Chase that he had discovered "unexpected opportunities for usefulness" in that position. In the very same correspondence, Smith asked for "permission to remove the Port of Entry . . . to Port Angeles," and told the Treasury Secretary for the first time about his purchase of 25 acres of land there, intending to make it his permanent home.[16]

While Smith supposedly had resigned retroactive to September 30th, he well knew correspondence took eight to ten days to travel across the country by Pony Express. During the first week of October, before sending his letter of resignation, he sent a number of reports not merely defaming Port Townsend, but now specifically singing the praises of "Cherbourg"/Port Angeles, Smith's favorite sheltered harbor 40 miles to the west. His official report of October 4, 1861, for example, referred scornfully to "The collection of huts known as Port Townsend," and challenged the area as being "not a good harbor . . . inconvenient as a distributing point (and) badly

situated." He then haughtily recommended that Chase simply transfer the Port of Entry to Port Angeles on Chase's own authority, something "which may be done by the Secretary of the Treasury, as Congress have (sic) never legislated on the subject."[17]

Smith's resignation from the treasury post seemed to have little impact on his job security; however, all attempts to document official reaction to it have met with failure. Existing records conflict as to what action, if any, was taken by Chase when Smith's letter arrived. Evidence suggests that the Secretary of the Treasury backed his Ohio friend to the hilt; he must either have ignored the resignation or rejected it, for Smith remained on – at least as Customs Collector – in 1862.

During those first two months on the job, Smith continually had fed Chase and others a steady diet of lies about himself and his activities, to say nothing of his tall tales about Port Townsend and Port Angeles. Nevertheless, a skeptical person might be excused for viewing this apparent non-action on his resignation as another "coincidence." After his resignation, Smith conveniently was retained near his speculative land deal at Cherbourg, in a position of authority. The Treasury Department left a man in Puget Sound who had a positive gift for making enemies – who, in fact would soon antagonize seemingly half the residents of Washington Territory.[18]

Lest a reader perhaps think the several coincidences surrounding Victor Smith's actions are *just* coincidences, being conveniently framed into a plot 120 years after the fact, it should be pointed out that the notion of a conspiracy by a group of land speculators certainly crossed the minds of a few of Smith's contemporaries. Indeed, there were some people in 1861 close enough to the scene to spot what they considered to be the real motivation behind Smith's actions – and even to hint publicly that a certain clique was behind the proposed move of the Customs House to Port Angeles. The Victoria, B.C. **British Colonist**, for example, in a December, 1861 article, listed all of Smith's official reasons for wishing to relocate the Port of Entry, then, with editorial eyebrows raised high, asked why " . . . patriotic people of Port Townsend are anxious to relinquish their improvements to settle at Port Angelos (as it was sometimes spelled at that time)?" The **British Colonist**'s editor then insinuated rather sarcastically that " . . . the chance of a speculation in town lots has, of course, nothing to do with the matter. They are patriotic enough to disclaim . . . prospective return."[19]

During the first five months of his stewardship, Smith was not content with writing lengthy, inflammatory letters to friends in Washington D.C. Enter

*"Anti-Smith feeling ran high, and the skinny fellow
who "looked down his nose" at Port Townsend
would soon be hanged in effigy . . ."*

The North-West, then being published in Port Townsend by the Reverend John Damon, who was an avid supporter of President Lincoln. Quite soon after Smith arrived in Puget Sound, using his powers of persuasion with consummate skill (and greasing the byway with hyperbole, promises of lucrative jobs and a few outright lies) he succeeded in getting Damon out of town temporarily so Smith could recite for **The North-West**'s subscribers his own peculiar view of the world. He used the little newspaper for several editions, lambasting Lincoln, promoting Smith's favorite cause, Spiritualism, and in general, wreaking havoc upon Damon's editorial policies. Damon returned from the wild goose chases upon which he'd been dispatched by Smith and, regaining the helm of his paper, proceeded in subsequent editorials to blitz the customs man mercilessly. Mortal damage had been inflicted to the paper, however, and **The North-West** folded within a year.

Editorials, Enemies and a "Hanging"

Moving onward in his grand fashion, Smith then launched a letter-writing campaign to newspapers throughout the Pacific Northwest, and to a couple of daily papers down the west coast. He continued to vilify the existing Port of Entry and promote the Ediz Hook beachfront. Though he occasionally signed letters with a pseudonym, he dearly loved to see his own name, as well as his words, in print, and for months went about his task with great vigor.[20] The letters reveal that Smith apparently was trying to create a giant smokescreen, hoping to shroud his land-buying activities at Port Angeles. When he occasionally was pinned down by suspicious editors, such as John Damon, he didn't hesitate to tell outright lies. For example, in a wordy letter published in **The North-West** in January, 1862 — dissected thoroughly by Damon — Smith stated flatly that he had "no pecuniary interest in the town of Port Angelos, and shall never acquire one . . ." This despite the fact that he notified Secretary Chase in his October 5, 1861 resignation letter that he had purchased 25 acres of land and intended to live there. Moreover, he would soon begin aggressively buying virtually every claim established within the confines of Ediz Hook![21]

Meanwhile, other enemies came thick and fast, and in a remarkably short period of time Smith had antagonized most of Port Townsend's prominent residents. After canceling Dr. P. M. O'Brien's federal contract to run the Marine Hospital, Smith, on October 9, 1861, hastily transported by steamer all equipment and patients four miles down the beach to the government's recently-vacated military installation, Fort Townsend.[22] Smith promptly installed Dr. John Allyn as director of the hospital; he had met Allyn, a young dentist, during the last leg of Smith's trip to Puget Sound and, exercising typical Smith-like snap judgment, had promised the man a job. Then, still not content with the merits of such a tidy arrangement, Smith forced Allyn to kick back $100 per month out of his salary to a New York paper supported by Smith. Smith then began collecting rent from the government for use of its own building![23]

Details of the treasury man's continuous barrage of letters to newspapers inevitably filtered back to Port Townsend over the next few months. Coupled with Smith's arrogance and his impetuous move of the Marine Hospital, they created almost universal enmity toward him. Anti-Smith feeling ran high, and the skinny fellow who "looked down his nose" at Port Townsend[24] would soon be hanged in effigy (January 11, 1862), from — appropriately enough — the Customs House roof.[25]

Meanwhile in Port Angeles . . .

While Victor Smith cranked out his strange correspondence and plucked bureaucratic strings from his Port Townsend office, the sheltered little enclave at False Dungeness had been plodding through a relatively uneventful year. Certainly the most important news of 1861 was the establishment of an official U.S. Government Post Office on February 28th. Because the speculative land company formed earlier had adopted the name, the postal area was designated "Cherbourg."[26] Local resident Joseph Frazier, a friend of Dr. P. M. O'Brien, was appointed the first Postmaster.

Vital news, such as the April 12, 1861 firing on Fort Sumter by Confederate troops, starting the American Civil War, or the Battle of Bull Run, which foretold a lengthy conflict, took weeks to seep into the tiny community. The war was far away.

In the fall of 1861, Cherbourg/Port Angeles witnessed its first store, a trading post operated by Samuel Stork, Smith's brother-in-law. Stork had traveled west with the Smith entourage, arriving in Port Townsend in July.

In December 1861, Smith journeyed to Cherbourg aboard the Revenue Cutter *Jefferson Davis,* and saw for himself the gorgeous harbor resting there.[27] His promoter's eye discerned that it was all he'd heard about and was indeed a once-in-a-lifetime opportunity. This little jewel would have to be handled in just the right way if it were to be a profitable venture for all concerned; it could be molded in the manner recommended by Isaac Stevens. It would be a city like no other in the nation: A National City, "built" by the federal government; and he, Smith, would be its leader. All that was necessary was for the President to set aside the land as a Federal Reserve, then have the federal government itself go into the townsite business — i.e., have federal auctioneers sell lots from that reserve to the general public. By doing so, according to the alleged Stevens/Smith/Chase conspiracy theory, Uncle Sam could make some money to finance the war while constructing a model city, and Smith and his colleagues could reap a profit, too!

The Collector kicked the campaign to promote this marvelous idea into high gear, and the year 1862 thus became a lively one in Olympic Peninsula history — as well as a vital one to the overall history of Port Angeles.

Allegations . . . a Grand Jury
. . . a Change of Residence

In January 1862, Smith ordered some crewmen from the U.S. Revenue Cutter *Shubrick* to begin clearing land at Cherbourg, and to start moving his household furniture there. All the while, he doggedly continued sending letters and reports to anybody he thought would read them. In one, published in the Olympia, (Washington) **Standard** February 8th, he described Port Townsend as ". . . a rotten borough whose people fared so sumptuously on the spoils of government that their eyes stuck out with fat."[28]

In his official capacity as treasury agent (since his resignation never was accepted officially) Smith turned up the heat even more by again recommending to the Treasury Department in February that the Marine Hospital be moved from the Fort to Cherbourg 40 miles westward. He added, as an inducement to do so, that the contractor was "willing to accept $3,100 less per year if such a move were approved." No record exists as to whether the

hospital's contractor, John Allyn, had been consulted prior to Smith's generous offer.[29]

By this time, however, the folks at Port Townsend — led by an enraged John Damon — had begun writing a few "reports" of their own. In a January 1862, editorial in **The North-West,** Damon referred to Smith as " . . . a Federal-fed parasite, who, in consideration of some scavenger work for his friend Salmon P. Chase, has been foisted upon us."[30] Other disgruntled Port Townsendites likewise were beginning to level heavy broadsides at Smith, in the form of letters to officials in Olympia (the Territorial Capital), and Washington, D.C. Along with the charges criticizing Smith's arrogant behavior, Damon and the other letter writers made specific accusations concerning Smith's alleged corrupt administrative conduct. He was said to be quilty of "defalcations" (embezzling), later said to have reached the sum of $17,000.[31]

Yet, as though to prove to the world that he was unafraid of anything or anybody — or any group of bodies — Smith, in February 1862, circulated critical remarks about Washington Territory's 3rd Judicial District Grand Jury, saying among other things that its decisions were unduly influenced by Mr. E. S. Fowler, prominent Port Townsend businessman. Greatly upset, Fowler and the members of the jury immediately started a formal investigation of the treasury agent. Soon after it began, though, Federal Judge Ethelbert P. Oliphant informed them to cease and desist, since a Washington Territory Grand Jury could not legally investigate the conduct of a Federal officer.

Smith seemed totally oblivious to such things as nasty editorials, Grand Jury probes or snide comments. Such accusations were merely pesky little irritations which he brushed off so he could concentrate on bigger game! And his indifference to the tumult seems to have been well justified, for the fusillade of claims and counterclaims, charges and countercharges had no discernible effect on official Washington. Chase, with unwavering faith in Smith's reports regarding the unsuitability of Port Townsend, formally recommended to the U.S. Senate's Committee on Commerce on March 6th that the Port of Entry be transferred from Port Townsend to Cherbourg.[32]

Smith, in what may have been an exaggerated report to the Treasury Department, on April 9th boasted that the proprietors of Port Angeles townsite had authorized him to say they would place their entire property in his hands for a war fund, with not a single lot to be reserved by the company. Presumably, the lots would be sold to the public, for Smith went on to say that after $50,000 had been obtained in this fashion, the group wanted to be reimbursed for its expenditures.[33]

Later that month, on April 22nd, Chase acknowledged receipt of a proposed law entitled "An Act to change the location of the Port of Entry for the Puget Sound collection district from Port Townsend to Port Angelos." In recommending its passage, his note to the Senate Commerce Committee neatly summarized everything he knew about the Puget Sound Customs District — i.e., everything Victor Smith had told him. Chase said "Port Angelos is much better adapted to the purposes of a port of entry than Port Townsend, on account of its superior location, being much nearer the ocean and commanding the Straits of Fuca, (sic) and the shipping to and from Victoria, and also on account of its better harbor, there being no good and safe accommodation for vessels at Port Townsend."[34]

After living in "the rotten borough of Port Townsend" for almost a year, the Victor Smith family moved to Port Angeles sometime early in 1862 (no exact date could be obtained). Smith's wife Caroline Prentice Rogers Smith thus — apparently — became the first white woman in the town.[35]

Smith the Land Baron

In addition to the other troubles he had fomented, Smith had been practicing a little nepotism. Much to the dismay of Port Townsend job-seekers, his relatives and friends were reaping the benefits of Smith's appointive powers: Brother Henry was on the government payroll at Port Angeles, and George Smith, Victor's father, was keeper of the Tatoosh Lighthouse on the Peninsula's West End.[36] J. W. Watson, a friend who had traveled west with Smith, was, according to **The North-West**, drawing pay as an inspector, while actually cooking for the Smith family. Damon claimed Watson was receiving a cook's wages — while Smith pocketed the rest![37]

Truly, the Puget Sound Collector of Customs was a whirlwind of activity. And there was more. In addition to official duties, writing letters and reports and making federal appointments, he was simultaneously doing something even more significant: He was now trying to acquire almost every piece of property inside Ediz Hook.

Smith's strenuous efforts to gain complete control of property lying within Port Angeles' sandspit began in 1860 while still in Washington, D.C. and continued following his July 30, 1861 arrival on the Peninsula — at exactly the same time he was carping about Port Townsend's poor location. With an interest in the Cherbourg Land Company already in his possession,[38] he solidified his position within a few days of his arrival by meeting with the firm's principals to explain the benefits of the Customs House transfer.[39] He must have had second thoughts on the matter, however, for six weeks later, in October, he decided he might be endangering his job as Customs Collector by maintaining a pecuniary interest in a private firm. Officially, he bowed out of the townsite company, but, with the consent of the others, retained the right to repurchase his interest at some future time. Then he methodically started buying as much land as he could in Port Angeles.

Though actual deeds of sale could not be found — it is believed they do not exist — to verify all of Smith's purchases, the treasury man, according to Dr. P. M. O'Brien, bought a claim from Lieutenant J. M. Selden, of the Revenue Cutter *Jefferson Davis*, and soon thereafter acquired one-fourth of a share (the other three-fourths being owned by O'Brien, William Taylor and John White) of John Mason's claim to an Ediz Hook beachfront lot.[40]

On April 29, 1862, Smith purchased from Lt. J. W. White, 7/40ths of the total beach land controlled by the townsite company, for $2,000[41] and asked Dr. O'Brien and Edward "Ned" Stanton (sometimes spelled Staunton) if their lots were for sale. Though the reply was negative, Smith later bought William Taylor's claim. According to the Port Townsend physician, this purchase meant that the company was no longer a viable entity, that O'Brien's own interest "was a myth," and that Smith had now "secured every interest except mine and (Joseph) Frazier's . . . had the entire control and would exercise it if the company sought to interfere with the townsite."[42]

Dr. O'Brien's illuminating account of the Cherbourg Land Company dealings brought out still another plot-like "coincidence" — with a definite Washington, D.C. connection — a link between Smith and one Hosmer G. Plantz, private secretary to Secretary of the Treasury Chase. A lengthy letter from O'Brien to Governor William Pickering says that in March, 1862, at the same time Chase was formally recommending to a U.S. Senate Committee that the Port be transferred, Smith purchased and was given a deed to M. H. Frost's claim, with the deed conveyed to Smith in the name of H. G. Plantz! Whether the purchase was indeed one Smith made for a high-echelon confederate back in Washington, D.C., or an act of subterfuge to lock up for himself more of the townsite property, cannot be determined. According to a later description of that same transaction, as told by Surveyor General Anson G. Henry to President Abraham Lincoln, the deed to M. H. Frost's land was conveyed "first in the name of Mr. Chase, and subsequently of Mr. Plantz . . . to whom

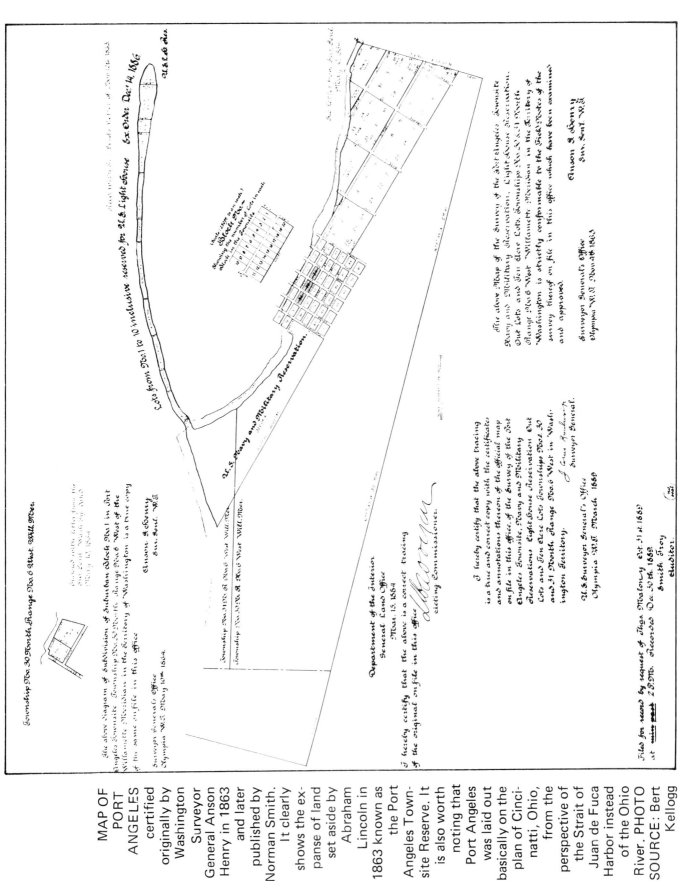

MAP OF PORT ANGELES certified originally by Washington Surveyor General Anson Henry in 1863 and later published by Norman Smith. It clearly shows the expanse of land set aside by Abraham Lincoln in 1863 known as the Port Angeles Townsite Reserve. It is also worth noting that Port Angeles was laid out basically on the plan of Cincinatti, Ohio, from the perspective of the Strait of Juan de Fuca Harbor instead of the Ohio River. PHOTO SOURCE: Bert Kellogg

and Smith the conveyance . . . now stands recorded."[43]

Smith Goes to Washington, D.C.

Having personally secured most of the land involved in the development scheme, Smith set out for Washington, D.C. in May 1862.[44] He was determined to achieve a couple of key objectives: Secure official approval of the Customs House transfer to Port Angeles; and, if at all possible, have the President establish the area around Ediz Hook as a federal reserve — the first giant step toward Smith's ultimate goal of making Port Angeles a National City.

He succeeded on both counts.

Port Townsendites, disgusted with Smith's selfish actions and arrogance, conjectured that the Customs Collector had been called to Washington, D.C. to answer their charges against him — or, even better, that he'd absconded with federal funds and would soon be headed for prison. **The North-West** waxed eloquent, glorying in the departure of this "high-toned scoundrel" who had chosen to pursue a "damnably dishonest course." Editor Damon chortled gleefully that Smith was "checkmated at Washington by telegraph, and if he goes there . . . will be locked up as a felon."[45] Seldom has the process of wishful thinking reached such heights. The Customs Collector was far from through.

From Smith's vantage point, his three-month visit to Washington, D.C. would have to be considered a smashing success. With very little effort, he refuted his enemies' charges against him to the satisfaction of Salmon Chase. Smith was in the nation's capital on June 6th when the land lying inside Ediz Hook officially was designated Port Angeles by the U.S. Post Office Department.

Later, within a two-day period in mid-June, he achieved his other two goals. On June 18th, subsequent to the Senate Commerce Committee's strong recommendation, the Congress of the United States enacted legislation transferring the Port of Entry from Port Townsend to Port Angeles. The very next day, President Lincoln signed an executive order setting aside 3,520 acres of land at Port Angeles as a military and lighthouse reservation. Some of the land — 10 acres — was strictly for lighthouse purposes, but the rest was to be used as a military, or townsite reserve. Smith and his cohorts had cagily used for their own purposes a well-known but previously unused policy of the War-poor North — that of stimulating land development in order to produce taxes and revenues with which to pay military debts. He easily persuaded the President — with substantial help from good friend Chase — that development of a model city and sale of federal land at Port Angeles

would generate a huge profit for the lean federal treasury.[46]

Word of Congress' action reached Port Townsend about two weeks later, and the shock was, of course, stupendous. The residents' sense of loss quickly gave way to outrage and frustration, and Victor Smith was, more than ever, condemned as a villain. Damon and **The North-West** were almost apoplectic, claiming the town had been betrayed by the federal lawmakers — especially, coming as it did, on the heels of an apparent scandal uncovered among the Customs House records during Smith's absence.

A "Warm" Welcome Home

It will be recalled that Smith had departed Puget Sound for the nation's capital in May; his departure sparked a chain of happenings culminating August 1st at Fowler's Dock in Port Townsend in an event, which, but for its ominous possibilities, resembled good old-fashioned slapstick comedy.

As he was preparing to leave in May, Smith realized there was nobody in the town whom he could trust to take charge of the Customs House in his absence. Records conflict as to exactly how Smith arrived at his ultimate choice,[47] but Lt. James H. Merryman, an officer from the Revenue Cutter *Joe Lane,* did assume the post of Deputy Collector, assisted by William Chalmers. Merryman's three-month stint as Collector was somewhat eventful, for his analysis of the records revealed what appeared to be a serious shortage of funds — "defalcations," he termed them — as well as the fact that Collector Smith had never been bonded, a requisite for retaining the position. Merryman immediately notified the Treasury Department in Washington, D.C. of his twin discoveries and, in view of the gravity of the situation, thoughtfully sent a copy of the report directly to President Lincoln. Before either letter arrived at the nation's capital, however, Victor Smith had completed his business there and had left for home totally victorious, armed with letters of commendation from Chase. He also was alleged to be carrying one million dollars in Treasury Notes to be disbursed in Puget Sound.[48]

In Port Townsend, Merryman's well-publicized story of Smith's "defalcations," coupled with the stunning news of the Port of Entry transfer, assured the Customs Collector a "warm" welcome upon his arrival there. However, a writer of fiction could not have conjured a more bizarre reception.

Fowler's Dock . . . and a Port of Entry is Moved

The zany details of Smith's farcical encounter with Merryman August 1, 1862 on Fowler's Dock have been told and re-told. Suffice it to say that

Smith disembarked, ordered the Customs records returned to him, and was refused by the young officer (who quite properly doubted Smith's authority). The Collector, in a huff, returned to his ship and had the five cannons of the *Shubrick* aimed shoreward, threatening to bombard Port Townsend unless the records were given to him at once. Merryman capitulated, the records were tossed into boxes, and the *Shubrick* sailed with them out into the harbor.

For all practical purposes, the Port of Entry had been moved!

Smith, realizing he had the momentum, moved fast, before official response to his actions could descend upon him. He sailed to Port Angeles, dropped off the records there, then quickly returned to Port Townsend, where he leased the Hastings Store (a second Customs House, no less) and placed two trusted associates in charge of it, as deputies.[49] According to letters written by Governor William Pickering, Smith had the huge iron safe removed from the old Customs House to the aging cutter *Joe Lane*, de-commissioned that vessel on the spot, and had it towed to Port Angeles. Then, accompanied by Lieutenant J. E. Wilson, he took the *Shubrick* to Olympia, gave orders that the *Eliza Anderson* was forbidden to carry mail anymore, and on August 10th conferred with Governor Pickering himself. The two federal officers were informed by His Excellency that a legal inquiry into their activities was about to begin, and, if the governor found any laws had been broken, he would place all wrongdoers under safekeeping.[50]

Smith — a Man on the Move

Naturally, the entire incident was highly publicized throughout the northwest, and on August 11th, Pickering and his Board of Inquiry went to Port Townsend to begin an on-the-spot investigation. As a result of this probe — added to other charges by Port Townsend residents — a Grand Jury convened in Olympia and indicted Smith on 13 counts, including resisting arrest, embezzlement and unlawfully purchasing public land.

Before the trial began, however, the Collector exhibited the true gambler's instinct for the jugular by pulling a few aces from his sleeve. Pickering's group of officials had no sooner left Port Townsend when Smith, on the *Shubrick* and towing the *Joe Lane*, slipped into Fort Townsend. He loaded the entire Marine Hospital, patients and all, onto the aged cutter, towed the whole thing back to Ediz Hook and anchored it there to serve as the hospital until a building could be constructed. Still in high gear, he then converted the frame structure built by Roberts and Riley into a temporary Customs House.

By this time, Smith realized he was a wanted man. Pickering's Board of Inquiry, not knowing what else it could or should do, had issued a warrant for the arrest of Smith and Lt. J. E. Wilson, charging them with "assault with intent to kill" for the cannon incident. Territorial Marshal William Huntington had in fact made strenuous efforts to serve summons' on the two men while the *Shubrick* lay a mile out in the Port Townsend harbor. But Lt. Wilson prevented the Marshal from even talking to Smith. The warrant was read aloud to Wilson but he refused to acknowledge it, then ordered Marshal Huntington from the vessel. Later that evening, when the marshal returned to the cutter, according to an official report by the Commander of Fort Steilacoom, Huntington's small boat was unable to even approach the larger, steam-driven craft because Lt. Wilson, probably under orders from Smith, kept the paddlewheel churning huge waves. Wilson then hauled the anchor and sailed lazily away![51]

Smith was unable to slow his frenzied pace, however, for shortly after the *Shubrick* cannon incident, Lts. White and Merryman and Captain Chaddock of the *Joe Lane* were "ordered to go to Washington."[52] The Collector apparently felt he should tell his side of the Fowler's Dock episode before those gentlemen — especially Merryman — presented their stories.[53] On August 13, 1862, therefore, Smith once again turned the mail route over to the "Old Anderson" and departed Puget Sound, leaving behind rumors that he was on his way to San Francisco and would soon return to Washington, D.C. It would be weeks before his whereabouts and his actions could be determined, but when he once again surfaced, the light must have begun to dawn on Port Townsend's people that they were dealing with an extraordinary scoundrel indeed! Smith had hurried to San Francisco on August 13th because he wanted to arrive before the steamer *Pacific* — which carried the infuriated Lt. Merryman. When the young man disembarked, Smith had him arrested on the spot, charging *him* with embezzlement and fraud. Thus detained, Merryman could not file his report immediately, and Smith's version of the encounter at Fowler's Dock would certainly arrive in Washington, D.C. first.[54] Smith had again — at least temporarily — patched another gaping hole in his armor!

The Trial . . . and Help from Washington, D.C.

The Collector, of course, knew he would have to surrender to the charges against him, and did so in Olympia, on September 10th. Long-suffering Port Townsend residents, whose outrage had soared to new heights, naturally were elated to see their sworn enemy ostensibly at their mercy, about to go on trial.

". . . though they had not yet slipped a noose about
Victor Smith's neck, they never quit trying to do so!"

They eagerly anticipated its beginning. Moreover, they chuckled, they had sent detailed charges to Washington, D.C., "which cannot be looked over."[55] The entire situation had become so emotional, in fact, that an editorial in **The North-West** pondered the possibility of Washington Territory's seceding from the United States if the confusion surrounding Smith and the Customs House was not soon resolved.[56]

The results of Victor Smith's trial turned out to be considerably less than the joyful event his enemies hoped it would be. "Twenty-five or thirty respectable men" testified against him, according to **The North-West**, and the Grand Jury did, indeed, return a bill of 13 indictments charging him with embezzlement, felony, theft of government property and unlawful purchase of lands.[57] The indomitable Smith, however, was able to explain the money shortages ("fund transfers"). All but four of the charges were dropped, and Smith was eventually cleared of those.[58]

Then, adding insult to injury, shortly after the trial ended another special agent of the U.S. Treasury, Thomas Brown, stepped ashore at San Francisco, having been sent by Chase to investigate the *Shubrick* affair. For several months, he traveled extensively up and down Puget Sound, gathering information, whitewash brush clutched firmly in hand. **The British Colonist**, in Victoria, said it was visited in December by Brown, who informed the editor that "a careful investigation of the charges . . . had completely exonerated (Smith) . . . from any irregularity."[59] The U.S. Solicitor General later fired off a peremptory order to the Territorial District Attorney, effectively stopping any other proceedings.[60] United States District Attorney Paul V. Hubbs was heard to murmur that Brown's investigation "consisted mainly of shrugging his shoulders and saying he was satisfied that the charges . . . were not true."[61] Port Townsend's thoroughly whipped citizens smelled a rat, but knew they had lost this round. There were many more battles to be fought, however, and, though they had not yet slipped a noose about Victor Smith's neck, they never quit trying to do so! The crew of the *Shubrick* officially moved the Customs House to Port Angeles on September 30th, placing it on the land of Edward "Ned" Stanton.[62]

Shortly thereafter, Victor Smith established a permanent Marine Hospital at Second and Valley streets. Other settlers began drifting in, some with families. Among the most noteworthy of the early pioneers were Nicholas Meagher, C. W. "Wint" Thompson, Eben Gay Morse and Alfred Lee.

Port Angeles, the Second National City

Five months later, as a follow-up to his earlier executive order, the President signed a bill into law "for increasing the Revenue by Reservations and sale of Town Sites on Public Lands,"[63] thus placing the federal government squarely in the land speculation business. Seven days later, March 10th, the Act was formally applied to Port Angeles. Because this was the first time such legislation was used (it was to be applied only once more, to Anchorage, Alaska in the 20th Century), Port Angeles was forever assured the title "Second National City," right behind Washington, D.C.

The term "Second National City" occasionally has been misinterpreted to mean something more grandiose than is warranted. Stated simply, it means only that a certain geographical area of Washington Territory was "nationalized," or placed under federal ownership; land was merely taken from the public domain with the hope that it might be sold by the government to raise funds for a depleted treasury. The impressive plan failed miserably, and the whole idea ultimately died a natural death.

As applied to Port Angeles, the 1862 law set aside as a lighthouse and military reserve "a tract of land one mile wide and five and one-half miles in length, along the Straits (sic) of Juan de Fuca, contiguous to Port Angelos, in townships 30 and 31 N, ranges 6 and 7 West, Washington Territory, (to be) reserved as a townsite under the provisions of an Act of Congress . . ."[64]

Another victory for the founder of Port Angeles. His "National City" was a reality!

Smith is Fired . . . and Hired Again

By now, however, the tide was noticeably beginning to turn against Victor Smith. He was to win a few more skirmishes, but the bell was slowly tolling. By sheer volume alone, the hundreds of people throughout the Territory whom Smith had offended began to turn up the heat. Dozens of scathing letters were by this time inundating the President and other officials in Washington, D.C., and Governor William Pickering had amassed impressive evidence against Smith. Several Territorial officials were fiercely demanding his resignation, ships' captains published lengthy accounts of Port Angeles' unworthiness as a Port of Entry, and even lumber mill owners protested the location of the Customs House. Dr. O'Brien's letter to Governor Pickering laid bare the details of Smith's land purchase shenanigans and Lieutenant Merryman had filed his damaging *Shubrick* report in the nation's capital. Finally, the President's close personal friend — probably Smith's foremost enemy — Surveyor General Anson Henry, wrote Lincoln a letter pressing charges against, and demanding removal of, the collector.[65]

In any normal situation, this veritable mountain of charges against Smith would have finished him off. It nearly did, for early in May 1863, while Chase was out of town, Lincoln received a delegation headed by Anson Henry which "seemed to include everybody then in Washington, official and unofficial, from the Pacific Coast . . . (which) filed formal charges against Smith and called for his removal."[66] After a few days impatiently waiting for Chase to return, the President on May 8th usurped his Treasury Secretary's authority and personally fired the eccentric fellow from Puget Sound.[67] In a note to Chase, Lincoln stressed the "degree of dissatisfaction with him (Smith)," and asserted that it was "too great for him to be retained."[68] Chase, anxious to keep his man in Puget Sound, and angry over what he considered an infringement of administrative freedom, once again displayed his endless loyalty to Smith. He submitted a stiff, lengthy letter of resignation as Secretary of the Treasury, Lincoln, however, made an intense personal plea and persuaded Chase to stay in the post, then filed his letter away with the cryptic comment, "First offer of resignation."[69]

Chase's (and therefore Smith's) political clout became quite clear at that point, for even though the President signed the Collector's dismissal order, he immediately pacified his Cabinet head by signing another commission appointing Smith "special agent of the treasury department with powers of supervision over all the customs houses on the Pacific Coast."[70] For one of the last times, therefore, Smith won a battle. He remained in Puget Sound (yet another "coincidence") with what appeared to be even greater authority and powers than before.

A Town Takes Root . . . Almost

For Port Angeles residents, the year 1863 was a year of hope and excitement. Emotionally, as well as geographically, they were far, far away from bloody places like Shiloh and Antietam. They gave little thought to President Lincoln's stunning Emancipation Proclamation. In fact, they couldn't rouse themselves to excitement over anything that happened "back there," because too much was going on right under their very noses. Construction of a new Customs House and Marine Hospital at Port Angeles required many workers, and the town's future that summer looked very bright. The whole community seemed to buzz with activity, and its population grew steadily.

Victor Smith's machinations had apparently succeeded, and the man had, superficially at least, created a thriving, prosperous town with a real destiny. Those little "firsts" were routinely taking place which, when tracing a town's development, mark a clear trail: The first white child, Davis W. Morse, Jr., was born April 19, 1863. Later that year, on October 9th, the first official marriage in Port Angeles took place, when Charles W. Howard of Port Angeles and Miss Fannie S. Spelling of London, England, were married by Justice of the Peace Marcellus Huntoon. Dr. George Calhoun, in charge of the new Marine Hospital, became Port Angeles' first doctor.

Despite these encouraging signs, however, Victor Smith was still under great pressure, and his political nine lives were being devoured at a rapid rate. Unfortunately for the little settlement of Port Angeles, it was, in 1863, almost entirely dependent upon his survival. Yet, as if being tied to the collector's questionable coattails weren't enough of a burden, fate then dealt a cruel blow to Port Angeles' future.

The Flood

Though Port Angeles and the Olympic Peninsula are in a region relatively free of natural disasters, one such catastrophe occurred on December 16, 1863, while Victor Smith was out of town (a rather customary situation at this point in his career).[71] Unknown to anybody living below, about a year earlier, a landslide had occurred a mile up the gorge directly above Port Angeles' main buildings. The slide had created a logjam. A large earthen dam, which backed up against the hillside, filled to overflowing, with water trickling down the creek bed to the bay. It thus presented itself to the residents downstream as a normal flow, and nobody was aware of the danger deposited above them.[72]

It was shortly after suppertime, perhaps 6:00. Callie Smith had just finished the dishes and put the

> *"Suddenly they heard a tremendous, earthquake-like rumbling. Callie seemed to know a wall of water was hurtling down the ravine behind the house, about to smash into them. She screamed, 'Dr. Gunn, the water is coming!'"*

youngest to bed. According to Victor Smith's son Norman, who was seven at the time, he and his mother went to the door leading to the newly-built Customs House and an adjacent building, to call in the three men working there: Collector Dr. Lewis C. Gunn, Mr. J. M. Anderson and Captain William B. Goodell. Suddenly they heard a tremendous, earthquake-like rumbling. Callie seemed to know a wall of water was hurtling down the ravine behind the house, about to smash into them. She screamed, "Dr. Gunn, the water is coming!" Gunn jumped into his private office, but the Customs House itself, with Anderson and Goodell in it, was swept away in the raging torrent. Both men died.[73]

The Smith home was terribly damaged, but according to Norman, a "pile of lumber back of the kitchen held by two stumps, had divided the flood . . . (and) the force went on either side."[74] Other buildings, occupied by Mr. J. Everett, Mrs. Stocksand, Mr. Adams and Edward Stanton were hurled from their foundations, coming to rest hundreds of feet away or floating in the bay. The Rough and Ready Saloon, owned by Captain W. W. Winsor, and the Conklin House also were destroyed, although their occupants escaped with their lives.

The story has been told that a green chest containing hundreds of gold pieces and a large quantity of money was stolen from Victor Smith's home after the flood. An Indian named Wa Holthup and his friends were charged with the theft after several people swore they'd seen him carry a large chest into his house and break it open. Though Wa Holthup was sentenced to jail by the judge, none of the gold ever was found, and considerable doubt exists as to the story's validity. It is not likely that Smith was solvent enough to have retained such wealth in his home.

Norman Smith's colorful account of the flood relates but one anecdotal incident amidst the tragic events. He recalled that "Ned Staunton's building" was occupied by the owner and some of his cronies, who were playing poker when the water struck, badly disrupting the game and sweeping the house "off the foundation and (carrying it) bodily out into the bay without tipping over or injuring the men who were in it. Some boatmen rowed out and rescued

them. Staunton claimed he had the winning hand . . ."[75]

Throughout the Puget Sound area, news accounts of the tragedy expressed great sorrow for Port Angeles' loss, but true to form, the folks at Port Townsend were recalcitrant. One correspondent from that unforgiving borough reported "sympathy for the sufferers at Port Angeles . . . below par" and mentioned "numerous . . . reflections cast upon Victor Smith, wishing he had been crushed beneath the ruins."[76]

In retrospect, considering the town's size, the loss of life, property, cattle, out-buildings and personal belongings spelled almost total catastrophe for Port Angeles. Many of the Customs House records were destroyed, encouraging Port Townsend residents to intensify their demands for return of their Port of Entry status. Nobody listened though, for Victor Smith still prowled the waters of Puget Sound — and the cloakrooms of Washington, D.C.

Public Land Sale

While all these exciting events transpired, something of a more humble nature had been taking place during the latter part of 1863: The entire Port Angeles "Second National City" reservation was being readied for sale. Land adjacent to Ediz Hook was surveyed in accordance with the Act signed into law in March of that year, and upon completion of the work in November, the townsite plat was given official approval by the Surveyor General.[77] This set the stage for the actual public sale of land which Smith, Salmon Chase and many others expected would line the coffers of the U.S. Treasury. They were in for a bit of a surprise.

Announcement of the sale was made by the Territorial Land Office on March 19, 1864; the date was officially set for May 1st. Victor Smith had boasted, during earlier Cherbourg Land Company days, that all of the firm's property had been placed in his hands "for a war fund," and that when the public sale took place, only after the "gross sum of $50,000 shall have been realized . . ." did the proprietors wish to be reimbursed for their patriotic contribution.

Smith's dollar estimates, it turned out, were a

trifle exaggerated: At the end of the day on May 4th, exactly $4,570.25 had been received from the sale of 34 lots and 3 blocks — to just 22 different buyers![78] Only the urban and suburban lots of the townsite were sold, mostly to those who earlier had settled on them. Precious little property away from the waterfront changed hands. Later that year, two additional lots were sold, only one during all of 1871, and a long 12 years after that, in 1883, two more changed hands.

People just didn't want to buy land in Port Angeles, and for several good reasons. As noted earlier, much free land was still available throughout the west; the vast, undeveloped government reservation surrounding Port Angeles, with its massive trees and heavy brush, stifled growth plans of the most ambitious speculator. Furthermore, one couldn't even enter the land, for fear of being arrested as a trespasser, subject to expulsion and fine by the Land Office. Quite incidentally, the cost to the government of the survey and May 4th "public outcry" was a mere $37,800![79]

The public sale had been a public fiasco. Port Townsend's citizens used it as just another wedge in their efforts to retrieve the Customs House from Smith's clutches. Finally, in 1864, after much lobbying, they convinced the Washington Territorial Legislative Assembly to pass a memorial "praying Congress to remove the Customs House from Port Angeles to Port Townsend." It was to receive a favorable reception in Washington, D.C. and ultimate approval by Congress.[80]

The Lighthouse

Another important item in Port Angeles' development was the proposed Ediz Hook Lighthouse. Five thousand dollars had been allocated in the March 3, 1863 Reservation and Lighthouse Act for the building of a permanent beacon light at the tip of Ediz Hook. Construction had begun almost immediately, continuing through that year and the next.[81] The permanent lighthouse was to open two years later, in 1865, with George Smith, Victor Smith's father (and late of the Tatoosh Lighthouse), as its first official keeper.

Smith — a Beleaguered Man

By this time, Victor Smith must have thought the entire world was collapsing about his ears. He had indeed achieved his primary goal of creating a town, but almost nothing else in his life was going right. A mountain of charges had been leveled against him, all of them filed by countless enemies seeking his removal. Only by using his quick wit and sharp tongue (with considerable help from the U.S. Treasury

Department) had he survived two Grand Jury inquiries and several indictments. Every public official in Washington Territory, including the Governor, was after his hide. In Washington, D.C., President Lincoln, having fired Smith once, was again reeling under intense pressure for the man's permanent removal. Even Smith's old chum, Salmon Chase, had begun showing signs of disgust at Smith's erratic behavior. Two lawsuits, the record shows, already had been filed against him; Edward Stanton sued Smith for constructing the Customs House on Stanton's property (right in the middle of his potato patch!), and Lieutenant White alleged in court that Smith had unfairly deprived him of his land.[82] Now Smith was being humbled further by a third suit filed by William Chalmers, in which he demanded back pay for services performed at the Customs House during the *Shubrick* affair.

The President's old friend Anson Henry, who had worked so strenuously to secure Smith's earlier dismissal, was nearly fanatical in his efforts to get rid of the Collector for good. Faced with the bitter reality of ships' captains refusing to anchor in Port Angeles' harbor a minute longer than necessary to complete customs papers, Smith's fantasy regarding the town's profitable Port of Entry status was dissipating rapidly. Then came the flood, with its dreadful, demoralizing effect on the town. And finally, the eagerly-anticipated land sale — Smith's dream of a majestic "National City" luring thousands of homesteaders from afar — in ashes.

He did succeed in having another Customs House built after the Port Angeles flood. It was, after all, Port Angeles' raison d' être. A few other hardy souls clung to the Smith Dream, but precious few newcomers straggled into the shaken little community. A transplanted Port Townsender, James Dalgardno, opened a tavern. However, he was forced to operate under the watchful eye of non-drinker Victor Smith, could not attract many sailors, sold very little liquor and struggled for survival.

Remembering "Judge" Huntoon

Nevertheless, Dalgardno's place retains some significance, for it doubled as the courtroom for one of the more colorful characters ever to grace early-day Port Angeles: Justice of the Peace-Judge-Acting Coroner Marcellus Aurelius Brutus Huntoon. Descriptions of the man and his bizarre antics are vivid.[83] Somewhat dilapidated-looking, in seedy, ill-fitting clothes, the Judge peered out at the world through one good eye (he was blind in the other) and, with his craggy, bent-nose countenance, presented a fearsome figure as he dispensed western-style justice

"Victor Smith's power base within the Cabinet had vanished, and his enemies had a clear, open shot at him."

throughout Clallam County.

Despite the town's veneer of durability, Judge Huntoon, Dalgardno, Smith and the other settlers were only clinging to the remnants of a dream. Back in Washington, D.C., events were taking place which would, within a year, shred even the remnants and bury that dream for a long time. Treasury Secretary Chase, though still a member of Lincoln's Cabinet, was priming himself for another run at the Presidency. Lincoln remained patient during the brief campaign, but it was to be the final embarrassment he would accept from Chase. A ground-swell of popular support for the Union and Lincoln ensued, Chase's aborted attempt was bungled by his lieutenants, and the man's Cabinet days were numbered.

Salmon Chase Resignation

When Chase offered the President another resignation, it was accepted.[84] Thus, even though Lincoln would later appoint Chase the Chief Justice of the United States Supreme Court, Victor Smith's power base within the Cabinet had vanished, and his enemies had a clear, open shot at him. The Territorial Legislature's Resolution to move the Customs House back to Port Townsend was being given serious consideration by Congress, and there was no longer a powerful voice present to calm the multitudes.[85]

The *Golden Rule*

As the Civil War began to grind toward a close, Victor Smith, still a Treasury Agent, went to Washington, D.C. with his family for Lincoln's March 4, 1865 inauguration. They were still on the east coast (Smith in Washington, his family visiting with friends in Rhode Island) on April 9, 1865, when the war ended — and a scant five days later when the President was assassinated. Shortly thereafter, Smith received a new assignment and on May 25th he and his family boarded the steamship *Golden Rule* for San Francisco. His immediate destination was the sub-Treasury in that city, where he was to deliver three million federal dollars and a large quantity of government bonds; all were to be exchanged for gold sorely needed by the war-impoverished Union. The journey was to be the last bizarre episode in which he would take part.[86]

Many, many stories have been told about the last voyage of the *Golden Rule*; some of them clash over important facts. All that is known for certain is that, five days out from New York, the steamer found herself 20 miles off course, and that she struck Roncador Reef in the Antilles Chain. The 600-plus passengers and crew were safely removed to a small, nearby island, but there suffered terribly from exposure to the sun. They survived on hard biscuits, bird eggs and water for a few days, until being rescued by two U.S. steamships, the *Huntsville* and *State of Georgia*. Impaled on the reef, however, the *Golden Rule* was bashed to pieces by heavy surf; wreckers soon stripped her clean. And . . . the $3,000,000 mysteriously had disappeared.

There are conflicting details, however, about Smith, the *Golden Rule*'s Captain Denny and the missing money. Passengers aboard the steamship told sordid tales of a drunken Captain Denny and members of the crew consorting with illicit companions. Having "lost their prudence," they ignored warnings that the ship was off course and in grave danger.[87]

Another account ignored the cause of the wreck, but described Victor Smith's heroic efforts to protect the money in his custody. This tale alleges that he stayed with the stricken vessel as long as he could, then courageously stood guard over it until a government cutter arrived to get him and the treasure — only to find when the safe was retrieved from the depths that it was empty![88]

Yet a third version sketches a tangled web of intrigue, beginning when Smith and another treasury agent, Rufus Leighton, boarded the *Golden Rule* with the money and bonds. Soon after boarding, Smith discovered that Montgomery Gibbs, a Treasury Department spy, was a passenger. Gibbs was apparently one of countless post-Civil War southern espionage agents enmeshed in the hotbed of Washington, D.C. politics, conspiring and scheming, still intent on harassing the Union in any way possible — but most of all intent on getting rich.

Smith apparently viewed Gibbs' presence with alarm. Evidence suggests that Captain Denny and Gibbs teamed up and began a thorough ship-wide search for the safe containing the money, unaware that it was in the hold, being transported as common freight. Smith, in this version, gallantly pretended to the conspirators that he had the safe with him in his cabin, and even drew a derringer, threatening to kill the first person who entered. Later, after the ship wrecked, Smith watched his family and other passengers being rescued — the last time they would see him alive — then stood guard over the wreck until a revenue cutter arrived and the safe could be retrieved from the hold. According to this version, it was found jimmied open, all money gone, bonds floating below decks and in calm water nearby. Gibbs and Denny already had been rescued, and it was later noted by some of the passengers that the two men gave undue attention to a box they insisted contained ship papers.[89]

Whichever tale is accepted, the money was never recovered, prompting endless stories that Smith somehow snared the fortune for his own use. Such a phenomenon is deemed most unlikely.

BROTHER JONATHAN. Artist's conception of the *Brother Jonathan* which sank July 30, 1865 off Crescent City, California, carrying 166 passengers — including Port Angeles founder Victor Smith — to the bottom. PHOTO SOURCE: Bert Kellogg

MEMORIAL erected by the California State Park Commission commemorating loss of life in the 1865 wreck of the 1,359-ton *Brother Jonathan*. PHOTO SOURCE: Del Norte County Historical Society

The *Brother Jonathan*

It is known that Smith contracted Panama Fever during his adventure on Roncador Reef, and was still sick when he arrived at San Francisco. After recuperating somewhat, he boarded the steamer *Brother Jonathan* on July 28th, and finally headed for his Puget Sound home. He never made it. The sturdy, 1,359-ton vessel, which recently had been damaged in a collision (ironically, while carrying Smith's family up to Victoria ahead of him), and which the captain had warned was overloaded, ran into a fierce storm just off Crescent City, California, on July 30, 1865. She split her bow open on an uncharted rock, lost several lifeboats filled with people, and went down within 45 minutes, carrying 166 people to their deaths. Only 19 people – eight passengers and 11 crewmen – survived the disaster.

Victor Smith's body was never found. Ironically, his last and most dedicated enemy, Anson Henry, also was aboard the ill-fated ship, and died with Smith.[90]

Port Angeles – the Ghost Town

Thus did Port Angeles witness the passing of its founder. Victor Smith had, through means both fair and foul, nurtured a dream far beyond the ordinary and stamped his mark indelibly upon the little town. With his death in 1865, the glitter that might have been Port Angeles' immediate future flickered and all but died. People began leaving the area, and soon the little school which had been operating since April closed.[91] Even with a Customs House functioning on the shore and a brand-new lighthouse twinkling near the end of Ediz Hook, gloom began settling within the bones of the community like a malignant disease.

Callie Smith remained, though, and threw herself into the raising of her brood. Certainly she needed no further calamities in her life, yet Mother Nature saw to it that she would agonize through yet one more terrible ordeal. In November of 1865, barely 24 hours after giving birth to her fifth child, Victor Rogers Smith, fire destroyed the home in which the Smith family lived. She was forced out into the snow, carrying the newborn babe and herding the four little ones to a neighbor's home for refuge. Shortly thereafter, they found themselves totally dependent on the dubious charity of Victor's sister Cynthia. Unable to bear Cynthia's cruelty toward her and her children for very long, Callie soon had a small house built on Ediz Hook, near Victor's father George, the keeper of the light.

Callie Smith remarried in 1869, to Samuel Atkinson, and, though later divorced from him, appears to have lived out her life in a cheery, Christian-like manner, earning the complete respect of all who knew her.

Increasingly, though, others began to desert the area, and when, in September of 1866 the Customs House was returned to Port Townsend "with raucous and salty jubilation" in that town, virtually everybody abandoned Port Angeles. It took on the dreary, wind-swept, morose appearance of a ghost town.[92]

Smith's Legacy

What of Victor Smith and his actions? The significance of what he did? This strange, troubled man did not live long enough to see his National City built, and during his brief four years in Puget Sound engendered so much hatred that his enemies nullified what few good deeds he performed almost before they had been accomplished. Nevertheless, he had an enormous impact on Port Angeles' long-term development. Not only did he leave behind the warm, intelligent Callie Smith, but several children as well. Among the latter was the influential Norman, who left his mark on the town during the early days of the 20th Century. Victor Smith's political manipulating made Ediz Hook the permanent site of a lighthouse which has been up-dated continually and has aided navigators in the Strait of Juan de Fuca for more than 100 years.

Moreover, and perhaps more important, he was the prime mover in the creation of a Government Reserve at Port Angeles which spelled trouble for awhile but in the long run was beneficial to the community. Reserve status, expected by Smith to enrich all parties involved, tied up the land in and around Port Angeles for nearly 25 years! Certainly there was no influx of people as there was in other western towns; nobody could even enter the Reserve legally, let alone buy property therein. Conversely though, as we shall see in Chapter Three, some of that same land – primarily because it had been legally knotted for more than two decades – would later be purchased cheaply by George Venable Smith (no relation to Victor) and serve as the site of the Puget Sound Cooperative Colony, a group as fascinating as it was vital to the maturing town of Port Angeles.

History's final verdict on Victor Smith might indeed be a harsh one, yet perhaps it should be tempered with understanding and at least a touch of pragmatism. It seems certain that he, along with others, plotted to create an important town which they could run for their own selfish purposes.[93] Nevertheless, Smith unquestionably was one of the key figures around whom the city of Port Angeles evolved. Whatever his faults or ulterior motives – there were plenty of both – Victor Smith was certainly the catalyst who succeeded in focusing attention on Port Angeles as a site of future importance.

FOGBELL ON EDIZ HOOK. The pyramidal bell-house and fogbell in this photo were adjacent to a lighthouse constructed on Ediz Hook during Victor Smith's tenure as Customs Collector in Port Angeles. The bell, weighing 3,150 pounds, warned sailors of their proximity to the shoreline, and remained in continuous use until 1909. Clockwork machinery automatically rang the bell every 15 seconds, but during extreme weather conditions, it could not be heard at any appreciable distance offshore. At those times, therefore, a steam siren could be pressed into service, with a rowboat used to haul water from the downtown Port Angeles area for the boiler. PHOTO SOURCE: Bert Kellogg

CAROLINE THOMPSON MORSE LEE, member of one of Port Angeles' very earliest families. Born July 8, Caroline was married to Davis W. Morse, Sr., who died shortly after the family's arrival here in 1862. She bore three children to Davis Morse — including Davis W. Morse, Jr., the first white child born in Port Angeles (April 19, 1863). After her marriage to Alfred Lee — with whom she had three more children — the family settled at the mouth of the stream now bearing that name. Caroline Lee died June 15, 1916. PHOTO SOURCE: Bert Kellogg

ALFRED LEE. One of Port Angeles' earliest settlers, Lee came to Port Angeles in 1862. After marrying Caroline Morse, widow of Davis W. Morse, Sr., Lee purchased from Silas Goodwin a home, pre-emption rights and improvements to property at the mouth of a stream slightly west of Morse Creek. That stream became known as Lee's Creek, and it still flows just outside Port Angeles' eastern city limits. Alfred Lee also served as Justice of the Peace in the fledgling community. He died in 1890. PHOTO SOURCE: Bert Kellogg

The Little Town Sleeps

With its founder gone, its population diminished and little positive future lying before it, Port Angeles was to doze for about 18 years, until the early 1880s. Its few residents eked out a living via trading, or, as in the case of Victor Smith's friends and relatives, through government paychecks. The importance of the town was, in fact, so minimal that the 1870 census taker apparently didn't bother making a personal visit to count heads. No exact population figure for that year can be determined, because all those listed as citizens of Clallam County are shown in such a way that they appear to be living in "Port Townsend P.O., Jefferson County."[94]

During Port Angeles' 18-year slumber, the crackling vitality of this young nation became more apparent; the very gait of its people quickened noticeably. In fact, as the little community lay dormant, the fibre of life in America was being altered forever. Electrifying changes were taking place, permeating almost every strata of society. En masse, Americans everywhere but in remote places like Port Angeles seemed to be priming themselves for a feverish, headlong dash toward the 20th Century.

America's assets — and ultimately her geography — changed when "Seward's Folly" resulted in the purchase of Alaska from Russia in 1867. Her political system was angrily threatened from within by the impeachment of Andrew Johnson and later, from without, by the assassination of President James Garfield. Her technology would be forever revamped by Andrew Carnegie's introduction of the Bessemer basic steelmaking factory, and her cities began bulging at the seams with immigrants whose members would ultimately exceed 20 million.

And still Port Angeles slept.

Finally came several stimulants which would serve to rouse Victor Smith's little town — and all the wild west. Beginning with the completion of the Northern Pacific Railroad, and with the country riding the crest of a fantastic land boom, there was a massive influx of settlers into the Pacific Northwest area. Many of them began casting covetous glances toward Port Angeles, and the sleepy little community finally awoke with a start!

Chapter Three: 1883 — 1889

The Puget Sound Cooperative Colony

*"Let the many combine in cooperation
as the few have done in corporations."*
—Colonists' Motto

During 1883, life in the little hamlet of Port Angeles went on, but at a sluggish pace. Its residents probably took little note of Thomas Edison's invention of the radio tube, or of the opening of the famous Brooklyn Bridge in New York.

However, subtle signs of Port Angeles' awakening were present. The U.S. Government had established a Signal Station in town (1882),[1] and a small store which doubled as the Post Office was opened by Postmaster Davis Waterman Morse. His uncle, Eben Gay Morse, was busy constructing the Central Hotel (later known as The Globe),[2] and increasingly, travelers stopped to look over the area on their way to and from Victoria. Over the next few years eight town lots were sold, Morse's hotel was finished, the large Merchant's Hotel (originally known as the

Olympian House) was built at Front and Laurel Streets,[3] and the town definitely began marching at a more rapid pace. One would like to think this was due to the energy and imagination of Port Angeles' citizenry. Such activity, however, was nothing more than a ripple effect from numerous ulterior events coming to focus on the Pacific Northwest.

For many reasons, the year 1883 proved to be the start of a great westward thrust of people. General business conditions throughout the young nation were quite good, a truly amazing land boom was about to begin, and the railroad was opening up vast stretches of the west. The impact of all this on Washington Territory (it would become a state six years later) was dramatic: Washington's population during the 10-year span beginning in 1883 was to

EARLIEST PHOTO OF EDIZ HOOK. This 1884 snapshot is the earliest such photo of the Port Angeles area known to be in existence. Pictured is the very base of the Spit, where today's Crown Zellerbach paper mill is located. Just out of the photo to the right was a Clallam Indian village and longhouse. PHOTO SOURCE: Bert Kellogg

quadruple — from 75,000 to 337,000! All of these factors — prosperity, the railroad, land boom and regional population increase — seemed to converge on the Puget Sound area, concentrated especially in Seattle and Tacoma. In combination, they bred working-class turmoil, which in turn led to the formation of an idealistic, communal society destined to have a tremendous influence upon Port Angeles for years to come.

Enter the Chinese

Seattle and Tacoma were still quite young communities in 1883, just emerging from rather primitive, pioneer conditions. Both cities, becoming more industrial by the day, attracted large numbers of skilled and unskilled laborers. Chinese, originally imported to work on railroads and in California canneries, settled in the area in significant numbers. There were not as many Chinese in Washington Territory as there were in California or adjoining Oregon;[4] nevertheless, anti-Chinese feeling was soon running high along the entire Northwest coast. Frustrated, unorganized, caucasian laborers were afraid their jobs and wages would be adversely affected by the Orientals. Labor organizers, some of them radicals

advocating violence, leaped at the opportunity, and in a remarkably short time, racism was the catalyst which unified many diverse labor groups. One such group, well-disciplined and with strong leadership, began to think of ways to escape the confusion — as well as the Chinese — so they could embrace other worthwhile causes.

Origins in Seattle

George Venable Smith, a prominent California lawyer who had moved to Seattle in 1884, was the Seattle City Attorney in 1885. Because of his position, he was deeply involved in city politics. Even more significantly, he was entangled with the "Chinese Problem," and had become one of the leaders of the anti-Chinese movement. Obviously sympathetic to whites, Smith went so far as to preside over meetings of radical labor agitators — even permitting some of the sessions to be held in his offices. After surviving conspiracy charges and an attempt to disbar him, he and several other leaders of the anti-Chinese element, including one Judge Peter Peyto Good, became enthralled with the idea that a utopia of sorts could be established in Puget Sound. Judge Good, as a result of trips to Mexico and Guise,

CENTRAL HOTEL, 1886. Built by Eben Gay Morse, the Central Hotel (later known as The Globe) was the town's first formal lodging house for travelers. It was located on the south side of Front Street, between Laurel and Oak Streets, and was opened for occupancy in 1884. PHOTO SOURCE: Clallam County Museum

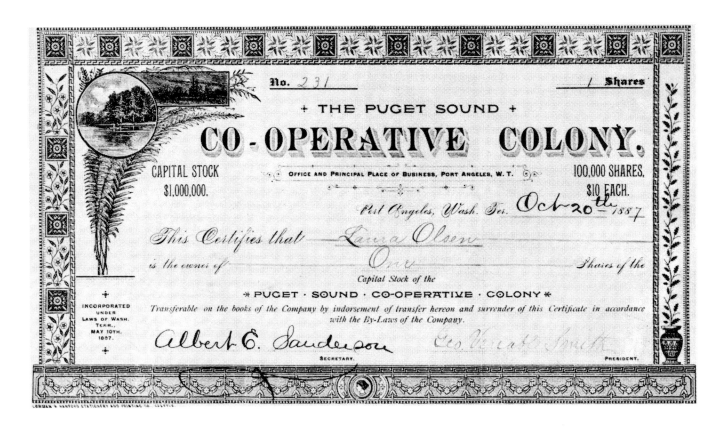

CAPITAL STOCK of the Puget Sound Cooperative Colony. Worth $10 per share to a purchaser, such stock represented part ownership in the unique colony venture which contributed so much to Port Angeles' early development. PHOTO SOURCE: Bert Kellogg

France, was infatuated with the idea of reform and cooperative, communal living, George Venable Smith became his primary organizer and promoter.

Smith and other organizers of the "Colony" idea saw it as the perfect way to avoid the devastating effects of low-wage Chinese competition and other economic ills infecting the Seattle economy. They visualized the Colony as a beautiful, model city, with its very cornerstone the theme of cooperative living. Cooperative homes, cooperative hotels, cooperative industries — all were part of the plan. Free medical care, no unemployment, no taxes and lifelong security were seen as attainable goals. When Good succeeded in firing promoter Smith's imagination, the plan took root. Thus was born the Puget Sound Cooperative Colony.

First Officers . . . Resistance
to the Movement . . . A Site

Original meetings of the Puget Sound Cooperative Colony were held in October, 1885, when specific plans were drawn for the establishment of the Colony. Shortly after the Seattle anti-Chinese riots of February 6th and 7th that year,[5] Peter Good, the original ideaman for the colony, died. The group, however, went ahead with a formal announcement

of the society's formation. Officers were elected (John Knoff, President; George Venable Smith, General Managing Agent)[6] and publicity was distributed outlining methods of financing that would be needed to make a commune work. The society even published a booklet detailing the proposal, and describing similar experiments around the world.[7]

Resistance Encountered

As with many new concepts, resistance was encountered. The Seattle business community vehemently condemned the Colony as nothing more than radical socialism, and tried to link it with that hated labor reform group, The Knights of Labor (which, interestingly, welcomed blacks and women as members — but excluded bankers, lawyers and gamblers!). Corporation-backed newspapers publicly attacked the Colony, denouncing its members as traitors and as pawns of the International Workingmen's Association (a radical group organized by Karl Marx in 1864 which advocated violence). Many others on the sidelines calmly assessed the experiment as a venture which, luring only fanatical cranks, was doomed to fail. Nevertheless, by early 1887, the fledgling organization was claiming that its membership was 500, that it had $15,000 cash and had already selected a

FRONT STREET IN 1887. With Port Angeles just beginning to awaken from a 20-year "slumber," this somewhat dreary view of Front Street was taken in 1887 when the population is thought to have been 39. Litter on the streets existed because at this point in time there were few horses or wagons in town. Development was limited strictly to the beach area, with most of the land south of that section closed to settlement under an order signed by President Abraham Lincoln June 19, 1862. PHOTO SOURCE: Bert Kellogg

ONE OF THE EARLIEST KNOWN PHOTOS OF DOWNTOWN SECTOR. With hundreds of Puget Sound Cooperative Colonists beginning to clear ground about one mile eastward, "downtown" Port Angeles was comparatively bleak, as demonstrated in this 1887 photograph. Peabody Creek is shown meandering through the middle of the street, between the Globe Hotel (on the left) and the Merchants Hotel at Laurel and Front (on the right). An open trough running through the center of the picture was the city's first water "system," stretching from Peabody Creek to the Morse Dock at the north end of Laurel Street. PHOTO SOURCE: Bert Kellogg

site for the venture (though kept a secret). Such claims soon attracted the attention of investors.

George V. Smith traveled to California, then on to the midwest, publicizing the Colony, seeking members and selling stock. On May 4, 1887, 35 member-delegates convened in Seattle, and drafted Articles of Incorporation and Bylaws, rendering it official. The Colony incorporated with capital stock of $100,000, issued 100 shares with $10 par value each, and elected Smith its new President (succeeding John Knoff), along with eleven Trustees to run the affairs of the corporation.

The New Site . . . Settling in . . . The First Newspaper . . . Resentment in "old" Port Angeles

Port Angeles was then identified as the proposed site. Trustees revealed that 22 members of the Puget Sound Cooperative Colony already were living there, having arrived in small groups late in 1886, and early in 1887. In addition to 200 acres of timber land they had acquired, the newcomers were developing 25 blocks of land bought a year earlier from Norman Smith, son of the town's founder (no relation to the

Colony's very own George V. Smith). The site chosen for actual development was a short distance east of "downtown" Port Angeles, at the mouth of Ennis Creek on property now owned by ITT Rayonier, Inc.

By the Fourth of July, 1887, there were 239 colonists living at the Port Angeles site, with 400 more to arrive later in that year. The first two Colony babies were born on April 29th and June 8th of that year.

Lodging temporarily at a west end hotel, most of the new Colony arrivals were quick to sense a certain antagonism on the part of the older Port Angeles community. However, because there was so much to be done merely to make the Colony livable, little interaction took place at first.

Starting by clearing a more accessible roadway than the existing beach trail, George Venable Smith and his well-organized unit soon cleared land, planted crops, felled timber and built buildings. The Colony newspaper, **The Model Commonwealth**, (founded May 21, 1886), was freighted in from Seattle and began publishing immediately, emphasizing the Colony's motto, "Let the many combine in cooperation as the few have done in corporations." They

THE GEORGE GALE HOME on Front Street between Vine and Albert Streets in Port Angeles, circa 1900. Gale arrived in Port Angeles in October, 1887 as a member of the Puget Sound Cooperative Colony. He was the original platter of what is now Gales Addition, a familiar Port Angeles neighborhood. PHOTO SOURCE: Clallam County Museum

THE MODEL COMMONWEALTH.

LET THE MANY COMBINE IN CO-OPERATION AS THE FEW HAVE DONE IN CORPORATIONS.

Vol. 2, No. 24. PORT ANGELES, WASH. TER., FRIDAY, NOVEMBER 18, 1887. $1.00 Per Annum.

OBITUARY.

DIED AT CHICAGO,

Nov. 11th, 1887,

FREE SPEECH !!!
FREE PRESS!!!

Rights of Americans Peaceably to Assemble and Discuss their Grievances !!!

Rights of Americans Against Unreasonable Search and Seizure Without Warrants !!!

Rights of Americans to a Fair Trial and Impartial Jury !!!

THE ANARCHISTS DEAD.
STRANGLED UPON THE GALLOWS.
They Died with Great Fortitude and Bravado.

Parsons, Spies, Fischer and Engel were hanged at Chicago Nov. 11th, at noon. The condemned men met death with heroic firmness.

At 10:30 o'clock Parsons, Fischer and Spies

ASKED FOR TWENTY MINUTES

each on the gallows in which to make speeches. The sheriff did not immediately return an answer to the question. Fischer than began singing the Marseillaise hymn in which the other prisoners joined. The voice of Fischer seemed round and full but quivering just a trifle. The reporters pressed close about the door of the cage and listened till the deep tones died away into silence. The song lasted two minutes. Adjutant General Vance of the state militia came into the jail at 10 o'clock and was closeted with the sheriff. Chief Deputy Gleason appeared with some papers which he declared were simply the official notice of the commutation of Schwab and Fielden.

The manuscript which Spies, Parsons and Fischer spent a portion of the morning in preparing were in part

WRITEN STATEMENTS,

the nature of which would not be divulged by any of the officials. These were delivered into the hands of Clerk Price, who turned them over to the sheriff, and this official locked them in his personal safe. It was stated by the sheriff that Spies, Parsons and Fischer have in addition written letters which he had also locked up securely. Parsons' letter was addressed to his wife and children, that Fischer goes to his wife, but the address on that of Spies the sheriff refuses to divulge. It is supposed that Parsons sent Nina Van Zandt. Before 10 o'clock

knowledge of the bombs and intimates plainly that the signers consider Lingg a monomaniac. Fischer wrote a statement in which he said he could not understand the affair at all. He could not believe Lingg intended to take the lives of the jail officials, who had treated him with so much kindness, nor did he think a man of Lingg's courage had decided to commit suicide.

Lingg's Suicide.

Louis Lingg, one of the doomed anarchists, blew his head off with dynamite in the Chicago jail on the morning of the 10th. How he secured the material with which the deed was committed is a mystery. The scene in Lingg's cell after the explosion was ghastly. Teeth, bits of jawbone, shreds of flesh and blood were scattered all over the narrow compartment A little trail of blood marked the way over the stone flagging to the room where Lingg was carried. Within fifteen minutes after the explosion Fischer, Parsons and Engel were taken from their cells and searched in the jailer's private office. All their clothing was taken off them and new suits were given them. The sheriff says Lingg was stripped and carefully searched yesterday and the day before. The news of

LINGG'S DREADFUL DEED

Created the most profound excitement at the sheriff's office and throughout the entire city. The suicide presented

A MOST HORRIBLE SIGHT.

The lower part of his jaw was completely torn off and his thick auburn hair matted with blood. His cheeks were torn out and hung down in jagged pieces on his neck. His teeth were knocked out, his gums torn away and but a slight stump of a tongue appeared protruding from his mangled throat. In the upper part of

FOR THESE WE MOURN !!!

Dr. Gray went into the prisoners, bearing in his hands three wine glasses and a bottle of Jarvis brandy, with which to brace up the men. All of them partook of the stimulant. Fischer continued to make a display of bravado. Soon after

SINGING THE MARSEILLAISE,

he spoke to Turnkey Stubbin and said laughingly, "When I get to heaven I will put in a good word for you." When Fischer awoke this morning he turned to one of the officers and said, "I dreamed about Germany last night," then he relapsed into silence for a long period. Following close upon the telegraph report from Gov. Oglesby that he had decided once for all, the greatest bustle and excitment prevailed in the jail office, but Spies in his cell continued writing uninterruptedly; and the others remained qually undisturbed, notwithstanding the confusion that marked the beginning of the end. The rattling of chairs, tables and benches continued for several minutes, but by 11:05 there began to fall a hush in the conversation among the crowd that sank almost to a whisper. The bare whitewashed wall was lost in painful comparison with the

DARK BROWN GALLOWS,

with its four noosed ropes dropping ominously near the floor. A gleam of sunshine shooting through the window at this instant fell on the corner of the death machine, and in a slight degree relieved its sombre hue. The chief bailiff began at 11:10 to call out the persons summoned as jurors and bringing them forward to whose countenance had a peculiar glisten totally unlike the ashiness of Engel's heavy features and in strange contrast with the dead lack of color in the pinched lineaments of Parsons. The once, jaunty vivacious Texan came last, a withered ten years since the day and hour scarcely twelve months before when he tripped lightly into the court before Judge Gary and declared that he was ready to be tried at once for his life. The minute his feet touched the scaffold Parsons seemed to completely loose his identity and to feel that his spirit was no longer part of his body. He, as an American, seemed to realize to the full extent he must die in a manner to impress, if possible, on all future generations the thought that he was a martyr. He was by far the most striking feature of the gallows picture.

THE SQUAT FORM

of Engel's alongside with his wide-jawed face made a hideous contrast to Parsons. Fischer, a head and shoulders taller than the other three, made his only occasional looks of too evident bravado more notable than might otherwise be, a sorry disadvantage compared with the stately coolness of Spies. The latter's exhibition of quiet, thorough nerve far surpassed as a wonder the behavior of any of his comrades. Four burly deputies standing to the rear of the four condemned men began with-ped upon their heads and pulled quickly down to the neck, shutting off the view of each as completely and with less warning than does the camera cloth of a photographer.

THEIR LAST WORDS.

August Spies was the first of the four doomed men to make use of his wits. In tones of intense spirit the man who wrote the famous revenge circular hissed out between his tightly clenched teeth, "There will come a time when our silence will be more powerful than the voices they are strangling to death." The last syllable of Spies' concluding words, hoarse with suppressed passion, had not reached an end when Engel, raising his voice, wildly cried, "Hurrah for anarchy." Fischer caught the fire of the utterance and still more loudly exclaimed, "Hurrah for anarchy" adding, "This is the happiest moment of my life." There was a silence like the grave, broken up by the slow, measured intonation of Parsons, like a white-robed priest before the alter of sacrifice, not as a dying request, but rather like a commander he sounded forth, "May I be allowed to speak?" Then with slow entreaty came "Will you let me speak, sheriff Matson?" There was another agonizing pause, the muffled shroud broke out in hollow accents, "Let the voice of the people be heard." part of the jaw bone a terrible gap was torn out from the inside. All of the thumb of the left hand with which he had touched off the explosive in his mouth was torn open. When the explosion occurred all the Anarchists in the prison were on their feet in an instant and every one of them looked stunned and frightened. Jailor Foltz at once gave orders to have every one of the cells searched.

The agent which had served Lingg to accomplish his deadly work is a small fulminating cap, a little over an inch long. It had been filled with fulminate of mercury and a small fuse, which is usually attached to these instruments of death, had been touched off by Lingg at the time the reporters thought he was lighting a cigar. When Lingg committed the deed he was lying on his face on his cot. After the affair, when he was searched, another candle was found, at the top of which, barely concealed by the ends of the wick, was a second fulminating cap. So it is supposed that Lingg's suicide was commited with a cap similarly hidden. The candles were furnished by the jail, so that the caps must have been put in by Lingg himself.

Bombs in Lingg's Cell.

A search of the cells occupied by the condemned Anarchists was made by the jail officials on the 6th, and four dynamite bombs were found in a box in Lingg's cell.

They were manufactured out of gas pipe, each being six to seven inches in

THE MODEL COMMONWEALTH. The November 18, 1887 issue of the Puget Sound Cooperative Colony's newspaper The Model Commonwealth. In this edition, the colonists, through their editor, roundly attacked the capital punishment inflicted upon four Chicago men for alleged criminal actions during the 1886 Haymarket Square riots. Colonists living in Port Angeles screamed their outrage that the so-called anarchists were hanged; most believed that the four had been executed more for their political beliefs rather than for specific actions during the riots. PHOTO SOURCE: North Olympic Library System

COLONY LUMBER MILL, Port Angeles' first real industry. Located on the present ITT Rayonier site, the mill shown in these two photos had the capacity to saw 20,000 board feet per day and provided lumber, laths, shingles and shakes for colony buildings. It was destroyed by fire near the end of the colony's corporate life.
PHOTO SOURCE: Clallam County Museum

COLONY BUILDINGS. Looking west from the beach near Ennis Creek, Puget Sound Cooperative Colony's East End Hotel on the right and the school in the center are shown in this 1887 photo. PHOTO SOURCE: Bert Kellogg

HOLLYWOOD BEACH IN THE 1880s. Looking east from a point approximating today's City Pier. The beach area, slightly east of what is now Railroad Avenue in downtown Port Angeles, was a favorite camping spot for Indians traveling the Strait of Juan de Fuca. PHOTO SOURCE: Bert Kellogg

brought in a sawmill from Seattle, and were soon cutting 20,000 feet of lumber a day, some of it sold, but most of it used to construct Colony buildings. Plans were made for construction of blacksmith and wagonmaker's shops, stables and other badly needed community ventures. Gardeners planted vegetables, fishermen fished, and, using clay found in the area, colonists produced bricks in a kiln near the dock.

All in all an auspicious beginning. It was a fore-taste of approximately one year of really successful Colony operations. The idea worked quite well . . . while it worked. Unfortunately, except for the euphoria which kept it humming that first year, the model city never really got off the ground.

As the colony sank roots near Ennis Creek, its members striving to achieve the ultimate in communitarianism, people in the "other" Port Angeles to the west did their best to ignore the newcomers. They never really trusted the Colony, generally disagreed with what they knew of the colonists' ideas, and most of all, resented the conceited, self-satisfied smugness that seemed to characterize this new breed of settler. Oh sure, some west enders nodded, they had to agree with a *few* things being said by the colonists. Radicals or not, those people sure were right in what they said

about the Chinese, weren't they? (The colonists' newspaper editor, in addressing "those who have experienced the misery of having this degrading and debasing element [Chinese] in their midst," said Port Angeles was "blessed, because it was as far removed from [this] vicious example as possible.")[8] Nevertheless, for the most part, the resentment against colonists continued throughout 1887 and 1888, intensifying almost daily because of what the west end viewed as inflammatory articles in **The Model Commonwealth**.

Then, on top of the typical "radical" items being published weekly, there was the newspaper's impudent response to the Haymarket Square Riot executions. A year earlier, on May 4, 1886, a large group of anarchists had been involved in a Chicago, Illinois, riot in which eleven persons died — including seven policemen. Many Americans blamed the affair on the Knights of Labor.[9] In November, 1887, amid the glare of national publicity, four of the supposedly guilty men were hanged. **The Model Commonwealth**, its front page heavily black-bordered, bitterly denounced the executions, describing them in the goriest, most explicit manner imaginable. Many colonists felt those rioters punished had suffered for

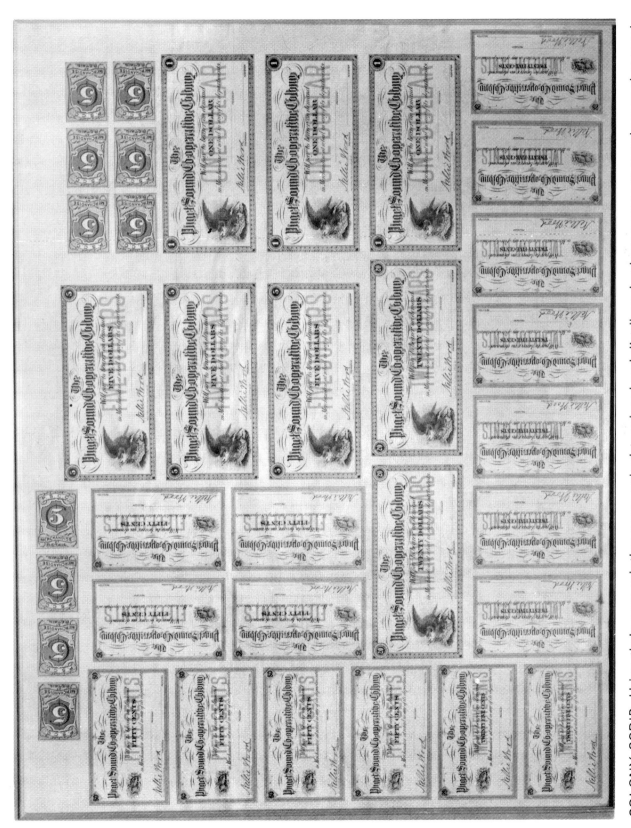

COLONY SCRIP. Using their own printing press, colonists printed and distributed colony money to members so that goods could be purchased from the cooperative-owned store. Lacking a hard dollar foundation, scrip was technically worthless, so the practice helped spark inflation. The entire colony structure began to unravel under the financial burden, and colony leaders ultimately were forced to sell off real estate holdings and other assets; eventually, they abandoned the project altogether. PHOTO SOURCE: Clallam County Museum

THE OPERA HOUSE completed in 1891, was built by cooperative colonists under bid to the City of Port Angeles. Scene of many of the town's "firsts," (the first flush toilet, the first County Fair, etc.) the Opera House served as the center of community life socially, politically and theatrically in Port Angeles until it was razed in 1923. Located on the south side of Front Street, the site later was occupied by the Olympus Hotel and is now the drive-through parking lot of Seattle-First National Bank. PHOTO SOURCE: Bert Kellogg

their political beliefs, rather than for actual crimes committed.[10]

Colony Money . . . Colony Problems

Frequently there were other, more personal, thoughts expressed in **The Model Commonwealth** which tended to rankle Port Angeles' conservative element. A few articles seemed to imply to the average reader that colonists were atheists and believed in free love (totally untrue).[11] One editorial even suggested that marriage was no longer a viable institution! Many newspaper comments criticized the need for money, claiming it was merely a capitalist tool. Later, as if to emphasize that point, colonists actually printed their own scrip (an action which some historians suggest hastened the demise of the

experiment). In reality, scrip was simply a Promissory Note, which meant the Colony owed the bearer goods. Later, when the economy of the group faltered, value of the scrip plummeted and a few lawsuits were filed by members asking fair compensation for the printed Colony currency.

Broadening men's minds and refining their cultural interests were two tenets of the grand design envisioned by George Venable Smith and Judge Good. Their followers were, by nature, ripe for creative ideas and reforms; indeed, Colonists routinely achieved difficult goals simply because they didn't know such things were supposed to be difficult. Moreover, if somebody had tried to point it out to them, they wouldn't have listened! Colonists formed a 22-member Cornet Band late in

COLONY SHIPYARD located at the mouth of Ennis Creek in Port Angeles. One of the Cooperative Colony's most ambitious projects, the shipyard, while operated solely by colonists, completed one major shipbuilding project: The *Angeles*, a 58-foot propeller-driven schooner. Later, after the shipyard was sold, the schooners *Lydia Thompson*, the *Jessie*, the *Ella Johnson*, the *R. Eacrett* and others were christened there. PHOTO SOURCE: Bert Kellogg

1887, then constructed the Pioneer Theatre, the first endeavor of its kind in Clallam County. Their first program, offered on October 22, 1887, was a "laughable, shadow pantomine entitled 'Conspiracy in a Hash House.' " (Colonists, however, *really* titillated their 19th Century Victorian audiences by advertising the next production as "That rich and racy Vaudeville . . . 'The Loan of a Lover.' "[12])

Opera House

Encouraged by their success with Pioneer Theatre, colonists then won a contract to begin building the Opera House in — of all places — the west end of town! This grand edifice, which took four years to build, was to be the heart of Port Angeles' social life for over 30 years, and itself was the site of a few "firsts" for the town. Rather pretentious, the Opera House was ornamented in front, displayed a square tower on top, and had the highest flagpole in town. Furthermore, it enabled theatergoers to look out through the first plate glass windows seen in Port Angeles. Later (wonder of wonders!), it boasted the town's first flush toilet! For years, it remained the only flush commode in the city, and the ingenious little device came to be known as the town's "show

place." Port Angelens, in fact, found it to be such a novelty that the toilet "saw practically 24-hour service."[13]

Colonists' Impact on Port Angeles

In fact, looking back at the Puget Sound Cooperative Colony's several years of operation, it becomes obvious that an impressive list of Port Angeles "firsts" must be attributed to it. Though critics often accused them of being agnostics and atheists, colonists had a religious bent; in fact, records demonstrate that the First Congregational, First Methodist, First Baptist, Saint Andrew's Episcopal and the first Catholic churches were all founded by the colonists. They built the first sawmill, the first schoolhouse and the first office building in town. The first — and only — Opera House was their doing, and of course, they started the first newspaper, **The Model Commonwealth**. In later years, even though it was declining as a unit, the Colony inaugurated the first eight-hour work day and the first genuine Health and Old Age Insurance in the entire Olympic Peninsula region. Colonists even designed and constructed several ships — including the 60-ton steam schooner, The *Angeles* — in their Ennis Creek shipyard.[14]

FIRST CHURCH IN PORT ANGELES. Built in 1889, the First Congregational Church building still stands at its original location at First and Vine Streets. Now listed in the State Register of Historical Places, the building became a real estate agency in 1976 and was still being utilized as such at the time this book went to press. PHOTO SOURCE: Bert Kellogg

GEORGE VENABLE SMITH one of the founders of the Puget Sound Cooperative Colony, a group prominent in early Port Angeles history. After the demise of the colony, Smith maintained a thriving law practice in Port Angeles, became a probate judge, later Clallam County Prosecuting Attorney and City Attorney from 1904 till his death on September 26, 1919 at the age of 76. PHOTO SOURCE: Bert Kellogg

EARLY SANITATION FACILITIES are clearly demonstrated in this photo of the "beach house" at the colonists' East End Hotel, circa 1888. Perched at the end of a ramp leading from the hotel, the lower portion of this unique outhouse was cleansed regularly by the rise and fall of the tide! PHOTO SOURCE: Bert Kellogg

Education, too, ranked high on the Colony's list of priorities. With almost a third of the group's number under the age of 16, Colonists became a definite force behind the expansion of Port Angeles' educational facilities. Miss Ione Tomlinson (later to become the second Mrs. George Venable Smith) taught a 25-member kindergarten class, believed to be the first one in Washington. It lasted only two years but apparently sparked west end Port Angeles residents to construct Central School. Three Colony members had been elected to the School Board in November 1887, and adult education programs and trade classes quickly sprang up in the district. Though the Colony concept would prove unworkable and eventually disappear from the local scene, this kind of unique, innovative thinking was infectious and left a distinct mark on education in Port Angeles.

Demise of the Colony

After all the sunshine, however, came the rain. By mid-1888, the Colony was already unraveling from within, as basic weaknesses in its idea and structure came to light. For one thing, it became evident immediately that promoters had "oversold" the idea to the public; too many people arrived too soon. And, though farmers, woodsmen and fishermen were the kind of workers needed (men "who understand the handling of ax, pick and shovel," as one observer put it[15]), a goodly number of the newcomers were tradesmen, children and other nonproductive individuals. Dissension among the leaders soon flushed to the surface. The group's first elected

president, John J. Knoff, had moved to Port Angeles in the spring of 1887 but quickly was disillusioned by what he perceived as scheming and land speculating by George V. Smith. Knoff was the first to crack the Colony's veneer of unity when he returned to Seattle with a group of followers just three months after his arrival.

The twin utopian themes of cooperative spirit and true democracy began to disintegrate early-on as corporate officers exercised strict control over affairs of the Colony, while worker-stockholders could only simmer and stew at their lack of influence.

So, after a little more than one full year of operation as a unit, during which time there was much political jockeying, the group elected a new corporate Board of Directors.[16] George Venable Smith was not reelected to his position of leadership (he was succeeded by Thomas Malony) and some original ideas on unity and cooperation — realized to be impractical — were abandoned in favor of more realistic ways by which the Colony should be operated.[17] Board leadership continued to change for the next couple of years and so did the philosophy and goals of the proposed utopia. Colony business ventures expanded, real estate transactions were initiated, and the basic, communal system sought by the group's founders was altered forever. Though it was to function as a corporate body for several more years — and, indeed, register the important achievements mentioned earlier — The Colony's demise as a social experiment was inevitable.[18]

Its death should not have come as a surprise, for,

MINERVA TROY. Daughter of Cooperative Colony surgeon Freeborn S. Lewis, Minerva Troy became one of Port Angeles' most outstanding citizens. Married to John Troy (who later became Governor of Alaska), she maintained great interest in art, music and drama throughout her lifetime in Port Angeles. Minerva Troy died August 31, 1960. PHOTO SOURCE: Bert Kellogg

despite the splendid people involved, their lofty ideas, hard work and impressive accomplishments, this marvelous social adventure was after all, based on the premise of utter cooperation among human beings. Stripped of its rhetoric, cooperation with all neighbors in all facets of day-to-day life seemed less palatable when colonists faced the cold, hard facts of human nature. Even deeper, perhaps the very core of the problem, the Puget Sound Cooperative Colony had been created by dreamers naive in critical areas of leadership. They knew little of sound management practices and practical, day-to-day techniques of supervision and were incapable of stabililzing a

venture so deeply rooted in idealism. Then too, with leadership changes, the overall direction of the Colony changed dramatically in a short time. Soon, people who had joined the utopian effort because it promised social welfare and anti-capitalistic reforms, found themselves swept up in conventional land speculation deals — just ordinary residents of a typical western town.

By 1889, lawsuits from within the ranks threatened to annihilate all that had been accomplished; many members were openly calling the whole thing a failure. Beginning on April 6, 1889, the Colony's cows had to be sold, corporate assets were auctioned and the brickyard ceased operations. Then **The Model Commonwealth** was sold to A. H. Howells, who moved it to the west end of town and changed its name to the **Port Angeles Times**. Finally, people began to leave the Colony confines in great numbers.

With the decline of the experiment, many of its people, however, decided to settle down in "old" Port Angeles. Marriages among colonists and west enders were taking place routinely by 1889, drawing the two factions inexorably closer together.[19] Colonists who stayed continued to contribute immensely to the city's growth. George Venable Smith became a civic leader and in 1888 was the first judge elected in Clallam County. The respected Minerva Lewis Troy later ran for a seat in the U.S. House of Representatives (2nd Congressional District) in 1922 — the first woman from this state to do so.[20]

If Victor Smith was Port Angeles' founder, it must be acknowledged that the Puget Sound Cooperative Colony was the town's most important early promoter. For the colonists, whether they meant to or not, publicized the area's many advantages to the world. Then, to a man, they set out to develop that area in a proper fashion. Platting and selling residential developments, setting the wheels of industry in motion, educating those who would be educated — even establishing a newspaper — the group greatly and favorably affected Port Angeles.

In the final analysis, the Colony's people probably represent its most signifcant long-term impact on Port Angeles. Although it had been formed during a time of anti-Oriental fever — indeed, its very creation was the result of such behavior — the Puget Sound Cooperative Colony became a reality because of clear-thinking liberals of that day who, generally speaking, made sincere efforts to recognize the rights of individuals.[21] They risked all in the name of a social experiment and were pioneers in the true sense of the word.

Chapter Four: 1889 — 1893

From Good Times to "Hard Times"

"I know (it's a counterfeit bill), my lad, but it is all we have . . . and it's doing a good job!"

— Tom Watson,
Port Angeles resident,
when informed that money
in his possession — the only
cash in town — was phony.

There were few real tears shed for the demise of the Colony. But then, folks living in these parts didn't incline toward wearing emotions on their sleeves. Many important, exciting things had occurred in the world over the previous three years — completion of both the Eiffel Tower and Statue of Liberty and notable inventions such as the Steam Turbine, Dirigible and Fountain Pen — all of which had little noticeable impact on Port Angelens. Seattle's great fire (65 blocks burned during 1889) did cause a commotion of sorts because of its proximity to Port Angeles, but the great loss of life in Pennsylvania's tragic Johnstown flood barely rated sidewalk conversation.

Residents just didn't have time for that sort of thing: Other vital events were by this time filling their thoughts from morning till night. Why, just a few weeks before the decade dawned (November 11, 1889), President Benjamin Harrison had proclaimed Washington the 42nd State of the Union! Residents of Port Angeles must have been impressed with the formality of such a declaration, for in that same year, in an obviously civic mood, they dug a well for the town pump at Front and Lincoln Streets, and formed the city's first Board of Trade and Chamber of Commerce. Both commercial bodies were to undergo substantial reorganization (the Board in 1892, the Chamber in 1894), then go on to perform creditable long-term service to Port Angeles.

FRONT STREET LOOKING EAST, 1890. This close-up of Peabody Creek running down the middle of the street is indicative of the ramshackle nature of Port Angeles as the "Gay Nineties" decade began. Eben Gay Morse's Central Hotel, later the Globe Hotel, is seen on the right. Just left of center in the picture is the "hog back" trail leading up Front Street out of the downtown section. PHOTO SOURCE: Bert Kellogg

FRONT STREET ENDING AT LAUREL. This photo, circa 1890, shows Front Street ending at Laurel Street. The large building in the center is the Olympian House, later the Merchants Hotel. PHOTO SOURCE: Bert Kellogg

A "Land Grab"

The year 1890 was a truly significant one in Port Angeles history. By then, with the Colony and the town drawing closer and forming a more united community, two remarkable, interrelated events — evolving nationally for years — converged on Port Angeles. Together, they would influence the town tremendously.

First, the nationwide land boom, begun about six years earlier, had reached new heights by 1889. It seemed to explode in Port Angeles with the force of a bomb, for when it hit town — still land-locked by Government Reserve and with no forseeable way to expand its borders — prices on available property surged upward dramatically and the population soared over 3,000.

The most spectacular consequence of the reserve-induced land squeeze was the unorthodox method Port Angeles citizens chose to ease the pressure. It became a story unique to Port Angeles and one displaying Yankee Ingenuity at its finest: Port Angelens merely conducted a real, honest-to-goodness land rush on Uncle Sam's property!

Founder Victor Smith's government reserve, signed into law by Abraham Lincoln in 1862, had inadvertently become a monster. The approximately 3,000 acres (no exact figure is available, since not all reservation property was put up for sale), still closed to settlement and choked with immense Douglas Fir, were an immovable object virtually caging the town and thoroughly restricting its development. An Irish lawyer named John C. Murphy moved to Port Angeles from Olympia in 1890, viewed the captive area and took note of the fact that numerous requests to free the land had gone unheeded. He therefore began a somewhat boisterous campaign to break the reserve.

Murphy devised a plan of action designed to force the Government's hand: Move onto the reservation en masse and, in an orderly fashion, stake claims and set up housekeeping in a tent or shanty (to "prove up" the land, or verify that it was being homesteaded). Under Murphy's direction, the reserve jumpers marched quietly into the woods on the Fourth of July, 1890, and began platting equal-size lots. The aura of patriotism surrounding this important date could not have been lost on the intrepid squatters. None knew what action the Government would take; all risked being arrested for trespassing. Nevertheless, they stayed and began a vigorous letter-writing campaign to officials in Washington, D.C. and Olympia.

In the minds of the land jumpers that memorable July Fourth, there was certainly no question the reserve had been breached, if not officially broken. And Murphy's plan worked! They were to live in the forest illegally as squatters for almost three years, but Congress eventually would concede right of ownership to them, opening the reserve to public sale.

PRESS EXPEDITION. This map shows the route of the Press Exploring Expedition, sponsored by the Seattle *Press* newspaper in 1889 and 1890. Six men, led by James H. Christie, became the first group ever to cross the Olympic Mountains, naming thirty-six peaks during a rugged, six-month journey. A detailed account of that expedition was published in the Seattle *Press* July 16, 1890.

The explorers started their trek in Port Angeles December 8th or 9th, 1889, (the two leaders' reports differ on this point) arriving in the harbor aboard the steamer *Evangel.* Seeking detailed information about an alleged trail up the Elwha River, they questioned Norman R. Smith and other community leaders, and a few days later embarked on their tortuous journey. The trail-blazing expedition officially ended on May 23, 1890 upon their arrival in Seattle by boat from Aberdeen. Members of the remarkable expedition were James H. Christie, leader; Charles A. Barnes, historian; John W. Sims, John H. Crumback, Christopher Hayes and Dr. Harris B. Runnalls.

The SHORTEST RAILROAD IN THE WORLD!

FIFTEEN FEET LONG –ATOP THE ROCK BLUFF

NEAR LAKE CRESCENT, CLALLAM COUNTY, Wash BUILT BY NORMAN R. SMITH TO HOLD THE PASS IN 1890

RIPLEY'S BELIEVE IT OR NOT

RAILROAD FEVER. Perhaps nothing so signifies the term "Railroad Fever" as did the 15-foot-long railroad constructed by Port Angeles promoter Norman Smith in 1890. Built near Lake Crescent, a few miles west of town, Smith's bizarre, one-man effort to "hold the pass" so that a railroad company could link up with it from the west, was so newsworthy that it later appeared in the famous Ripley's "Believe It Or Not" Column. PHOTO SOURCE: *Port Angeles Evening News,* March 7, 1938

The "Iron Horse"

The second important condition to touch Port Angeles at this time was the railroad. Nineteenth Century Americans were obsessed with the Iron Horse. It seemed to infect cities and promoters throughout the country like a virulent disease; getting one's town connected to the "outside" world was surely a goal worth fighting for. Throughout the Pacific Northwest, promotional hoopla was especially intense, with many ambitious little communities practically tumbling over one another in their eagerness to become the westernmost terminus of the Northern Pacific. Seattle, Tacoma, Mukilteo and the then-bustling town of Port Crescent[1] saw themselves as logical terminals for tracks coming up the Cowlitz Corridor (a hodge-podge of wagon roads and water routes between Portland and Olympia); Port Townsend's aspiring promoters were confident their town

was an even more logical locale. Port Angeles, however, was bitten the hardest. Residents here, once victimized by railroad fever, seemed to apply a new dimension to the term "die-hard." Over a span of 27 years, no fewer than *14 separate railroad promotions* took place in the community, virtually all of which received community financial support. Later we shall look at some of them and their impact.

Though the land jump was undoubtedly the town's most exciting single event of 1890, others occurring that year reveal that, as the decade of the "Gay Nineties" opened, Port Angeles began to take itself very seriously. The beach village, straggling from Oak Street on the west to the Colony site on the east, visibly began to take on city airs.

Port Angeles — The City — The County Seat
Listening to Murphy's inspired oratory, with their numbers increasing daily and with a railroad expected

FIRST PORT ANGELES CITY COUNCIL. Elected in June of 1890 were (front row) T.J. Patterson, City Clerk, and J.F. Meagher; (second row, standing), E.H. Foster, Donald McInnes, John Dyke, Mayor, W.W. Gray and D.P. Quinn. PHOTO SOURCE: Bert Kellogg

practically any moment, Port Angeles citizens in 1890 were in a mood to flex their muscles. In a June public assembly, townspeople chose their first Mayor (John Dyke) and City Council (E. H. Foster, Donald McInnes, W. W. Gray, D. P. Quinn and J. F. Meagher), with election results being certified to the Secretary of State in Olympia on June 11th. Thus was the city officially incorporated.

Mayor Dyke and the Council met almost continuously for weeks, posting official proceedings of those sessions with the Board of Commissioners at the County Seat in New Dungeness. Then, coldly assessing the town's larger population, the Council persuaded the Board of Commissioners to determine where the County Seat should be. (New Dungeness was in 1890 the oldest town in the county, but smaller than Port Angeles.) A general election was held on November 4th, with the three populous areas of the county — Port Crescent, Port Angeles and New Dungeness — all voting on the county seat location. Because Port Angeles was the acknowledged pop-

ulation center, the outcome was never really in doubt (in fact, hardly anybody at New Dungeness bothered voting, believing that a County Seat could not be transferred so casually). The final tally was Port Angeles 687, Port Crescent 293 and New Dungeness 7.

Following the election, three or four days went by without the County records being shipped from New Dungeness. Some Port Angelens, their imaginations wandering far afield, viewed this as an ominous sign that New Dungeness intended to fight to retain its County Seat status. There was wild talk that bitter Port Crescent folk had sided with those from New Dungeness and together were planning a bloody battle to the finish. Clearly, a fierce struggle was imminent. So, amidst much talk of "expected hostilities," and "bring (ing) the records . . . to Port Angeles . . . by violence if necessary," and even "battle formations," a 25-man armed posse gathered in classic western style. The posse rode on horseback to New Dungeness and descended upon the lone figure of

VIEW OF FIRST STREET, CIRCA 1891, taken from Second and Valley Streets. It was at this time that city officials were first trying to fill in some of the town's beachfront. With much of Front Street on pilings, dirt was being shoveled from surrounding hillsides by hand, loaded into mine cars and hauled to the end of the street near Valley Creek. The old West Dependable building (a parking lot on the northwest corner of Front and Oak Streets when this book went to press) is the large building with the false front near the left edge of the photo.
PHOTO SOURCE: Bert Kellogg

CITY HOTEL. Construction of this grand, three-story hotel began in 1891, but records indicate that it officially opened for business on the south side of Front Street between Lincoln and Laurel, on August 15, 1892. One year later, in June of 1893 its name was changed to the Hotel Arlington, and by 1915 it was called the Hotel Angeles. The old City Hotel was torn down in 1929. PHOTO SOURCE: Clallam County Museum

THE CANNING COMPANY was established in Port Angeles in 1891, on a dock west of today's Boat Haven on Marine Drive. One of the largest employers in town during the 1890s it was owned by Mary Easter until she sold it on May 31, 1895 to Mr. J.W. Hume of Astoria, Oregon; Hume renamed it the National Packing Company. Later, (1902) the plant became the Manhattan Packing Company (owner, C.J. Farmer) and counted among its employees were perhaps 20 Chinese, a source of discomfort to townspeople. Newspapers report that it was a matter of genuine pride to Farmer and to city officials, that the plant employed "no more heathen" than were absolutely necessary to operate the plant! PHOTO SOURCE: Bert Kellogg

County Auditor Smith Troy. Not only did Troy offer no resistance, but the invaders found virtually every resident of the town calmly singing hymns at Sunday Church services (gallant warriors all, posse members at first imagined the hymn-singing to be some sort of weird, preliminary war dance!). Troy wondered aloud what had taken the men so long, then graciously helped load the records onto wagons for a triumphant, song-filled ride into Port Angeles![2]

It would seem that western style justice in 1890 also embraced a somewhat biased view of the eternal War of the Sexes. In those days, a man was conceded to be Lord and Master of his household, and any time a recalcitrant woman dared to step over that invisible line to threaten his position . . . well there was always a sympathetic judge nearby to explain the law to her.

That, at least, was the case when a man appeared before Justice L. T. Haynes that year, charging his wife with threatening "to kill him by cutting out his liver and eat(ing) the same." The witness was angry — but far more frightened — for, as he testified, his wife was "mean enough to do it." Justice Haynes took one look at the woman, nodded his agreement, and immediately bound her over to Superior Court under $500 bond![3]

* * * * *

Until bonds could be floated, corporate licenses were the only source of revenue available to the new City Fathers in 1890; nevertheless, with a brand new city to organize, Dyke and his Council moved swiftly. They levied a $500 annual license fee on the many saloons in town, established Assessment District No. 1, then made plans for immediate grading and street filling. A zig-zag stairway was ordered for the steep hillside at First and Oak Streets. Ten-foot-wide sidewalks were set for Front Street and twelve-foot walkways for First Street. Following this early decisive action, however, the six men required five months to agree on the width of Front Street itself. Finally, in November, it was set at 80 feet, which meant that ten additional feet had to be removed from all property on the north side of the street; owners were given all of ten days to move their buildings!

On December 2nd the first regular election of the newly-formed city was held. Willard Brumfield was elected Mayor over John Dyke, and by a vote of 199-9 voters advanced Port Angeles from township status to third class city status.[4]

By the end of 1890, Port Angeles' citizens could look back upon a productive "boom" year. Besides the city's incorporation and the many improvements ($2 million in real estate transactions and 200 new buildings!), three significant groups were formed that year: One fraternal, one financial, and one that appeared to be speculative. They were the Masonic Lodge (April 29th), the First National Bank (launch-

PORT ANGELES ON THE BRINK, 1892, during the building boom sweeping the west — and just after the Port Angeles land rush which ultimately broke the Reserve. Within a year, Congress had conveyed to the land jumpers the right of ownership, the town's population ballooned from 500 to 3,000, some 200 buildings were constructed, and a water system and electricity became available. PHOTO SOURCE: Bert Kellogg

ed late that year with capital of $50,000, B. F. Schwartz, President)[5] and the Union Pacific Railroad, which had, during 1890, secured a franchise and installed an agent near its newly-constructed dock at the foot of Lincoln Street. This last was the first tangible evidence that railroad mania had come to roost in Port Angeles.

Finally, after laboring many years to vindicate his father's actions concerning the Customs House, Norman Smith secured approval from Congress on August 30th to have Port Angeles made a Sub-Port of Entry. No doubt he anticipated great economic benefits for the town from this action, but little of substance occurred during the years ahead.[6]

The year 1891 began on a somber note with the January death of Victor Smith's widow, Mrs. Caroline Smith. Several other notable events occurred in the young city that year. The first steam-operated electrical plant was started, Captain L. Simonsen's Salvation Army began conducting meetings in town,[7] and the United States Weather Bureau assumed control of Port Angeles' weather telegraph system from the U.S.

Signal Corporation. A Citizens Association, formed by promoter Colonel James Coolican, published a little brochure entitled "Port Angeles Illustrated." Before closing the books on his first official city administration, Mayor Dyke and his five-man Council divided the community into three wards, requiring that two councilmen be elected from each, with another at-large. This meant a seven-person council would be elected later that year. Gales Hook and Ladder Company was organized, colonists finished building the Opera House, and a Catholic Church was erected on Lincoln Street (later purchased by the County for use as a courthouse).

Of far greater significance, however, on March 3rd President Grover Cleveland opened the federal reservation and gave squatters prior right to settle on and homestead two lots (50 x 140-feet each),[8] on which they could show proof of homesteading and later acquire title. (Twentieth Century realtors might like to note that all lots on the reserve were appraised at $5.00 each!) Sportsmen also got into the act: The "Port Angeles Base Ball Club" was organized, with

H. B. Crockett, as manager.[9] As 1891 neared its end, Norman Smith was elected to his first of two one-year terms as Mayor, on December 8th, and word reached town of a major gold strike at a place called Pike's Peak, in Colorado.

Continuing its notably steady progress, Port Angeles in 1892 displayed a newly-acquired cultural side when the new Opera House was filled for two consecutive nights for "Chimes of Normandy." Funds raised from the opera paid for a large (8 x 10-feet) painting of Port Angeles harbor by "Count" Gustav Kallang; the painting was Port Angeles' entry in Chicago's World Columbian Expedition one year later. In 1892, the first brick house in Port Angeles was constructed. It was erected on 6th Street, between Cherry and Oak, by Mike Geraghty, using bricks manufactured in his own brickyard. Also in 1892, the County Medical Association was founded locally on March 3rd, Andrew Jacobsen discovered Olympic Hot Springs west of the city limits, and the steamer *Matilda* was built.[10] Near the end of Norman Smith's first term, he and his colleagues again divided the town, this time into six wards, each represented by one councilman, with a seventh at-large.

Of little note in 1892 – but an event of long-term importance to the city – was a poster printed and widely circulated, advertising Port Angeles as the "best harbor on the Pacific Coast." It was this poster which brought Gregers Marius Lauridsen to Port Angeles. As we shall see, Lauridsen was to have a weighty impact on the town.

In September of 1892, a colony of The Grand Army of the Republic (G.A.R.)[11] from Michigan arrived aboard the steamer *Garland*. Among them was Ismael Filion, his son and his brother – men who were to own and run a sawmill (known affectionately as "The Grand Army Mill") in Port Angeles for many years. Wages from the Filion mill and the monthly pensions of $10 and $15 received by G.A.R. members were to be the primary sources of funds in the cash-poor city of Port Angeles for over 20 years!

It was also in 1892 that the road between Port Angeles and New Dungeness (near what is now the city of Sequim) was built. Cursed by travelers because it was not surfaced with crushed rock, the roadway maintained a layer of dust sometimes a foot thick and in the rainy season was a sea of mud!

Eighteen-ninety-three was a significant year in United States history. The Great Northern Railway completed its cross-country trek all the way to Washington State, the nation returned to the Gold Standard, Johns Hopkins Medical School was founded and the first Ford motor car was tested. Elsewhere in the world, Roentgen's X-Rays and an anti-diphtheria serum enhanced the world of medicine, and Marconi's wireless telegraph dramatically improved the communications field.

Nevertheless, most old-timers did not recall 1893 with great fondness. Especially old-timers in Port Angeles, Washington. Residents of the little town vividly remembered it as the year of a great snowfall and . . . another depression, this one usually referred to simply as "hard times."

Snow started falling in downtown Port Angeles January 27th and fell every day until February 7th, dumping 75.1 inches on the young community. And it was cold. During that 12-day span, the extreme lowest temperature ever known in Port Angeles – 1 degree below zero – was recorded (January 31st).

In other events, later that year: Alexander Sampson, one of Port Angeles' earliest settlers, died; the *Lydia Thompson*, 92 feet long, with a 22-foot beam, was built at Fred and Rex Thompson's shipyard;[12] and a spectacular, fatal shooting took place on the northwest corner of Front and Laurel Streets, involving two prominent local citizens, Judge S. P. Carusi and Dr. L. R. Herrick. (Herrick died, Carusi was acquitted – "self defense" – and soon thereafter ran for reelection!)[13]

Then, despite the onrushing business panic that seemed to be throttling the entire country – destined to persist for three to four years – two brief flurries of industrial excitement occurred. One was a move to manufacture turpentine using local wood products. (One Port Angeles editor chortled "if . . . fir stumps can be . . . converted into turpentine, we will have another industry . . . for which we have unlimited raw material. The invasion of the East by Puget Sound turpentine will be as overwhelming as the red cedar shingle.")[14] The other, more than a little zany even for those wild times, advocated the mining of gold from beneath the streets of Port Angeles![15] The first venture proved to be unprofitable and the second was declared illegal.

The depression, by now enveloping much of the world, had begun to suck the United States down into one of its gloomiest economic periods in history. Real estate values plummeted, shipping was paralyzed from coast to coast and very little construction took place. Virtually all capital investment was frozen and those banks which didn't fail were able to lend money on only topnotch collateral.

Certainly such momentous events impacted heavily on Port Angeles, and for several years real cash ranged from scarce to nonexistent. In fact, the sight of valid United States currency on the town's streets was a much-talked-about event. The story is told that a counterfeit bill – either $5 or $10 – was practically the only money circulating throughout Port Angeles for a long time. When the bank finally

ANOTHER VIEW OF FRONT STREET looking west in 1892, featuring the "hog back" path on the left. First dock shown on right was located at the foot of what is now Lincoln Street (the thoroughfare had not yet been cut through to the beach). Beyond that is Morse Dock at the north end of Laurel Street. The Holly-wood Beach area (lower right), now occupied by the Red Lion Bay Shore Inn, was at that time a popular camping ground for Indians traveling the Strait. PHOTO SOURCE: Bert Kellogg

caught up with it and informed Tom Watson, its current owner, that it was phony, Watson replied, "I know it, my lad, but it is all we have . . . it's doing a good job!" — *and the bill continued to circulate!*[16] Whether true or not (some who lived through those times said they didn't believe there was *that* much money circulating!), the tale graphically illustrates Port Angeles' precarious financial picture in 1893.

However, that old familiar friend Yankee Ingenuity, reared its head once again when a resourceful Port Angelen and his unique monetary plan helped the town through its financial woes.

OLDEST BUSINESS IN PORT ANGELES. The Johnson and Bork Paint Store has been operating continuously since January, 1892, and is still doing business at the northeast corner of Front and Lincoln Streets. Charles Bork and Herman Johnson opened this business in the Mallette Building between Oak and Laurel Streets, across from what is now Port Angeles City Hall. Shortly after the turn of the century, the two men moved their business to its present location. PHOTO SOURCE: *Port Angeles Evening News*

G.M. LAURIDSEN, standing at left in this photo, came to Port Angeles in 1892. Reputed to be the town's first millionaire, the astute Lauridsen started with a grocery store and later turned to real estate and banking. Upon his death, most of Lauridsen's fortune was allocated to charitable purposes. The Lauridsen home shown here still stands atop a hill at Second and Lincoln Streets. PHOTO SOURCE: Bert Kellogg

Lauridsen Money

Port Angeles' dwindling population was left virtually alone and deserted when the hard times of the not-always-so-Gay Nineties landed. Living in an isolated community, those people remaining had to work hard just to stay alive, most eking out a living by hunting in the thick woods or by fishing and clamming. The only money in town was that being generated by the sale of cedar shingles and by the G.A.R. pension checks. Port Angeles' only bank had failed in June of 1893 and local businessmen were forced to carry out normal bank functions — including cashing checks (at a discount, naturally, since what little currency there was had to be shipped in from Seattle).

Such was the setting for one of the more amazing chapters in Port Angeles' — and the nation's — financial history.

Gregers M. Lauridsen was a reputable store owner who acted as broker for practically all the shingle mills then operating in the county. Mill owners shipping their products to big export towns such as Port Ludlow or Port Hadlock could always expect a 90- to 180-day waiting period before payment was received. Many of them, therefore, were forced to borrow large sums from the astute Lauridsen just to keep their doors open. A good businessman, the store owner also generously offered credit to the mill workers so they could buy groceries, hardware and other goods at his store. Eventually, even Lauridsen's considerable resources were strained and it was then he conceived of an ingenious device with which he

LAURIDSEN MONEY. Coins and paper money shown here were stamped and printed respectively by Gregers M. Lauridsen shortly after the failure of Port Angeles' only bank in June, 1893. The country was in a severe financial panic, and cash was scarce. Lauridsen, a Port Angeles grocer at the time, began lending both money and credit at his store. He ordered aluminum coins from a catalog store, had his personal stamp put on them — and simultaneously began printing paper bills. "Lauridsen money" worked well in the isolated community for over ten years but eventually was taken out of circulation by the U.S. Treasury Department. PHOTO SOURCE: Pete Capos and Clallam County Museum

EARLY PHOTO OF FIRST STREET in Port Angeles, circa 1893, showing the First Congregational Church, Old Central School and the First Methodist Episcopal Church. The First Congregational building is still in use, though not as a church. Old Central later became the Washington School, and is now the site occupied by the United States Postal Service building. The First Methodist Church building was sold to the Central Labor Council in 1929 and was torn down in April, 1932. PHOTO SOURCE: Bert Kellogg

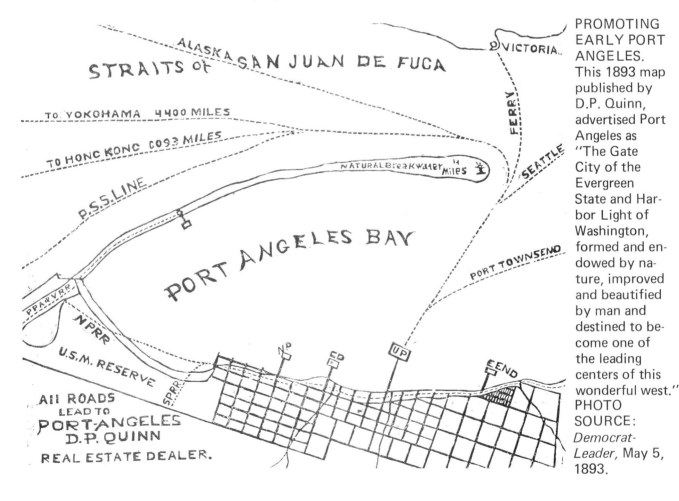

PROMOTING EARLY PORT ANGELES. This 1893 map published by D.P. Quinn, advertised Port Angeles as "The Gate City of the Evergreen State and Harbor Light of Washington, formed and endowed by nature, improved and beautified by man and destined to become one of the leading centers of this wonderful west." PHOTO SOURCE: *Democrat-Leader,* May 5, 1893.

TAKEN FROM THE HARBOR, this excellent photo of a bustling Port Angeles was taken about 1893. Though the government Reserve had by this time been "broken," one can still see from this shot, the heavily forested area running south from the waterfront. Immense Douglas Firs and dense foliage, coupled with "reserve" status conferred earlier upon Victor Smith's "Second National City," had prevented any significant development until 1890. At that time, squatters moved onto the land and staked out lots, ultimately forcing the federal government to open it for public sale. The First Baptist Church is seen on the hill at Second and Oak Streets; the City Hotel at extreme left, and the Merchants Hotel to right of center, above boat. PHOTO SOURCE: Bert Kellogg

COUNT GUSTAV KALLANG painting of Ediz Hook now hangs in the Clallam County Museum. Kallang, an itinerant artist, was paid $200 by townspeople for the eight-by-ten foot painting, selected as Port Angeles' entry in the 1893 World Columbian Exposition in Chicago. To pay for the painting and the wide, gilt frame in which it is enclosed, townspeople sponsored dances, masquerades and other social events. Chief fund-raiser was an elaborate production of the opera "Chimes of Normandy" in the Port Angeles Opera House. PHOTO SOURCE: Bert Kellogg

could minimize bookkeeping, help keep the crippled local economy alive and still maintain personal financial stability.

Lauridsen began manufacturing his own money.

By itself, the simple expediency of printing one's own cash and stamping personalized aluminum coins — both of which G. M. Lauridsen did — is not historically rare. (Indeed, in Port Angeles itself, the Puget Sound Cooperative Colony had by this time been producing currency, and it was in limited use.) What made "Lauridsen Money" stand out from other such currency fads was the obvious fact that it worked.

For 10 long years, tokens and paper money ($5 and $1 bills; 5 -10-and 25-cent coins) manufactured by G. M. Lauridsen enjoyed wide circulation and complete acceptance throughout the Olympic Peninsula from Port Townsend to Neah Bay — backed only by the sterling reputation of its creator. Given originally to mill workers so they could purchase staples in his store, "Lauridsen Money" (or "Port Angeles Money" as it was also known) increased available working capital in the county and always was redeemable at face value as though it were real Uncle Sam cash. The end came when a naive Port Angeles woman tried to use it to buy stamps at a Seattle Post Office. The Treasury Department was notified and a subsequent inspection resulted in discontinuance of the practice. All "Port Angeles Money" was recalled and Lauridsen, who candidly admitted to his actions, was counseled but not punished in any way for engaging in his 10-year "competition" with Uncle Sam's valid currency.

Most local historians who have analyzed the situation credit Lauridsen's clever idea with being the key element in easing the town over an incredibly bad financial period.[17]

Perhaps the city's only real bright spot during 1893 occurred in August, when Port Angeles residents received official notice from the Government that the reserve land, which had for so long gripped the town, would be put up for sale at a time of their choosing. Citizens chose January 1, 1894 . . . and then it all sank in. They knew with dead certainty that the mammoth risk they'd taken three-and-one-half years earlier had paid off. It was over and they, the squatters, had won!

The great day arrived, the first day of the year. United States Land Office Registrar William D. O'Toole (pressed into service as auctioneer) offered a congratulatory speech, then presided over an opening day which featured pomp and circumstance. Just before the auction started, those who had broken the reserve presented themselves to Mr. O'Toole, gave affidavits and provided witnesses verifying that they had improved the land; then after paying a small fee, they were handed the precious deeds to their property. The public auction began, lasted until January 22nd and culminated two days after that with a stupendous, three-hour speech by Mr. O'Toole setting forth for his bored audience a monotonous litany of statistics and pertinent data accumulated during that time. Some lots (1,760) remained unsold, but they later were deeded to out-of-town buyers.

Summarized, the grand affair — including sales made subsequent to the January 22, 1894 closing — brought in a total of $57,718.00.[18]

Chapter Five: 1894 — 1913

Railroad Fever and the Turn of the Century

"Nothing dampens the ardor of a true railroad promoter."

— Patricia Campbell
**A History of the
North Olympic Peninsula**

By 1894, Port Angeles folk had grown accustomed to talk of a railroad coming to town. Six years earlier, while the Colonists were still publishing their newspaper, a feeble attempt to get something started had been made by an obscure firm calling itself The Port Angeles and West Shore Railroad Company. It published an advertisement in **The Model Commonwealth**[1] offering stock for sale, and was but the first of 14 separate attempts — virtually all of them undercapitalized and speculative — to lure a mainline railroad to Port Angeles, seeking to link the town with the great metropolitan centers of the country.[2]

Another period of frenzied excitement had taken place in 1890 when three promoters, Iris Clapp, John Lutz and A. R. Coleman, secured tacit approval from the Northern Pacific to run track from Port Crescent (west of town) through the Olympic Mountains south to Grays Harbor. Their Port Crescent and Chehalis Railroad Company was vigorously promoted, but again, no funds . . . no rails. When a third company, the Port Angeles and Central Railway, crumbled for lack of a cash foundation later that same year, one would think promoters might have begun exercising caution. And they probably would have, had the next ride on the rails not come so close to working. It was the Union Pacific's effort which was to instill the notion among townspeople that a great transcontinental railway would soon wind its way into town.

The Union Pacific Railroad Company had begun moving into town a few months earlier, and in 1890 proceeded to do something no other promoter's

REAR ADMIRAL LESLIE A. BEARDSLEE, Commander of the U.S. Navy's Pacific Fleet. The fleet was an annual visitor to the Port Angeles harbor for almost 40 years, beginning in 1895. Beardslee, an avid fisherman, often fished Lake Crescent, west of town. Two species of trout peculiar to that body of water had never been named, so Beardslee sent samples of both to the Smithsonian Institution which, after examination, designated them the Beardslee and Crescenti after the Admiral and the Lake respectively. PHOTO SOURCE: Bert Kellogg

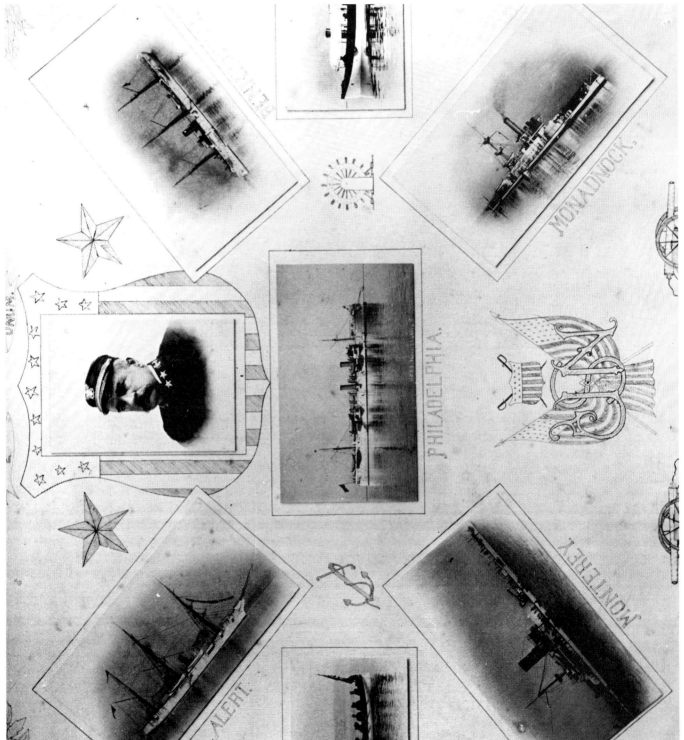

PARADE ON FRONT STREET. Looking east on Front Street, circa 1895, military personnel parade through downtown area. Most were probably sailors from the Pacific Fleet then stationed in the Port Angeles harbor. Some, though, might have been local residents, who were Civil War veterans, for the Grand Army of the Republic (GAR) boasted many members in the Port Angeles area, and conducted an annual Memorial Day parade. PHOTO SOURCE: Clallam County Museum

FIRST GRADUATION CLASS. The six scholars shown here were Port Angeles' first High School graduation class, in 1895. Attending classes — all grades, one to twelve — in the Old Central School, the six men received the bulk of their High School instruction from O.A. Tiffany, who doubled as School Superintendent. The six graduates were: (seated) Roy McClinton, George Meagher and Edgar McCormick; (standing, left to right) Frank Cram, A.N. Taylor and Ray McLaughlin. PHOTO SOURCE: Clallam County Museum

COLONEL JAMES S. COOLICAN, extreme left, shown here at a picnic near Morse Creek. The energetic Coolican was a real estate promoter who longed to make Port Angeles the center of commercial activity on the west coast. Among other things, he published a pamphlet advertising Port Angeles as "The Gate City of the Pacific Coast." That pamphlet was responsible for luring hundreds of people to this area.
PHOTO SOURCE: Clallam County Museum

pipe dream had accomplished: It presented a specific plan of action — and actually *brought money!* Operating an office in Port Angeles for two years, there was not even a hint of a local stock sale, huckstering, or schemers beating the bushes; the aroma was that of stability rather than speculation. In addition to the office, the well-heeled railroad giant installed Major R. R. Harding as its agent, and built a dock for ocean-going vessels at the bottom of Lincoln Street. One of the Union Pacific's subsidiaries, the Oregon Navigation Company, even placed a ship, the new side-wheeler *George E. Starr*, on a daily run from Port Angeles to Port Townsend. Prosperity reigned. Real estate sold and resold at inflated prices and just about everybody knew the boom was here to stay.

Wrong.

When the 1893 Panic began choking the nation's economy, the Union Pacific — which already had spent millions of dollars running lines from eastern cities to Olympia — abandoned plans for Port Angeles, opting instead for Seattle and Tacoma. The Port Angeles office closed, the firm's agent left town and many Port Angelens were stunned, finding themselves to be what G. M. Lauridsen later described as "property poor."[3] Though a terrible blow emotionally, residents could at least breathe a sigh of relief that no local capital departed with the Union Pacific. Port Angeles would not be quite so lucky over the course of the next nine such attempts.

These railroad promoters were tenacious but naive. Even though this was a boisterous era, when all things seemed possible and even the wildest schemes were calmly taken as inevitable, some of these men, it seems, just could not differentiate between fact and fantasy. They tried again and again and again, even though most couldn't even grasp the magnitude of the transcontinental projects they sought to attract. Their promotions failed for that very reason.

Nevertheless, though railroad tracks would not wriggle their way along the Strait into Port Angeles until well into the 20th Century, the irresistible lure of the rails did something else: It brought to this area some highly intelligent, imaginative men who wouldn't take "no" for an answer and who were relentless in pursuit of their goals. These men would provide guidance and initiative in the years ahead, solidifying the town's place in 20th Century America. Men like James S. Coolican and M. J. Carrigan joined others such as Norman Smith and G. M. Lauridsen to form the city's core of leadership for many years.

Carrigan, Coal . . . The County Fair

Promoter M. J. Carrigan, in 1894, deviated somewhat from his favorite realm, railroads, to elicit

MADGE NAILOR. This photograph of the prominent Mrs. Nailor is thought to have been taken around 1900 when she was 20 years of age. Madge Nailor came to Port Angeles in 1887 with her parents, Mr. and Mrs. Lorenzo Haynes, members of the Puget Sound Cooperative Colony. Her family remained in the area after the colony disbanded, and Mrs. Nailor became active in community affairs. She was appointed Treasurer of the City of Port Angeles, serving in that capacity for 30 years, and was also one of the founders of the Clallam County Historical Society. Mrs. Nailor died March 9, 1976 at age 96. PHOTO SOURCE: Bert Kellogg

from local residents a genuine interest in coal mining. Port Angeles' newfound enthusiasm for this mineral had been roused earlier that same year when Norman Smith, Lewis Levy and Major William F. Hooker

FIRST CLALLAM COUNTY FAIR (1895) was held in the Opera House, and featured this imposing pyramid of canned salmon arranged by Port Angeles' own National Packing Company. The cannery, established four years earlier, was one of Port Angeles' steady employers for years, retailing "American Flag" salmon throughout the west. At the time this photo was taken, John Hume was the company's manager. PHOTO SOURCE: Clallam County Museum

THE ANGELES BREWING AND MALTING COMPANY, located at the mouth of Tumwater Creek. Built by Charles H. Hirsch and Fred A. Jensen in 1902, the brewery had a capacity of 6,000 barrels per year, and ran its own freight ship the *Albion* between Port Angeles and Seattle. PHOTO SOURCE: Clallam County Museum

THE *ALBION*, owned and operated by the Angeles Brewing and Malting Company, was rammed by the steamship *Chippewa* on August 4, 1910. Though there were no fatalities, the incident was frightening beyond belief, for on that day, the *Albion* was loaded with passengers — and dynamite! Among the Port Angeles passengers were the now well-known Ivor and Don Smith, being transported to Seattle with their mother, Mrs. William Smith. PHOTO SOURCE: Ivor Smith

ANGELES BEER SERVING TRAY. Angeles Beer was an excellent product, which its manufacturers marketed successfully throughout the Puget Sound area. As part of that marketing process, taverns were encouraged to serve the foamy liquid from colorful, humorous trays such as the one shown here. PHOTO SOURCE: Sandy Keys

PORT ANGELES BEER. Brewed by the Angeles Brewing and Malting Company on Valley Street, Angeles Beer was a popular beverage throughout the State of Washington from 1902 to 1920. Over 6,000 barrels were produced annually, most being shipped to Seattle and points east by the *Albion* a company-owned freighter. PHOTO SOURCE: Sandy Keys

BARREL FACTORY ON VALLEY CREEK, relied almost exclusively on the Angeles Brewing and Malting Company for business. The factory was forced to stop production in 1920 when the brewery closed. PHOTO SOURCE: Bert Kellogg

made a couple of attempts to get drilling started.[4] After attracting a few Ohio capitalists, Carrigan rounded up $10,000 locally to purchase a diamond drill, which, after many anxious weeks, arrived on October 18th. The speculators — assisted by what had by this time become a zealous group of townspeople — carried it to Tumwater Valley on the west side of town and there began drilling destined to reach 600 feet, biting all the way through sand, clay, boulders and gravel. No coal. No Ohio money . . . for coal or railroads.[5]

During 1894, despite the depression and railroad non-success — and a noticeably dwindling population — the town still managed to register signs of progress, as it opened Ocean View Cemetery and began the grading of Tumwater Hill from Second to Fifth Streets.[6]

Over the next several years, Port Angeles, much like dozens of other western communities, seemed to have settled into a work-a-day routine, interrupted only sporadically by the inevitable railroad flurries. The city welcomed new businesses, established or-

ganizations and, like the rest of the world, gaped in slack-jaw amazement at the first of the wondrous contraptions known as the telephone.

The first County Fair was held in the Port Angeles Opera House in 1895 in honor of Rear Admiral Leslie A. Beardslee of the *Philadelphia,* the flagship of the Pacific Fleet; (the fleet would later become a frequent visitor to these waters).[7] Elks Naval Lodge No. 353 was established one year later.[8] And amidst excited talk of the new, mammoth Klondike Gold Strike — destined to lure to Alaska and the Pacific Northwest many kinds of adventurous folk — M. J. Carrigan organized the Clallam County Immigration Association for the noble purpose of encouraging "a desirable class of immigrants to settle in Clallam County."[9]

One year later, President Grover Cleveland issued an executive order setting aside a large tract of land to be known as the Olympic National Forest. Also that year, Carrigan's group produced and distributed a pamphlet entitled "Port Angeles, the Gate City of the Pacific Coast;" the first hardware store in Port

Angeles, operated by Robert D. Willson, opened in a small Front Street building, and a promoter by the name of Michael Earles built the Puget Sound Sawmill and Shingle Company just a few miles west of Port Angeles. Earles would later do big things for Port Angeles itself.

Eighteen-ninety-eight was a year of lively expectations for both the nation and the ambitious little city along the Strait of Juan de Fuca. It was an action-packed time, with maturing, self-confident Americans clearly able to sense their approaching pre-eminence on the world stage. When the U.S.S. *Maine* was blown up in Havana Harbor in February, Spain was blamed (even though the country's culpability was never proved), war was declared in April and one week later the enemy's entire fleet of 10 vessels was destroyed at Manila, without loss of American life or damage to American ships. The brief Spanish-American War ended suddenly and in a surge of nationalistic pride.

Perhaps more important to Port Angeles residents in 1898, though, relief from the cash crunch was in sight. Hard times were almost over and it appeared they could once again get on with the vital business of linking up with the rest of the world. Improved communication was much on their minds. One citizen, C. J. Farmer, who operated a cannery in the west end of town (near what is now the Merrill and Ring, Inc. Timber Company), could not traverse the beach road at high tide and apparently suffered the pangs of loneliness. To alleviate them, he strung a line to the telegraph office downtown, quickly becoming the envy of his neighbors, for the line became, in effect, the luxury of a private telephone. Predictably enough, the cannery owner was soon deluged with requests from merchants wanting to tap in and, being an enterprising fellow, he soon bought a small switchboard with which to start an exchange. Ultimately the alert Farmer serviced over 100 customers with his line.

By the turn of the century, plans were under way to establish a city streetcar line (it never arrived) and for construction of a large wharf on the waterfront near Tumwater (to serve a planned shingle mill nearby). Moreover, a large brewery was being proposed by Frederick Antoine Jensen. Things were looking up!

Less than two years later, though, the entire country was reeling from the September 1901, assassination of President William McKinley,[10] and the ghastly shadow of a nationwide smallpox epidemic hovered over the land. Nineteen-oh-two started with Albert Smith, the City Health Officer, ordering vaccinations for everybody in town to prevent a local outbreak of the dreaded, often fatal disease. City Council members, feeling drastic measures were called for, banned all public meetings and ordered saloon crowds be dispersed by police. The Post Office was closed during mail distribution and all illnesses of a "questionable nature" were to be called to the attention of the City Health Officer on pain of fine, imprisonment or both.[11]

Then, as if the threat of pestilence weren't bad enough, rumor had it that Uncle Sam planned to take from the U.S. Lighthouse Reserve all land not actually needed for lighthouse purposes (this never happened, but the rumor was terribly upsetting in 1902).

The town's pendulum of fortune seemed to reverse itself, however, when the irrepressible Norman Smith filed Articles of Incorporation for his Port Angeles Pacific Railroad, again destined to kindle a railroad flap. Port Angeles' first phone company, The Angeles Telephone and Telegraph Company, officially opened, bringing the outside world just a little closer[12] and Angeles Brewing and Malting Company's building was erected at the mouth of Tumwater Creek. The brewery, which produced 6,000 barrels annually, used its own ship, the *Albion,* to freight the popular "Angeles Beer" to Seattle regularly. It was destined to last until Prohibition forced its closure.

"The Baron"

The year 1902 is also remembered in Port Angeles as "The Year of the Baron" – Baron Martin Von Schlosser. Telling Port Angeles folks he was from an old German family of nobility, the Baron quickly made a reputation for himself as a jovial, wealthy companion and a terrific party-giver. Fascinating stories were told about him and his soirées – culminating in a grisly tale about his reported death (he was allegedly killed by a bear near Lake Crescent). Much insulted because his friends hadn't even bothered to search for him during his prolonged absence, the Baron left town in a huff and some time elapsed before word reached Port Angeles that he had been jailed for stealing a $5,000 ring from a Detroit woman. Perhaps, it was rumored, Port Angeles citizens had actually been in the presence of a famous international swindler and fugitive from justice! Disappointingly though, at the trial in Detroit it was proved that before moving to the Northwest Baron Von Schlosser had been merely a chef in a St. Louis restaurant.[13]

Before the year ended, Congress passed a far-reaching piece of legislation, the National Reclamation Act, authorizing the Federal Government to construct great irrigation dams throughout the western United States.

VON SCHLOSSER BANQUET in the Merchants Hotel at Front and Laurel Streets. This photo, thought to have been taken in 1902, shows "Baron" Martin Von Schlosser at bottom left, hosting a banquet which was attended by virtually every prominent man in town. Von Schlosser was a jovial, easygoing "man of means," who entertained lavishly during his brief stay in Port Angeles. He claimed to be a member of the German nobility. Years later, however, Port Angelens discovered that he actually was a swindler and fugitive from justice, having stolen jewelry from a woman in Detroit before traveling to the Olympic Peninsula. PHOTO SOURCE: Bert Kellogg

RAILROAD CONNECTIONS were deemed necessary to the successful early day western town. After many fruitless promotions, Norman Smith's Port Angeles Pacific Railroad Company purchased a locomotive and shipped it to town aboard the steamer *Rapid Transit*. This unique photo shows the lokey being unloaded at the Morse Dock, February 5, 1903. PHOTO SOURCE: Clallam County Museum

"Norman No. 1"

Under the direction of partners Dr. Donald McGillivray and Dr. Samuel Whitfield Hartt (the latter a graduate of Johns Hopkins Medical School), General Hospital began operations at Eighth and Peabody in 1903. Conceived originally so the two physicians could care for the fleet stationed in the harbor, this hospital also served numerous logging camps and small shingle mills throughout the area.[14]

And then . . . another major resurgence of Railroad Fever. The tireless Norman Smith and his Port Angeles Pacific Railroad stoked the fires vigorously this time, raising hopes that Port Angeles' long-sought coupling with a major line was imminent. By the latter part of 1902, he had secured funds from Elmira, New York capitalists and begun the paperwork necessary to land his prize. Easily obtaining approval from City Council to pass over and along certain streets, the PAPRR actually began laying track up Tumwater Street in the spring of 1903. The community, so often discouraged in the past by similar affairs which fizzled, really began to buzz with excitement this time. Soon people were ecstatic, for Norman continued prodding and soon had driven his rails a full three miles through the woods into the valley. Then, looming before the very eyes of a skeptical town, its residents blinking in disbelief, there was a locomotive, the "Norman No. 1." A real railroad, at last!

Norman Smith and two others, E. B. Mastick (a former Colony Board member) and James Stewart, soon formed the Smith-Mastick Construction Company so they could lock up the contract to run tracks into western Clallam County. Smith even threw a fun-filled party aboard the train's flatcar — he had it fitted with seats — and transported about fifty people up the line to the stone quarry. Things looked too good to be true . . . and they were.

In October, construction halted and Smith's Elmira backers conducted a secret investigation of affairs in Port Angeles. Investigator, Frederick C. Chandler put nothing in writing but it is known that he was dissatisfied with certain transactions carried out by the principals. He returned to Elmira still carrying the $35,000 check given him to deposit if the situation appeared to warrant such action . . . and gave his report.

Money from Elmira evaporated immediately. Smith and his associates applied to the courts for receivership; the person appointed though, was none other than one of the principals in the Smith-Mastick Construction Company, James Stewart. He didn't keep his post. When word of the shady transactions came to the attention of Judge James Hatch, Stewart's appointment was terminated and he was

THE NORMAN NUMBER 1, shown rusting away near what is now the Port Angeles Boat Haven. Named for Norman Smith, son of Port Angeles founder Victor Smith, the locomotive was purchased and brought to town in 1903 to demonstrate the validity of Smith's Port Angeles Pacific Railroad. Smith laid rails three full miles up Tumwater Valley (now the Port Angeles Truck Route) and the Port Angeles Pacific Railroad smelled of success. However, as with almost every other railroad promotion that came to town, funds disappeared and the dream collapsed. The lokey was taken to Seattle in 1907, later dismantled, and sold for scrap during World War One.
PHOTO SOURCE: Bert Kellogg

APPARENTLY A G.M. LAURIDSEN IDEA, this "Bank of Prosperity" certificate made payable to Jessie Ayres and signed by Lauridsen, was one of many early promotions by local businessmen. Lauridsen, Colonel James Coolican and others worked tirelessly to sell Port Angeles as a future northwest metropolis. Little information exists as to how successful the "Bank of Prosperity" was. PHOTO SOURCE: North Olympic Library System

WESTPHAL COUNTY HOME on Mount Angeles Road. Hans (Henry) Westphal died August 20, 1902, leaving land and money for a home for the indigent. With additional money provided by County Commissioners, the Westphal Home was erected in 1904 and provided more than 60 years of service to the Port Angeles community. During the 1920s, it carried the unfortunate nickname "Pest House," when it served as a haven for patients with tuberculosis and other contagious diseases. Later, it was known as the County Poor Farm, and still later as the Port Angeles Nursing Home. The building was razed in 1966. PHOTO SOURCE: Clallam County Museum

THE *CLALLAM,* victim of the worst marine disaster in the history of the Strait of Juan de Fuca. On January 9, 1904, with a total of about 87 persons aboard (exact number unknown), the *Clallam* encountered a severe storm and lost her pumps. Built before the days of radio, she was unable to communicate her plight, became disabled, and drifted for almost 24 hours before going to the bottom between Dungeness and Smith Island. At least 55 people died in the storm-tossed waters. Seafarers of that day were fond of saying that the *Clallam* was jinxed, because she had been launched with her flag upside down! PHOTO SOURCE: Bert Kellogg

replaced by C. J. Farmer. Despite another last-ditch attempt by Smith to bail out the beleaguered company with money from a New York bank, it was too late. The receivership was closed, the engine known as "Norman No. 1" began to rust away and finally was scrapped during the First World War.

As 1904 got under way, all Puget Sound was horrified by the worst marine disaster ever to occur in the Strait of Juan de Fuca. On January 9th, the brand-new steamer *Clallam* encountered a gale while making a run from Seattle to Victoria, B.C., took on water and went down between New Dungeness and Smith Island. At least 55 people were lost in the tragedy — including *all* the women and children. The tally is probably inaccurate, for little attention was paid to a passenger list. Built at a time when ships were not yet equipped with radio, the 167-foot *Clallam* was nevertheless considered quite

safe. Its sinking resulted in the enactment of strict measures to protect passengers' lives on inland waters. The Canadian Pacific immediately started to run large ocean-going vessels between Seattle and Victoria, a policy still intact today.[15]

Later that year, word reached town that construction of a vast, dangerous project known as the Panama Canal was under way and that a delightful novelty item, the ice-cream cone, had been introduced at the St. Louis World's Fair. Closer to home, the Post Office Department thoughtfully provided the first two street letter boxes in downtown Port Angeles, Cooke's Prairie (later called Lincoln Park) was founded on 170 acres,[16] and Congressman Francis E. Cushman made a sincere effort to preserve a vital part of the Olympic wilderness by introducing a bill to establish a large preserve known as "Elk National Park." The project became controversial

Newspapers

The story of newspapering in Port Angeles, like the history of the town itself, is snarled and hectic. What follows is an honest effort to unravel the tangled assortment of openings, closings, mergers and re-mergers which zig-zag their way through Port Angeles' early years.

The Model Commonwealth, a weekly, started May 21, 1886 in Seattle and was brought to Port Angeles by the Puget Sound Cooperative Colony when it settled here one year later. It thus became the first newspaper in Clallam County. After dropping the word "Model" from its masthead, **The Commonwealth** ran for two years (or until the demise of the colony experiment), at which time it was taken over by Mr. A. H. Howells. Howells moved the paper's location to the 1889 version of "downtown" and began publishing it under a new banner, **The Port Angeles Times**. In a short time, however, he was bought out by two veteran newsmen, Arthur A. Smith and Horace White, who ran the **Times** until 1891.

During the fall of 1890, Col. R. H. Ballinger and his son Joseph had begun publication of a competitive weekly, **The Port Angeles Tribune**, managing it until April 20, 1892, when it merged with the Smith-White paper to become **The Tribune-Times**. (For a short time in 1892 — from January to August — **The Tribune-Times** ran as **The Daily Tribune**, thus becoming the first daily paper in Port Angeles.[17]) **The Tribune-Times** was destined to run as a weekly for 26 years, until 1918.

In May, 1892, shortly after **The Tribune-Times** merger, Mr. John W. Troy — who would later become the Governor of Alaska — founded **The Democrat** and one

year later merged it with a more recent arrival, **The Leader**, which the well-known promoter M. J. Carrigan had moved to town from Port Crescent. The offspring of this corporate marriage was christened **The Democrat-Leader**.

Even though several small papers opened their doors thereafter (and closed them with great rapidity[18]), no other significant changes occurred until 1904 when **The Olympic** was founded by a gentleman whose name would long be associated with newspapering in the Northwest: Edward Barton Webster. Webster, his father, son, daughter and daughters-in-law were for 65 years linked to the publishing of Olympic Peninsula daily papers.

In 1905, E. B. Webster bought A. J. (Andy) Cosser's **Democrat-Leader**, then merged it with his own **Olympic** to form the **Olympic-Leader**. (Cosser had bought the **Democrat-Leader** from Troy and Carrigan in 1896, with Troy remaining as editor for a few years; when he left for Alaska in 1898, Cosser became editor and publisher.) The newly-created **Olympic-Leader** would later gain considerable fame by bringing the first Linotype machine to the Peninsula; until that time all local papers had been entirely handset.

Port Angeles in 1906 thus featured two weekly newspapers, with the **Tribune-Times** and the **Olympic-Leader** (which later ran concurrently as the **Olympic-Tribune**) in direct competition. This situation remained virtually unchanged until 1913, when for several months the **Olympic-Leader** became a semi-weekly, couldn't make it and went back to weekly status. Serious competition for the two weeklies arrived in

E.B. WEBSTER, author, publisher and naturalist. Founder of the *Port Angeles Evening News* (now the *Daily News)* in 1916, Webster also wrote three books about the Olympics and developed the famous Klahhane Gardens near the Heart o' the Hills. There he grew more varieties of mountain flowers and plants than anybody on the Pacific Coast. After his death in 1936, a mountain peak, a flower and the gardens were named after him.
PHOTO SOURCE: Port Angeles *Daily News*

JESSIE TRUMBULL WEBSTER, a woman ahead of her time. Active in local affairs, Mrs. Webster spearheaded the campaign for Port Angeles' first public library — and later was instrumental in establishing a system of parks throughout the city. She was President of the *Port Angeles Evening News* for four years prior to her death in 1940.
PHOTO SOURCE: Dorothy Wenner

December, 1915, when entrepeneur Michael Earles and several other timbermen took over the equipment of a defunct weekly (**The Bee**) and founded the **Daily Herald**. Webster then made a strategic move: On April 10, 1916, he and Olympic-Tribune's A.A. Smith, while retaining ownership of and continuing to publish their rival weeklies, joined forced

to do battle against Earles' **Daily Herald**. Webster and Smith, consummate newsmen, began publishing their own daily and the evolution of a long-running, influential paper was complete: **The Port Angeles Evening News** was born.

This brief synopsis of newspaper publishing in early-day Port Angeles will be resumed in Chapter Seven.

FIRST AUTOMOBILE IN CLALLAM COUNTY, was a two-cylinder 1906 Buick with chain drive owned by James H. Gibson. Gibson bought the car in Seattle and transported it to Port Williams (just east of Sequim) on the steamer *Rosalie.* The sturdy old vehicle has been preserved, and is presently owned by Dr. Harlan McNutt, former Port Angeles resident. PHOTO SOURCE: Bert Kellogg

MATILDA C. COOPER, known affectionately as
"Auntie Cooper," well-known early Port Angeles
woman. Civic-minded and sensitive, Mrs. Cooper's
tireless work in 1894 persuaded federal officials to
donate land to the city for Ocean View Cemetery.
She also was one of the leaders in the formation of
the First Episcopal Church in Port Angeles, and in
1904 was instrumental, along with then-Mayor Freeborn Stanton Lewis, in obtaining congressional action
for the formation of what would later (1925) be
called Lincoln Park. PHOTO SOURCE: First Episcopal Church, Port Angeles

locally and failed; however, his effort did persuade
the State Legislature to pass a law prohibiting the
slaughter of elk for their teeth (a long-established
practice of poachers, who used the teeth to make
watch fobs!). Newspapers that year noted that the
city's new light plant was running smoothly and that
a new "Poor Farm" (real name Westphal County
Home) had been constructed three miles south of
town on property willed to the County by Hans
(Henry) Westphal, a rather eccentric German who had
come to Port Angeles as one of the early Colonists.
The Westphal Home would remain a comfortable
center for indigents for 36 years.[19]

Americans in 1905 were reading Upton Sinclair's
novel, "The Jungle," a stunning expose' of the meat-
packing industry. Most, however, had only a vague
understanding of the importance of Albert Einstein's

widely-publicized Mass and Energy Formula, $E=MC^2$.
In Port Angeles, it was the start of a rather calm
period. The most imporant events of the next two
years included: Congressional passage of a law
authorizing construction of a new $10,000 fog
signal (with a double dwelling adjacent to it) on
Ediz Hook (1905);[20] the opening of the Angeles
Monument and Building Company on Morse Dock
(1906); O. J. Morse's new Parlor Theatre on Front
Street (1906); and the issuing of a much needed
ruling from the U.S. Department of Commerce
ordering compulsory pilotage on Puget Sound waters
(1906).[21] That same year Port Angeles residents
nervously began wondering if their town might ever
suffer anything similar to the devastating April 11th
San Francisco Earthquake which killed 452 and
caused $400 million damage. Also, City Council
began exploring the possibility of building bridges
within city limits, and community leader Thomas
Aldwell began work on a unique building at First and
Laurel Streets — the first stone structure in town.

City Council passed an ordinance in 1907 which
established a Water Works and Power Plant for the
town, then set new rates for electric usage. This was
also the year the very first automobile — a 1906
Buick owned by James Gibson — was brought to
town. Freighted in from Seattle aboard a steamer
which landed at Port Williams (near present-day
Sequim Bay State Park), the horseless contraption
was fitted in front with a large American flag, then
driven by Gibson to Port Angeles, a distance of about
16 miles, in the dazzling time of one hour and ten
minutes.

The following year, roller skating was in its
heyday locally and Mother's Day was observed
nationally for the first time. Uncle Sam rebuilt the
Lighthouse on Ediz Hook, City Council granted a
franchise to the Angeles Railway and Terminal Line
(a subsidiary of the Milwaukee Railroad) so it could
run tracks into the city, and townspeople were
amused by the celebrated American illusionist, Karl
Germain, who performed at the Opera House.

Port Angeles residents were grateful their town
was shaken only slightly by severe 1909 earthquakes
which caused extensive damage throughout British
Columbia and Alaska. Although there was no damage
in Port Angeles, the **Olympic-Leader** described the
January tremors as the "most severe shock of earthquakes (in this area) since its habitation by white
men." Then, as word reached civilization that
Admiral Robert E. Perry had reached the North Pole
at Latitude 90° North, Mount Olympus National
Monument — 615,000 acres — was established on the
Peninsula and former Colonist Harry Coventon built
a covered bridge over the Elwha River west of Port
Angeles in order to take advantage of the new road to

ALDWELL BUILDING, FIRST AND LAUREL STREETS, built in 1906 with stone from the Tumwater Creek rock quarry. Three stories high, and with a basement, it was the first stone building in Port Angeles. The Aldwell Building survived a fire in 1929, then was weakened severely in a December, 1965 blaze; it was torn down one year later. PHOTO SOURCE: Bert Kellogg

Lakes Sutherland and Crescent.

In a somewhat lighter vein, the **Olympic-Leader** observed early in 1909 that the tug *Snohomish*, built for Pacific Coast life-saving duty, was scheduled for transfer from its post at Port Angeles to Cape Flattery. However, in May, the **Leader**'s editor reported a sudden change in orders. The *Snohomish* was " . . . to stay in Port Angeles, 60-odd miles from the Cape and will hereafter do its life-saving duty in that vicinity instead of Neah Bay. *Vessels about to be wrecked in the Pacific Ocean are requested and will be expected to go and get wrecked on the Port Angeles sand spit handy to the steamer.*"[22]

Routine maintenance and planning were on the agenda for Port Angeles in 1910. Not only did City Council have the mud scraped and removed from buildings and gutters along Front Street, but Councilmen for the first time, contemplated the serious problem of tides in Port Angeles bay. With the population increase and the construction of more buildings along the shore, tides had begun generating a serious health problem, keeping raw sewage from entering the water or washing it back onto the beach. To quote the **Olympic-Leader**. " . . . if allowed to remain longer, with the growth of the city . . . (this)

EARLY PHOTO OF THOMAS T. ALDWELL, taken when he was Deputy Collector of Customs for Clallam County. Born in Toronto, Canada on June 14, 1868, Aldwell came to Port Angeles in 1890, and for over 60 years, was deeply involved in civic and commercial activities in his adopted town. PHOTO SOURCE: *The Commonwealth*

ANGELES HOTEL. Taken around 1908, this is one of the earliest known photos of a well-known Port Angeles landmark. The Angeles later became the Olympic Hotel, and still later, the Port Angeles Clinic. It has been used as the main facility of the Y.M.C.A. since 1953. PHOTO SOURCE: *Olympic-Leader*

ANGELES ATHLETIC ASSOCIATION basketball team in 1909. The organization stressed that its rolls were open to "any young man of good moral character." Membership in the AAA was a one dollar entry fee, with 50 cents dues per month. PHOTO SOURCE: Clallam County Museum

SNOHOMISH. Assigned by the United States Coast Guard to Port Angeles in December, 1910, the *Snohomish* remained in the local harbor for seven years. A combination cutter, tugboat and rescue ship, the *"Sno"* was transferred to the United States Navy when this country entered World War I in 1917. She was mustered out of that branch of the service and back into the Coast Guard two years later. She then returned to Port Angeles, where she built an incredible record of rescues of ships and lives. She was decommissioned in 1934, and sold to a buyer in Seattle. In 1947, she was sold to the Argentine Government and renamed *Mataras.* PHOTO SOURCE: U.S. Naval Institute

would be a serious menace to health, threatening epidemics and resulting in conditions that could not be tolerated."[23] (This same problem was attacked vigorously by City Council a scant four years later.) Midway through 1910, the City Council granted Elwha Light and Power Company a franchise for construction of a hydroelectric power plant on the Elwha River, a structure which was expected to furnish Port Angeles with about 25 years of current for lighting and domestic purposes. One of Port Angeles' most prominent citizens, Thomas Aldwell, was the driving force behind this successful effort. He placed his reputation and virtually his entire fortune on the line to bring electricity to his adopted town, almost singlehandedly arranging financing and far-flung markets for the plant.

Then . . . a matter of grave importance to residents of Port Angeles and all of Clallam County: The Women's Christian Temperance Union stalked the

SOL DUC. The steamer *S.S. Sol Duc*, owned by the Island Navigation Company. This 16-knot, 189-foot-long vessel was highly regarded throughout Puget Sound because of its stately rooms and plush carpeting. It became a familiar sight to residents along the Strait of Juan de Fuca and in the Sound, making the Seattle to Port Townsend run from 1912 to 1928. PHOTO SOURCE: Bert Kellogg

LOWER ELWHA HYDROELECTRIC DAM, constructed by Thomas T. Aldwell and associates (1910-1912). After buying land around the Elwha Canyon for approximately 12 years, Aldwell, wealthy Canadian George Glines, Joshua Green, R.D. Merrill and Michael Earles secured a franchise from the City of Port Angeles and other power contracts — then obtained necessary capital from Chicago investors for construction. The dam blew out in October, 1912 but was rebuilt within a year. PHOTO SOURCE: Bert Kellogg

MICHAEL EARLES AND M.J. CARRIGAN in the foreground. Behind them in this 1913 photo, is the construction site of Earles' "Big Mill," where today's M & R Timber Company is located. The Earles mill started cutting lumber in 1914, and was one of the largest enterprises of its kind in the entire world. PHOTO SOURCE: Clallam County Museum

countryside, unleashing terrible attacks on the sworn enemy, John Barleycorn. All residents were asked to vote on the critical issue of whether the County would be "wet" or "dry." It was reported that saloon owners throughout the area suffered great mental anguish, but they need not have worried: By a healthy majority of 125 votes, the City of Port Angeles beat back the efforts of the prohibitionists "in favor of continued moisture."[24] (The County did the same by only "a couple of dozen to the good.")

The Port Angeles Commercial Club and the Women's Auxiliary were both formed in 1911, the latter promptly filing complaints with City Council about the lack of public restrooms. The ladies expressed their displeasure, too, about the state of disrepair of the Oak Street zig-zag stairway. And . . . still another railroad – the Olympic Peninsula Electric Railway Company – was planned that year by the energetic Thomas Aldwell. Track was expected to run from Lake Crescent to Port Ludlow. Ultimately, unfortunately, another fizzle.

With plans under way for construction of a Moving Picture Theatre and a Federal Building, Mrs. Jessie Webster of the Women's Auxiliary proposed in 1912 the construction of a library.

Thomas Aldwell's recently completed Elwha River Dam – a victim of some shoddy work by the contractor – failed on October 31st, blowing out 80 feet from the bottom and destroying most of the newly-installed electrical equipment. Aldwell, a man not easily defeated, immediately set machinery in motion to repair the dam's foundation and would bring the project to a successful conclusion just one year later.[25]

Strictly as a matter of economics, however, nothing that happened in Port Angeles in 1912 surpassed in importance a couple of mere conversations conducted during that year. Some of the town's shrewdest businessmen were putting their heads together, with the result that several long-sought, essential goals of the city were eventually achieved.

Three years earlier, Michael Earles, timber and sawmill operator extraordinary, had expressed a willingness to build the biggest sawmill in Washington if the Clallam County Board of Commissioners would give him a few specific tax breaks. The Commissioners demurred, feeling they could not legally make such a contract. However, in 1912, seeing the utter need for a large payroll in the city, 60 local merchants pooled their resources and gave Earles $33,150, with which he bought land for "The Big Mill." Earles' mill – built on free land – was the county's chief employer and bulwark of its economy for almost 20 years.

"THE LITTLE SHOP," a small restaurant located at the northwest corner of Front and Lincoln Streets, circa 1913. Owned by Anna B. Smith and Mae Brockhouse, the popular eatery became famous locally for Mrs. Smith's cornbread muffins — and for its restroom "fitted up with reading and writing desk, easy rockers, lounges, etc.," according to the *Olympic-Leader*. Note the City Ordinance on pole nearby. At a time when cows were still permitted to graze on city streets, the ordinance prohibited the feeding and tying of animals less than 20 feet from the corner of any intersection. PHOTO SOURCE: Clallam County Museum

Just as significant that year, a wealthy Seattle contractor named C. J. Erickson looked over the town and was soon captivated by its prospects as a railroad terminal. Lured to Port Angeles originally by a special agent of the Milwaukee Railroad (whose own interest was initially fanned by none other than Michael Earles), Erickson formed a business association with local residents G. M. Lauridsen and J. P. Christensen. This group, over the course of the next few years, would accomplish what no others had: They would link the town to the ever-expanding transcontinental railroad system.

In 1913, D. W. Morse constructed the first three-story concrete building in Port Angeles at the corner of Front and Laurel Streets. And the city's first public library — set up one year earlier in the cramped back rooms of the Commercial Clubhouse — moved to separate quarters at the rear of the Old Central School on First Street, where it was to remain for seven years. Also that year, C. J. Erickson, subsequent to pledges by local businessmen, advanced $23,000 cash to start work on the railroad right-of-way. By summertime, work on that essential preliminary was progressing well under the supervision of G. M. Lauridsen and his Chief Engineer, Charles Donovan. The Industrial Workers of the World (I.W.W.), however, then sent a couple of organizers — most called them "agitators" — to town to unionize the project. The I.W.W., whose members were known as "Wobblies,"[26] was a militant, socialistic labor organization, one of whose goals was to overthrow capitalism. "Wobblies" were known to use work slow-downs, wildcat strikes and even sabotage to achieve their goals, so when Donovan's right-of-way crew indicated they were afraid to continue working, the two agitators were unceremoniously dumped aboard the steamer *Iroquois* and advised to make their living elsewhere.[27]

Nineteen-thirteen also revealed a rather ugly side of several prominent Port Angeles residents (albeit common for the time) — a well-defined streak of racism. Editors of the **Olympic-Leader** and a number of important white citizens, most of them real estate brokers, stood not-so-tall that year when they unleashed a blistering attack against "undesirable Hindoos and Negroes." The large, front-page article they published featured both a signed petition and a scathing editorial asserting that such people "materially depreciated value of adjacent property and . . . injured reputations of the neighborhood." Introducing the negro into Port Angeles, the article continued, "is an insult to the intelligence of the people, (for) that problem has already spread far enough through the length and breadth of the country."[28]

However, the year did have its brighter side. The new high school was dedicated (February 21) and the Port Angeles Business College started operations at the corner of Vine and First Streets, offering "bookkeeping, shorthand, typewriting, penmanship and rapid figuring."[29] The two Eighth Street bridges, designed by City Engineer Charles Filion, were completed in July, a new Olympic Hotel was ready for occupancy by August, and City Council passed an ordinance setting the grade of Front Street above its existing level. Council then began negotiations with the Federal government to secure a long-term grant or lease on Ediz Hook for industrial purposes; these negotiations would culminate the following year in the signing of a 99-year lease.[30]

Thus Port Angeles, by the end of the year 1913 was completing a 30-year period of steady but sometimes irregular growth.

"This group (C.J. Erickson, G.M. Lauridsen and J.P. Christensen) . . . would accomplish what no others had: They would link the town to the ever-expanding transcontinental railroad system."

After awakening in the mid-1880s from its post-Victor Smith slumber, the Port of Our Lady of the Angels at the northwest tip of the continent finally began to blossom. Rail lines winding into the Puget Sound region brought with them many people, some of whom were promoters selling pie-in-the-sky projects . . . but also some who would provide years of solid leadership to Port Angeles. The Puget Sound Cooperative Colony moved into town, ultimately furnishing a nucleus of exceptional people who were achievers and totally fearless of the future. Port Angeles' growth was influenced by a great westward movement of the country's population and by its own dramatic 1893 "land rush" — the opening of the federal reservation. Electric power, telephones, automobiles, roads on which to drive them and the inexorable, final displacement of sailing vessels by steamers also impacted on the city by the Strait, helping to mold its destiny.

NEW EIGHTH STREET BRIDGES. Access to the city's growing west end was made easier with the construction of two new Eighth Street bridges in 1913. Coinciding with a surge of community growth and development, the bridges were designed by City Engineer Charles Filion and spanned both Valley Street and Tumwater Canyon. By 1982 standards, construction costs were relatively modest: a mere $29,544.99 for labor and the 820,000 board feet of lumber used. Both spans were used by travelers until 1936, when they were replaced by newer ones. PHOTO SOURCE: North Olympic Library System

S.S. City of Angeles —
Port Angeles Transportation Co.

THE STEAMER *CITY OF ANGELES*. Christened the *City of Long Beach* when it was built in 1906, the 125-foot long, propeller-driven steamer was renamed *City of Angeles* September 30, 1913 after she was bought by the Port Angeles Transportation Company. Later, the vessel was used as a ferry operating between Anacortes, Washington and Sidney, B.C. In 1938 she was sold for scrap. PHOTO SOURCE: Bert Kellogg

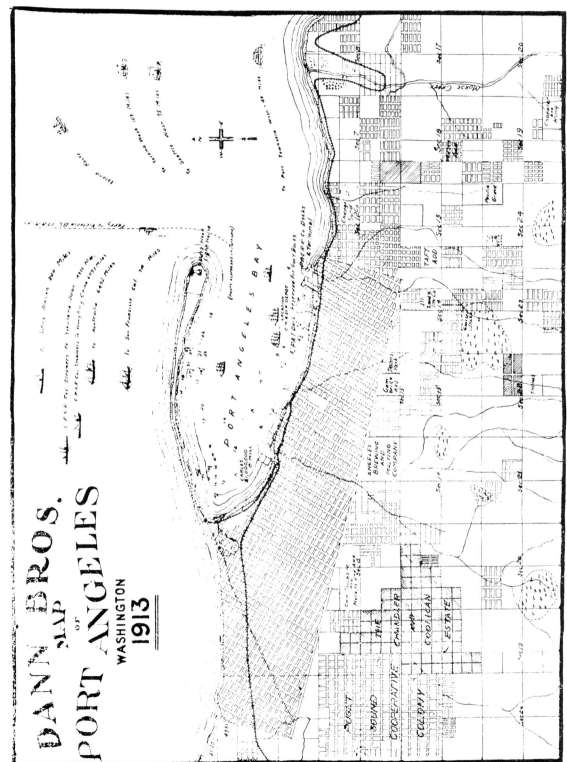

1913 PROMO-TIONAL MAP proclaiming Port Angeles' future status as "The Coming Coast City." The Dann brothers, who published the map, were local real estate promoters who, swept up in the fervor of the times, believed the city was destined to be the greatest shipping port in the west. They distributed hundreds of copies of this advertisement throughout the region. PHOTO SOURCE: North Olympic Library System

Like a gangly, rawboned youngster anxious about the future yet with the necessary strength and confidence to face it, the town in 1913 found itself standing on the threshold of a thrilling new era. Its 25-year uphill effort to establish rail linkage with the rest of the nation seemed to be nearing success. A sawmill of gargantuan proportions was already under construction by Michael Earles. City Council had just made a vital decision on raising and grading downtown streets. Negotiations with the United States Government to secure industrial usage of Ediz Hook were already under way. Tom Aldwell's Herculean, four-year effort to build an operable hydroelectric plant — the greatest construction job Clallam County had yet seen — was on the verge of completion.

And far, far away, Germany's Kaiser Wilhelm had begun making threatening gestures toward other nations, creating a hostile, warlike environment which would in a few years have a ghastly impact upon America and the rest of the world.

Chapter Six: 1914 — 1918

Municipal Progress, the Spruce Division and the "Great War"

"I sometimes wonder if I ever saw Port Angeles' **Present** *because so much of my time was spent seeing Port Angeles'* **Future,** *and as the future became present, I kept looking ahead."*

— Thomas Aldwell
in **Conquering the
Last Frontier**

Nineteen-fourteen. What an exciting time it was!

For the City of Our Lady of the Angels (conveniently observed with nearly 70 years' perspective as a guide), 1914 is now seen as an important, yet sad, peculiar year in the town's history and one highlighted by vivid contrasts. More importantly, 1914 clearly identifies the start of a new era in Port Angeles.

Little more than a pioneer lumber and shingle mill town for years, still flanked by massive forests, Port Angeles in 1914 had begun expanding its horizons. It had survived the many economic crises which devastated some other western communities, and showed every sign of becoming a solid, prosperous 20th Century city. One had only to look at Thomas Aldwell's soon-to-be-activated hydroelectric plant,

Michael Earles' lumber mill (known locally as the "Big Mill") just gearing up — the town's first major industrial plant — or Charles J. Erickson's imminent railroad hook-up to verify that economically, at least, Port Angeles was on the move. Yet, much like a stodgy old gentleman in a starched, button-down collar who comes face-to-face with a bearded hippie, some comfortable, time-honored customs began clashing with "new fangled," fresh ideas in 1914; living conditions that Port Angelens previously took for granted collided head-on with more modern tastes.

For example, cows were finally prohibited from roaming at will and grazing on downtown streets — a common sight in earlier days.

A COMMON SIGHT ON FRONT STREET well into the early days of this century, cows were allowed to roam under the law of "free pasturage." In fact, it was not uncommon to see local residents with pails and milk stools actually milking cows right on the street! Finally, after months of controversy, by a city-wide vote of 561-357 on November 10, 1914, cows were banned from the streets. PHOTO SOURCE: Bert Kellogg

Also, 1914 was the year Clallamites discovered that the automobile, while certainly a contemporary, fascinating device, also presented a new kind of hazard: The county recorded its first motor vehicle fatality on May 5th, when James Henderson (ironically, returning home from a funeral!) was thrown from his car and killed.

Raising the Streets

The disgraceful condition of downtown streets — at sea level and susceptible to tides which produced a pungent backwash of raw sewage — had been stoically accepted by townspeople for years. The persistent, nauseous odors, however, (described by one newsman as "The Curse of Port Angeles"[1]), — and the threat of planked streets being washed out to sea — finally prompted City Council to act . . . and the area was totally revamped. The regrading job performed was impressive, with the steep Front Street hill sluiced down with water pumped from the bay. Beach-level Front and First Streets and intersecting

thoroughfares were raised 10-14 feet for a distance of several blocks.

In August, the Clallam County Commissioners awarded a contract for construction of a new courthouse; two months later, on October 16th, the cornerstone was laid for this much-needed building.[2]

Progress on Three Fronts

However, the big news items for the year were the Dam, the "Big Mill," and the Railroad. Power generated by Aldwell's dam lit the entire town and was extended as far away as the United States Navy Yard at Bremerton. A totally unique project for that era, it was the only large-scale industrial operation of its kind in the west promoted from start to finish by a local resident.

Michael Earles' "Big Mill" was perhaps the most complete facility of its kind in the world in 1914. Not only did it produce a wide variety of tailored lumber (flooring, trusses, etc.) and maintain its own box factory, but the unique plant also boasted a cook

TOKENS worth five cents were stamped by Lou Harrington shortly after he opened his cigar store and newsstand. PHOTO SOURCE: Pete Capos

HARRINGTON'S cigar store and newsstand at southwest corner of Front and Laurel Streets opened July 1, 1913. Lou Harrington was the sole proprietor until 1920. He and partner Andy Giles then maintained a retail outlet at that corner until Harrington's retirement in 1945. PHOTO SOURCE: Clallam County Museum

house, bunk house (300-man capacity), fully-equipped store and a butcher shop; it was virtually a town unto itself. Earles' "long mill" was capable of sawing timber of 150 feet in length, and his shingle mill was a leader throughout the entire industry. The Earles payroll even included stevedoring crews which served ships from all points of the globe.[3]

Then there was C. J. Erickson's railroad. Tracks laid by Erickson stretched from Port Crescent (west of Port Angeles) to Port Townsend and in just one year would link townspeople with transcontinental rail connections for the first time. Under an ordinance granted by City Council in 1914, Erickson's railroad — ultimately acquired by the Milwaukee Road — was granted blanket approval to run track along and across all downtown Port Angeles streets east and west "as required."[4] For many years the railroad would haul logs to Port Angeles mills from the west end, then carry passengers, lumber and freight to the Port Townsend terminal. On return trips, passengers were transported as far west as Twin, Washington.

War in Europe

Unfortunately, though, the year 1914 had also nudged the United States one step nearer to what were by now full-scale hostilities in Europe. Just a month after Archduke Francis Ferdinand of Austria-Hungary was assassinated, war broke out (July 28th), and one after another the great powers of Eastern Europe tumbled into it. When Great Britain also declared war on Germany in August, the United States found itself virtually committed to the fray.

Kaiser Wilhelm's war also bred uncertainty and suspicion among neighbors in sociable old Port Angeles. Many long-term friendships were abruptly terminated as people of German descent were deliberately and cruelly ostracized from the mainstream of the community. In one especially ugly incident, a tall, distinguished immigrant, Colonel William A. Lange — known as "Professor" and a well-liked music teacher before the war — was confronted downtown by a hostile crowd and threatened with physical violence unless he publicly kissed the American flag. The old gentleman did so, but reluctantly, because of the embarassing circumstances. (Some headstrong observers maintained that he actually spit on the Stars and Stripes, but the allegation could not be proven.)

Through it all America's leaders worked hard to retain international neutrality. President Woodrow Wilson was in constant communication with the Germans, trying to make his peaceful intentions clear to them. He truly believed he had persuaded them not to attack vessels with Americans aboard. However, he was wrong, as he discovered on May 7, 1915,

FIRST PASSENGER TRAIN. On July 21, 1914, the Milwaukee Railroad Company launched its first excursion trip from Port Angeles heading westward to the Elwha River. Consisting of a locomotive and three coaches, the passenger train carried officials of the Railroad Company and local politicians. Fifteen months later (October 20, 1915), the Milwaukee carried its first passenger to Port Townsend. PHOTO SOURCE: Bert Kellogg

1914 Street Projects

AT THE START of the year 1914, remnants of Port Angeles' past were still very much in evidence. Not only did cows roam city streets, but Peabody Creek still ran down Lincoln Street and veered westward through the middle of Front Street, entering the bay in the vicinity of today's Valley Street. The first project to be undertaken in 1914 required tunneling through the "Hog Back" hillside at Lincoln Street between First and Front Streets, changing the course of Peabody Creek so that it would enter the bay near what is now the City Pier. The old east-west creek bed winding through the downtown business district was then filled to allow more construction there.

THE SECOND PROJECT undertaken that year was the Port Angeles Regrade. The steep Front Street hill and remnants of the "Hog Back" were dredged and sluiced into the business district, with dirt being captured as fill, thus raising the level of all downtown streets.

1914 PHOTO looking east from the corner of First and Laurel Streets in downtown Port Angeles. This interesting shot was taken from the area of present-day Laurel Street above the Conrad Dyar Memorial Fountain. Note the wooded area in the center of the photo where, as part of a massive street-raising program, engineers would later punch through the existing hillside, thus extending Lincoln Street northward to the harbor. PHOTO SOURCE: North Olympic Library System

LAUREL STREET LOOKING NORTH just before the streets were actually raised. Morse Dock at the extreme north end of Laurel Street is now the Coho Ferry dock. PHOTO SOURCE: Bert Kellogg

WATER PUMPED FROM THE BAY emitted powerful jets which sluiced away the hillside, pushing dirt down what is now the Front Street hill. This photo depicts sluicing of the hill looking west from Front and Chase Streets. PHOTO SOURCE: Bert Kellogg

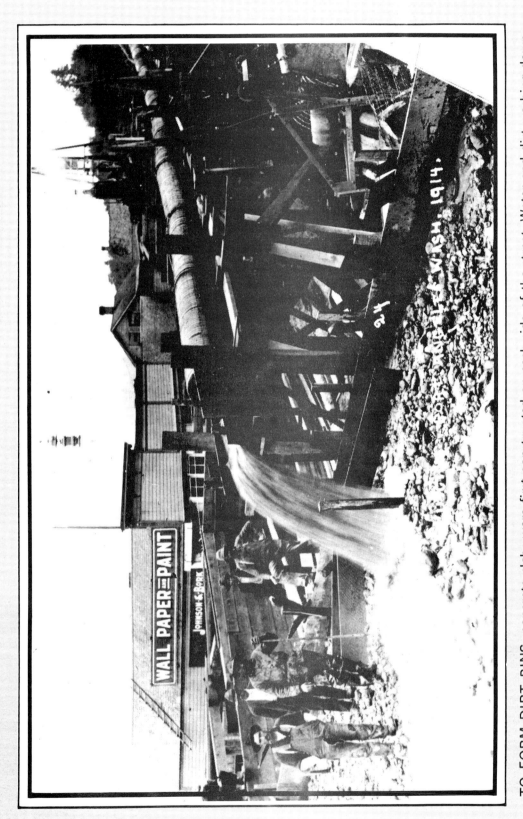

TO FORM DIRT BINS, concrete slabs were first constructed on each side of the street. Water and dirt washing down the Front Street hill tossed fill material into dirt bins in the middle of the street between the two walls. Shown here in a photo looking north from the intersection of Front and Lincoln Streets, is fill material being dumped into catcher bins.
PHOTO SOURCE: Bert Kellogg

TEMPORARY DAMS were made to contain fill material until it reached the desired level. One city block at a time was filled with dirt, at which time the dam would be shifted farther down the street. Looking east on Front Street, the sluicing operation is visible in the distance. The Opera House is the first building on right. PHOTO SOURCE: Bert Kellogg

LOOKING WEST along Front Street one can see how high buildings had to be raised to match the new street level. Some structures were torn down and rebuilt; in others the first floor became the "new" basement level. PHOTO SOURCE: Bert Kellogg

LOOKING NORTH ON LAUREL STREET from the hillside on the south side of First Street. Note that the city block leading down to Front Street had already been filled in, but buildings had not yet been raised. PHOTO SOURCE: Bert Kellogg

AGAIN LOOKING NORTH ON LAUREL STREET, from the same area as the photograph on page 115. Note that one building on the west side of Laurel (Lewis Levy Real Estate) and the sidewalk in front of the Aldwell Building (northeast corner on right) already have been raised, and that the dam has been moved farther north toward the north end of Laurel Street. PHOTO SOURCE: Bert Kellogg

LAUREL STREET LOOKING SOUTH. This scene demonstrates the kind of temporary damming of the streets that was necessary to fill them. Here, water is being released toward the harbor, leaving behind necessary fill material. The Merchants Hotel, seen on right, is the site of today's Great Northwest Savings and Loan Association. PHOTO SOURCE: Bert Kellogg

AFTER THE FILLING PROCESS was completed in 1914, it was necessary to let the dirt settle for several years. To allow this, streets were planked in 1914, and five years later they were paved. PHOTO SOURCE: Bert Kellogg

LAUREL STREET. Two years after the regrade projects, Port Angeles had begun to take on the appearance of a more "modern" town. Note planking on streets and absence of horses. Also, notice the street light, upper right. Moreover, this scene sharply illustrates the demise of sailing vessels and the certain onset of steamships as the predominant form of transportation in Puget Sound. PHOTO SOURCE: Bert Kellogg

FIRST CITY JAIL, shown in this 1914 photograph was located on west First Street near what is now Filion's Jewelers. Port Angeles' first jail tank was built in 1890 on the east coast, at a cost of $500.00. The primitive structure contained a steel "tank" 14' x 13' and served as the town's sole means of incarceration until 1915, when it was replaced by the County Jail building. PHOTO SOURCE: Bert Kellogg

when a German submarine sank the *S. S. Lusitania*, killing 1,198 people — including 128 American citizens who were aboard. Port Angeles residents, who had for years cheerfully joined the chorus of Americans wanting this nation to stay out of the war at all costs, finally began to realize that neutral status in such a volatile situation was folly. United States entry into the war seemed to be inevitable. Nevertheless, casting one worried eye toward the European Front and the other toward Woodrow Wilson, trying to gauge his conduct, Port Angelens went on with the necessary business of facing and solving their day-to-day problems. As with most human endeavors, they were destined to win a few battles and lose a few.

The first minor triumph took place early in 1915 when work began on the Ediz Hook roadway; simul-

taneously, Port Angeles was authorized by the State of Washington to accept Uncle Sam's 99-year lease for industrial use of the Hook.

The "Big Snow," Ediz Hook Lease
— and the landscape changes

Nineteen-sixteen was recalled by many as the year of the "Big Snow."[5] But it was also a time which marked cosmetic changes in and around Port Angeles. In January, a freak storm hit town, to be followed by more and more snow throughout that month and into early February. When it was all finished, a blanket of white stuff ranging up to six feet had paralyzed the little community.[6] Then, in rapid succession one large, new building was dedicated . . . and another, older one, lost. On May 5th, the new Elks Building on

THE PORT ANGELES GENERAL HOSPITAL at the northwest corner of Eighth and Peabody Streets in 1915. At the time this photo was taken, the hospital, headquartered in the renovated Old Germania Hall (also called Herman Hall) was undergoing renovations again following a serious fire the previous year. In 1915, it was being run by Dr. Donald E. McGillivray, who, with a former associate, Dr. Samuel Whitfield Hartt, had founded the first Port Angeles General Hospital in 1903 at the same location. The hospital shown here was destroyed by fire in 1922. PHOTO SOURCE: Bert Kellogg

Lincoln Street was opened, and three weeks later (May 23rd), a flash fire ravaged the Martin Sash and Door factory at First and Oak Streets. It was at this time, too, that a dreadful blaze leveled Michael Earles' renowned Sol Duc Health Resort west of town. Sol Duc was unquestionably one of the more prestigious health spas in all the Western Hemisphere. Though spread over a wide area, Earles' entire complex — sanitarium, hotel, commissary, bathhouses, powerhouse, laundry, cottages and other small frame buildings — was obliterated in the disaster.

Before 1916 ended, though, good news arrived from New York, when the philanthropic Carnegie Corporation granted Port Angeles $12,500 for a free public library — on condition that City Council provide both a suitable site and funds for annual maintenance. Council acted, and plans for the new building began immediately. Two years later, in 1918, construction would begin on Port Angeles' first genuine library building.

SOL DUC HOT SPRINGS HOTEL, Michael Earles' grand pleasure and health resort west of Port Angeles when it opened on May 15, 1912 (formal opening June 1, 1912). The noted resort boasted 165 rooms, each with an outside view. Steam heat, electric lights, telephones, and hot and cold running water greeted visitors to the Hot Springs; guests numbered 10,000 in its peak year. During the resort's short life span, its impact upon Port Angeles and the entire Pacific Northwest was enormous. The hotel shown here, and all surrounding facilities burned down May 16, 1916. PHOTO SOURCE: Bert Kellogg

BENJAMIN PHILLIPS, prominent Port Angeles banker shown at left here, shortly after the opening of the Port Angeles Trust and Savings Bank, on February 10, 1914. Five years later, in 1919, he took over the Citizens National Bank, and changed its name to the First National Bank. That institution was purchased by Seattle-First National Bank in 1976. Pictured with Phillips in this 1914 photo is Clifford Babcock, prominent Port Angeles businessman who later was elected Treasurer of Washington State. PHOTO SOURCE: James Phillips

Early Banking in Port Angeles

The history of commercial banking in Port Angeles is a checkered one. As with most towns in the early days of the wild west, Port Angeles banks had a tendency to open and close with mercurial speed. Several attempts to establish viable banking institutions had been made during the Gay Nineties and the early part of the Twentieth Century, but with few exceptions they failed to take root and, after varying lengths of time, suspended operations.

After the demise of the First National Bank (See Chapter Four, p. 66) and the gloom of the Panic of 1893, Harry E. Lutz organized and incorporated the Bank of Clallam County in April,

1895. Lutz purchased the assets and quarters of the old First National Bank, and opened with the following officers: President, Harry E. Lutz; Vice-President, George Y. Bollinger; Cashier, Charles E. Mallette.

The Bank of Clallam County continued until December, 1923, when it merged with the Washington State Bank under President G.M. Lauridsen. The Washington State Bank then operated continuously until failing in January, 1933.

Another, the Cain National Bank, also took hold, and remained solvent for about two years.[7] Then, via a convoluted series of stock purchases, mergers and name changes over a span of two decades, it evolved into the well-known First National Bank of Port Angeles.

John C. Cain founded the bank named after him in 1901, opening for business on the first floor of the old Opera House on Front Street.[8] A somewhat flamboyant, venturesome man by nature, Cain soon tired of the stuffy banking business — it really wasn't doing too well under his guidance anyway — so he sold his stock to some local men in 1903. The bank's new owners changed its name to the Citizens National Bank and hired the astute J. P. Christensen as their new manager. The bank prospered and when Port

Angeles' most prominent citizen G. M. Lauridsen, later became its president, its future seemed assured.

On February 10, 1914, though, competition arrived in the form of the Port Angeles Trust and Savings Bank, managed by an aggressive young fellow named Benjamin N. Phillips. Under his leadership the new bank gained wide acceptance in town, and just a few years later Phillips engineered a coup. In December 1919,[9] he purchased majority ownership of Lauridsen's and Christensen's bank, then successfully merged the two organizations, retaining the name Citizens

(continued on page 124)

LOCAL CURRENCY secured, printed and distributed by the First National Bank in Port Angeles in 1920s.
PHOTO SOURCE: James Phillips

(banking, continued)
National Bank.

Despite some grumbling by minority owners and the fact that they later opened a new institution — the Washington State Bank — on January 1, 1920, Phillips and the Citizens National Bank continued to prosper in the community. Later the name was changed to the First National Bank, remaining so until 1976, when it was purchased by the Seattle-First National Bank.

"BIG MILL." This is Michael Earles' Puget Sound Mills and Timber Company, photographed in 1914 when it was in full operation. Port Angeles' main employer for over 20 years, the "Big Mill" inventoried 15 million board feet of logs daily in the Port Angeles harbor, and was virtually a complete city unto itself. It was one of the few "long mills" in existence at that time and could saw timbers 150 feet in length. PHOTO SOURCE: Bert Kellogg

THE "COMPANY STORE." The Puget Sound Mills and Timber Company's retail outlet and offices in 1917. According to one Port Angeles newspaper, *The Peninsula Free Press*, Michael Earles' "Big Mill" pressured its employees into trading at the store — and that single men were "compelled to board at the company boarding house." Such allegations were vigorously denied by officials of the firm, but many Port Angelens firmly believed that Earles did indeed run an unsavory "Company Store." PHOTO SOURCE: Ed Gaul

TIN MONEY. An integral part of the Michael Earles Mill was the Company Store. Mill employees were "encouraged" to purchase staple goods here — and if they happened to be short of cash, "tin money," shown here, could be used as an advance on their paychecks. The special tokens were redeemable only at the Earles Store. PHOTO SOURCE: Clallam County Museum

America enters the war

By 1917 it was no longer possible for Americans to cast but one eye toward Europe. In just two years the general mood of the country had veered sharply from one of fervent neutrality to outright, hawkish patriotism, and the nation's complete attention had turned to war. In Port Angeles, except for the opening of the new two-story, red brick Lincoln Heights School January 9th,[10] virtually every newsworthy item occurring throughout the year bore military connotations. And on April 6th the inevitable happened: President Wilson and Congress officially declared war on Germany.

Port Angeles citizens responded predictably, and "in a spontaneous outburst of patriotic enthusiasm, added (their) pledge to the chorus of acclaim . . . going up all over the nation in support of the war decision."[11] One thousand and eighty-five local men eagerly marched to the Draft Board and registered for military service. (The "patriotic enthusiasm" of many, however, must have subsided somewhat by the time they arrived, for the record shows that more than half of them claimed exemption!)[12]

Almost overnight a Port Angeles Home Guard was formed and wartime harbor regulations were enacted requiring civilian boats to keep clear of naval vessels operating in the bay. Liberty Bonds went on sale, Liberty Fires blazed, and a local Chapter of the Red Cross was organized under the auspices of the recently established Daughters of the American Revolution (DAR). Residents were urged to cultivate every available plot of ground and begin raising vegetables for local consumption. By the end of 1917 Uncle Sam had issued a call for an enormous amount of spruce timber for airplane construction[13] — a fact that would play a vital role in America's war operations, *and* in Port Angeles economic history.

CATHOLIC CHURCH AND LATER COURTHOUSE for 23 years (1892-1915), this building stood atop a knoll at Second and Lincoln Streets. Though the hill is gone, the location is the approximate site of today's Port Angeles Branch of the North Olympic Library System. PHOTO SOURCE: Bert Kellogg

COURTHOUSE DEDICATION. Dedication of the Clallam County Courthouse at Fourth and Lincoln Streets, June 14, 1915. Elks Naval Lodge #353 coordinated the ceremonies, accompanied by a platoon from the Port Angeles-based Coast Guard Cutter *Snohomish*. An impressive three-story structure, the county's newest "seat" was built of red pressed brick and terra cotta, topped by a 16-foot square tower reaching to a height of 82 feet. PHOTO SOURCE: Bert Kellogg

GERMAN HALL at Fourteenth and Valley Streets, a popular social hall built by local residents of German descent. It opened January 1, 1915 and burned to the ground in 1919. PHOTO SOURCE: Clallam County Museum

The Spruce Division and the 4-L's

Military men in 1917 were convinced that the war in Europe would be won or lost in the air; enough planes overhead, they believed, would guarantee victory on the ground. They therefore made a decision to build more planes — and national significance was instantly bestowed upon the Port of Our Lady of the Angels. Spruce was considered to be the finest wood extant for construction of aircraft, Uncle Sam needed great quantities of it, and Port Angeles was literally the gateway to the sprawling spruce forests of western Clallam County.

At first, it was assumed that private industry would be able to provide enough lumber, but it became obvious almost immediately that spruce production was woefully inadequate. Desperate for the lumber, the War Department assigned one of its chief "troubleshooters," Colonel Bryce P. Disque,[14] the job of increasing output in the Pacific Northwest — and gave him broad powers to get it done. The way he did it was unique, for he created two separate, incongruous groups and forced them to work together toward a common goal: Winning the war. The two groups were the Spruce Division (an actual army unit comprised of soldiers-converted-into-loggers) and a government-backed, union-like organization of civilians known as the 4-L's — the Loyal Legion of Loggers and Lumbermen. Together, these two unlikely partners would have a heavy impact on Port Angeles.

A serious, no-nonsense administrator, Disque first analyzed the existing situation from his "outsider's" viewpoint and discovered utter chaos at many levels.

There was no representative union with which employers would even consider negotiating. Employers were intractable, clinging desperately to management prerogatives and insisting upon their right to maintain "open (i.e., non union) shops." To make matters worse, most mill owners in the region didn't even know what the actual specifications were for finished spruce, thereby rendering unusable most of what little they produced. Finally, as the coup de grâce, the I.W.W. (The Industrial Workers of the World, mentioned in Chapter Five) had recently called a crippling industry-wide strike which plummeted spruce shipments almost to the vanishing point.[15]

Disque quickly brought in 100 officer-organizers to tour all camps and mills in the Northwest, administering loyalty oaths and getting workers *and* employers to join his new organization. Union-like Locals, each with a grievance committee, were formed throughout the region, with members of the Locals later electing delegates to seven Districts. All seven Districts in turn answered to the Headquarters Council, presided over by Disque and his advisers. In 1918 the 4-L's even drafted a constitution. Its basic provisions, though — including a controversial "no strike" clause — were determined by Disque and his advisers.

Immediately after the embryo 4-L's was formed, Disque recommended creation of a special division of troops to be used in logging camps and mills. At his request the War Department began sending thousands of men to the Northwest. They were the first wave of the United States Spruce Production Corporation, better

known as the Spruce Division. Most of the soldier-loggers — ultimately they would number between 25,000 and 30,000 — worked at logging camps and mills; a few thousand, though, were assigned to building railroads, a fact of great consequence to Clallam County folks. All the soldiers lived under military discipline but received civilian pay for work performed.

It is safe to assume that the reluctant lumberjacks were very unhappy young men.

Civilian loggers thought at first that the soldiers had been sent to maintain order. When they discovered, however, that the unskilled doughboys were there to overcome a serious labor shortage, bitter resentment sprang up. The troublesome "Wobblies" saw them as union-breakers and didn't want them in camp. Then too, it was obvious these boys wearing combat hats knew little about the Pacific Northwest's wet woods and even less about logging. The soldiers' morale sagged, for most felt cheated. Here they were practically at the end of the earth, isolated and lonely, clambering over huge, slippery stumps every day, all the while being sneered at as "secondary soldiers" — yet still trying to sound heroic as they wrote to girl friends about dodging tree limbs in Washington rather than enemy bullets in France!

Eventually the Spruce Division became entrenched in bureaucracy and by the end of the war found itself wading knee-deep in controversy. In fact, after the armistice many responsible officials seriously questioned the manner in which Disque had administered the program, and a Congressional probe looked

into allegations of uneconomical, discriminatory practices; the probe was inconclusive. The 4-L's were also criticized, with their members often ridiculed as "Lazy Loggers and Loafing Lumbermen"[16] with "Little Loyalty and Large Loot."[17]

Nevertheless, though controversial and costly, Uncle Sam's strange journey into the realm of labor conscription and union organizing was considered successful by most observers. The Spruce Production Division and the 4-L's were able to point with pride to an impressive record of achievement, accomplishing much that squabbling labor unions of that day could not, and paving the way for reforms in working conditions within the logging industry. Army officers looked at the scene and were appalled at the terrible living and working conditions of civilian loggers. They flatly refused to submit their troops to such hardships, and made it mandatory that soldier-loggers and civilians be given clean mattresses, sheets, pillows, pillowcases and blankets regularly; no longer would woodsmen have to carry personal "bindles" from job to job. Then too, Disque's 4-L's forced industry-wide agreement on a minimum wage, an eight-hour day, 48-hour work week, and even establishment of a system of inspection for maintenance of reforms.[18]

The Spruce Division's long-term impact on Port Angeles and Clallam County was nothing short of spectacular, but not because of the amount of lumber harvested; that amounted to very little. Its real importance lay in the rail lines and capital improvements left behind. With up to 10,000 troops laboring, 45 miles of main

continued on page 131

SPRUCE DIVISION campsite during World War I near Lake Pleasant, in Clallam County's west end. PHOTO SOURCE: Bert Kellogg

Spruce Division, continued
line and 20 miles of railroad spur lines were laid throughout the county (at the staggering cost of $30,000-plus per mile!). Most of the tracks were built from Tyee (Lake Pleasant), along the north shore of Lake Crescent to the town of Disque, where it joined the Port Angeles Western Railroad (formerly the Milwaukee Railroad).

Disque's Spruce Division workers also built a large mill at the mouth of Ennis Creek, on the Klallam Indians' old potlatch site and connected it to tracks running westward into the forests. It was all very stirring . . . and everything was finished just in time for the end of the war. The Ennis Creek plant never opened — and the Spruce Division did not haul a single log over the Olympic Peninsula rail route!

But was it significant? Indeed. The Ennis Creek mill site with its critical rail connections would be the single most important factor in the Olympic Forest Products Company's decision, 11 years later, to move to Port Angeles. Olympic Forest Products — now ITT Rayonier, Inc. — saw the mill as an ideal location for a pulp plant, moved to town and became a bedrock fixture in Port Angeles, remaining so today.

U.S. SPRUCE CORPORATION MILL at the mouth of Ennis Creek. Built by the Spruce Division, construction was completed in 1918 just as World War I ended, and the beautifully-designed sawmill was never used. It stood empty from 1918 to 1929, when it was purchased by Olympic Forest Products. Today it is the site of ITT Rayonier, Inc. PHOTO SOURCE: Bert Kellogg

Just before the war ended in 1918, a grim Spanish Flu epidemic surged through the country, killing thousands, and striking Port Angeles with a particular vengeance. During the four-month period beginning October, 1918, the deadly germ swept back and forth through the isolated little community. Although no exact statistics could be found, it is known that several deaths were recorded in Port Angeles. And, there was one 48-hour period when almost 40 cases of flu were diagnosed; near-panic ensued. Mayor E. J. Walton and Health Officer Dr. Donald E. McGillivray ordered flu masks for all those traveling in public, then closed schools, theaters, churches and other indoor public meeting places, including dance halls and pool rooms (all this before McGillivray himself was confined to bed with the virulent disease!).[19] The ban was lifted just one day after the November 11th Armistice.

With the horrible fighting behind, Port Angelens mourned their dead (500 Clallam Countians served in the conflict, seven died),[20] sighed with relief, and welcomed home their doughboy heroes.

It was time to pick up the pieces left dangling a few years before.

Chapter Seven: 1919 — 1928

From Post-War Uncertainty to "Black Friday" on the Prosperity Express

"Peace itself is war in masquerade."
— John Dryden
Absalom and Achitophel

Shortly after America's entry into World War I, Paraffine Companies, Inc. of California broke ground for a boxboard mill near the head of Port Angeles harbor. Construction of the plant was suspended during hostilities, but it was finished early in 1919, and Paraffine began operations in mid-year with a one-digester unit.[1] Known locally for many years as "Crescent Boxboard" (Paraffine officials named it for Lake Crescent) and later simply as "Fibreboard," the firm was for a long time the only plant west of the Rocky Mountains with its own pulp mill and paper machines. By 1926, it was shipping 14,000 tons of wallboard, boxboard and egg fillers annually to markets around the nation.

Paraffine operated the Port Angeles mill until 1927, when its boardmaking plants and those of Crown Zellerbach Corporation were merged into the new Fibreboard Products Corporation.[2] As it continued to improve operations, Fibreboard's growth pattern spiraled upward and for years it was recognized as the steadiest producer in the entire boxboard industry. By the late 1960s, however, mounting freight costs (raw material had to be freighted in) and increasingly distant markets for finished products immersed the local mill in red ink. So, after 52 long years of admirable service to the Port Angeles community, Fibreboard's doors closed permanently on December 31, 1970.

A New Decade Brings Uncertainty

From all indications, the average Port Angeles breadwinner was a trifle skittish at the start of the

FIBREBOARD. Begun in 1917 and finished two years later, the Port Angeles plant of California-based Paraffine Companies Incorporated was originally called Crescent Boxboard, in honor of Lake Crescent. Following a 1927 merger with Crown Zellerbach, it became the Fibreboard Products Corporation, or simply "Fibreboard." Ranked among the leading producers in the industry, the factory along Marine Drive manufactured wallboard, boxboard and egg fillers for over 50 years. Escalating freight costs and increasingly distant markets caused its downfall, however, and Fibreboard closed its doors permanently on December 31, 1970. PHOTO SOURCE: Bert Kellogg

1920s. He was downright apprehensive about the future of the timber industry (and by extension, of the town), and longed to stabilize his life in this beautiful, remote part of the country. Yet several unknown, unsettling factors created grave doubts as to whether this could be done.

For one thing, a large sawmill company, Bloedel-Donovan, headquartered at Sekiu, in Clallam County's west end, was in 1920 negotiating the purchase of millions of dollars worth of Clallam County timber, and nobody knew whether the sale would be culminated or what was to happen if it were.

Moreover, by this time it was obvious to woodsmen that first-growth timber would ultimately be depleted. What would happen then? Would there, could there ever be a real market for second-growth timber?

Then too, rumors were flying that somebody was going to take over the deserted, never-utilized Spruce Mill on Ennis Creek — but nobody knew why.

Even the future of Port Angeles' major money-maker, the "Big Mill," was clouded, for owner

Michael Earles had passed away in 1919.

As the years went by, however, such concerns evaporated one after another like dew in the morning sun.

Bloedel-Donovan did indeed buy enormous tracts of land in the west end of the county, logged it heavily and maintained steady payrolls in and around Port Angeles for years. Second-growth timber came into its own as one of the soundest investments in the United States economy. The Spruce Mill site, with its all-important railroad link to Clallam County forests, eventually would become a beehive of industrial activity. Earles' mill stayed open, was later sold to the Charles Nelson Company and remained a money-maker until 1930. The Nelson Mill, Crescent Boxboard and other manufacturing and logging operations kept the local economy pumping steadily, and for most of the decade — some call it the most exciting in this nation's history — Port Angeles, as a city, strutted with confidence. During this time, perhaps more than in any other, the community displayed an essential character trait of the true pioneer: The innate ability to sink roots, survive and mature.

FIRST AIRPLANE IN PORT ANGELES. Landing on Front Street between Oak and Valley, on July 11, 1919, Lieutenant J.D. Clemence of the Royal Flying Corporation and L.L. Grant of the American Aircraft Corporation, treated local residents to an exhibition of their flying skill. PHOTO SOURCE: Bert Kellogg

Washington Pulp and Paper Company/ Crown Zellerbach Corporation

During the First World War a Canadian paper firm owned by two brothers, James and George Whalen, analyzed Port Angeles' favorable geography — proximity to timber, hydroelectric power and water transportation — and decided it had great future potential as a pulp center. They therefore began making specific plans to open a mill in town.

Though the Whalen brothers secured a splendid lease on property at the base of Ediz Hook and later shipped in a quantity of equipment with which to begin operations, uncertain markets caused by wartime conditions delayed construction of the pulp and paper mill. Months dragged by and townspeople began to get impatient. They wanted action. City Council considered canceling the Whalens' lease. Meanwhile, the clever Tom Aldwell, President of the Commercial Club, was seeking outlets for electricity generated at his power plant on the Elwha River. Late in 1919 therefore, after several sputtering starts — and with all parties being goaded mercilessly by the forceful Aldwell — things began to happen. The Whalens' interests were bought by a newly-created Zellerbach Paper Company subsidiary, the Washington Pulp and Paper Company. On January 26, 1920, a contract was let for construction of the plant and soon thereafter ground was broken for the large mill. Construction was rapid, and before Christmas that year (December 14th) two reels of standard newsprint were produced: The much-needed plant was off and running.

Washington Pulp and Paper gradually acquired title to more than 52,000 acres of timberland in Washington and would later buy Aldwell's Olympic Power dam, transmission lines and power plant. In 1927, the firm built a second, larger dam in Glines Canyon farther up the Elwha River.

By 1982, the Port Angeles plant was one of 16 pulp and paper mills in the sprawling corporate structure of the largest paper manufacturer on the Pacific Coast, Crown Zellerbach Corporation.

EXCELLENT PHOTO of Lincoln Street believed to be taken in the early 1920s. Seen are the Carnegie Library, Roosevelt High School, the Clallam County Courthouse, the Audett Hotel and the Angeles Cooperative Creamery. PHOTO SOURCE: Bert Kellogg

MASONIC TEMPLE on Lincoln Street, as seen in this photograph taken shortly after it officially opened Tuesday November 22, 1921. PHOTO SOURCE: Ed Gaul

Politics, "The Port," Prohibition . . . and Progress

In a November, 1920, special election, Port Angelens voted heavily in favor of a new Commission form of government; later (December 20th), they elected H. Maurice Fisher the town's first Mayor-Commissioner, along with George W. Kuppler and John Hallahan, Commissioners.[3] The hard, vital news of 1920, though, could be none other than Prohibition. The Eighteenth Amendment to the U.S. Constitution, prohibiting the manufacture, sale, transporting or possession of alcoholic beverages, went into effect. (The Eighteenth Amendment had been proclaimed a year earlier, January 29, 1919, and would be enforced by the controversial Volstead Act.) Legal questions about the law which would render America "dry" for 14 long years, had kept it bottled up in the courts. But on January 5, 1920, the Supreme Court upheld all of the law's major provisions, and Prohibition was here![4]

The Angeles Brewing and Malting Company, at Third and Tumwater Streets, toppled soon after Prohibition took hold, but most of the inhabitants of this rugged seaport town, self-sufficient to a remarkable degree, merely shrugged their shoulders and ignored it; to Port Angeles folk , it was seemingly irrelevant whether the nation was wet or dry. They hitched up their pants and marched through the '20s in notably energetic fashion, their eyes riveted on the future. New companies came to town, community service groups emerged, and even the city's landscape took on a healthy new look. Resthaven Hospital at 5th and Peabody (with the first electric dishwasher in town) and the Carnegie Library at Second and Lincoln (finished two years earlier)

both underwent expansion and modernization in 1921. And even as the imposing Masonic Temple at 7th and Lincoln was being dedicated (November 22, 1921), the wheels were placed in motion for construction of hotels, apartment buildings, a creamery, a new First National Bank Building downtown, and the Washington School on East First Street. All would be completed the following year.[5] (Washington School, however, would not be ready for occupancy till early in 1923.)

In a late-developing election campaign which was hardly noticed by many residents and belied its future significance to the region, voters by a 2-to-1 margin created a Port District for Clallam County in November, 1922.

Also, during the early '20s, Community Service groups such as the Rotary Club, Knights of Columbus (Council No. 2260), Kiwanis Club, Camp Fire Girls, Boy Scout Council and Wolf Cubs (forerunner to Cub Scouts) were formed, and with these, the very heart of the community was further strengthened.[6]

There were a few episodes of racism (the Ku Klux Klan counted many prominent Port Angeles men as members of its powerful, local Klavern — in fact, two huge rallies were conducted at the Masonic Temple in 1923) and some scattered violence among moonshiners and rum runners during the awkward Prohibition era, but serious problems in Port Angeles were unusual.

Two notable achievements in the field of education occurred in 1922. Both the Jefferson and Lincoln Schools were dedicated. At evening ceremonies held November 23rd, the new Jefferson Elementary School, standing "on a beautiful, commanding spot on Twelfth Street just east of Lincoln

REACTION TO PROHIBITION in Port Angeles was typical of that around the nation. Here Fred Rice, Sheriff's Deputy in charge of liquor control, sits in front of a collection of stills behind the Clallam County Courthouse in 1923. Moonshine mash was uncovered in sheds and shacks throughout the County; an operable still was even found located in the old, abandoned Bellevue School in October, 1923. The apparatus pictured here was melted for its copper value, and the salvage money was given to Beacon Bill Welsh's Christmas collection for the needy. PHOTO SOURCE: Clallam County Museum

(Street)" was formally opened.[7] Two weeks later, at Lincoln School, at Ninth and C Streets, a new addition to that building — a "Community Hall" — was officially dedicated by school board representatives.[8]

One week after the Lincoln School ceremonies, Doctors D. E. McGillivray and Walter Taylor opened a new $2,500 ward on the west side of the Port Angeles General Hospital (formerly called the Olympic) at Sixth and Jones Streets. The two men had reopened at that location after a May 25th fire had destroyed their previous medical facilities on the northwest corner of Eighth and Peabody. The new ward at Sixth and Jones, along with other improvements to the building and some new equipment added by McGillivray and Taylor, greatly enhanced medical coverage for residents of Port Angeles and the entire Olympic Peninsula.[9]

During 1923, two important financial institutions were chartered in Port Angeles. On March 16, 1923,

the Port Angeles Savings and Loan Association was granted a charter by the State of Washington, thus becoming the first savings and loan association on the North Olympic Peninsula. Just two weeks later, on March 31st, the Lincoln Savings and Loan Association received similar authorization to operate within the state's boundaries. (Eleven years later, upon receiving its federal charter, the Lincoln would change its name to First Federal Savings and Loan, the name under which it was still operating in 1982.)

By 1923, local businessmen felt the need for some healthy outdoor recreational facilities, so they formed the Port Angeles Golf and Country Club. In 1924, with mill manager Norman B. Gibbs the prime mover, the club bought 120 acres of land from screen actress Dorothy Dalton, and etched a fine, nine-hole golf course into sloping hills on the east side of Port Angeles. The course witnessed its first round of golf in 1925.[10]

EARLY PHOTO OF THE PORT OF PORT ANGELES. On November 8, 1922, city voters created the Port of Port Angeles District. Its authority covers the entire length of Clallam County's shoreline — thought to be the largest such shoreline responsibility of any Port District in the contiguous United States. The hammerhead type crane shown in this 1926 photo had a five-ton capacity at a ninety-five-foot radius and was so designed and equipped that it could handle lumber, coal, sand, gravel and sulphur ore. When installed, the "Brute Crane," as it was called, was the largest of its kind in commercial service on the Pacific Coast. PHOTO SOURCE: Port of Port Angeles

The Port of Port Angeles

The November 1922, election creating the Port District was a momentous occasion for Clallam County, since it officially established the Port of Port Angeles as a Municipal Corporation of the State of Washington. The Port's coastal boundary line was set as that of Clallam County — which is believed to be the longest shoreline responsibility of any Port District in the contiguous United States.

Three Commissioners were voted into office in that 1922 election: Hans J. Bugge, Nat Hawkins and George Lamb. The three held their first session January 8, 1923, with Hawkins (who later became City Clerk) being selected as the Port District's first President, and Lamb its first Secretary.

Early in 1925, the Port District Board appointed William J. Murphy as the first Port Engineer; two years later he became its first Manager. Soon, the competent, hardworking Irishman had guided a Comprehensive Plan of harbor improvements to adoption. Later it was revised and funded with a $440,000 bond issue authorized by Port District voters. All of the bond money was used to acquire land, erect Port Terminal Number One, dredge the harbor, drive piles for bulkheading, and in general anchor the Port District as a solid, vital force in Port Angeles' history.

An important first move made by Port officials was construction of Terminal Number One, a project which was completed August 1, 1926: Jutting northeast into the harbor from the shore between Valley and Tumwater Streets, the terminal was 150 feet by 550 feet;[11] it afforded captains of steamers and sailing vessels ideal facilities for commerce on the North Olympic Peninsula.

Commissioners really began to hit their stride in 1941, though, when Peninsula Plywood first organized. Courted avidly by Board Members, Port Manager Henry Davies and the omnipresent Thomas Aldwell (himself a former Port Commissioner), Peninsula Plywood — nicknamed "PenPly" — founders Oscar Groth and Carl Stromberg decided to build their Cooperative plant in Port Angeles. Commissioners filled a large site adjacent to Port headquarters, negotiated a lease with the ambitious young promoters, then secured voter approval of a bond issue so a log pond could be excavated for the firm.

From that time forward, the diverse activities of the Commissioners, extending as they do throughout the vast Port District, have in some way touched virtually every resident of Clallam County. From corporate development to boat havens, from log yards to airports and from international trade to Industrial Parks, Commissioners and their staffs have made things happen. Both onshore and off, Port Planners over the next four decades developed new facilities, purchased others and continued to improve and enlarge those they already had.

Construction of the Boat Haven along Marine Drive (in 1931) had offered boaters some shelter, though it was unsatisfactory at best, providing no real protection against northeast storms. Maintenance costs were high over the next decade, so by 1941 plans were being made for a new design; World War Two interrupted all activities.

In Volume Two of this

THE STEAMSHIP *GLYMONT* shown here, from the Charles Nelson Shipyards in Port Angeles was the first vessel to call at the Port dock in 1925. PHOTO SOURCE: Bert Kellogg

work we will discuss in detail the further development of the Boat Haven, improvements to existing terminals, construction of new piers, the airport and the Port's involvement in international lumber markets.

CHARLES N. WEBSTER, prominent newspaperman in Port Angeles. Charles Webster was named Editor, and his sister Beth became President, of the *Port Angeles Evening News* in 1936, upon the death of its founder, E.B. Webster. Twelve years later, in 1948, when Beth also passed away, Charles became the newspaper's President. In addition to his journalistic and civic endeavors, Mr. Webster also established Radio Station KONP (*K O*lympic *N*ational *P*ark) in 1945. After a lengthy illness, Charles Webster died April 20, 1969. PHOTO SOURCE: Esther Webster

Newspapers

(Continued from Chapter Five)

E. B. Webster's **Port Angeles Evening News**, with roots stretching back to the first newspaper **(The Model Commonwealth)** and tracking its way through most of the weekly papers which had opened and closed their doors since that time, put its first edition on the streets April 10, 1916. Garnering first-rate people from the time it opened, the **Evening News** gained wide circulation and soon had **The Daily Herald** on the ropes. (It should be noted, though, that **The Daily Herald** had been seriously damaged by the departure of

its able business manager, Jack Campbell, the 1918 retirement of its editor, Arthur V. Watts, and the 1919 death of Michael Earles.) In 1920, Elmer E. Beard, prominent newsman from Vancouver, Washington, (by way of Alaska) purchased the **Daily Herald** and breathed new life into it. The new life was temporary, however; Beard's **Herald** lasted only until May 12, 1923, when the **Port Angeles Evening News** bought it lock, stock and barrel — then closed it forever.

A. A. Smith sold his share

of the **Evening News** on April 21, 1919 — E. B. Webster obtaining controlling interest — and the other shareholders, William Welsh and John Schweitzer, later sold their interests to the Webster family. From that time until 1971, the Websters ran the **Port Angeles Evening News**. According to local writer Virginia Keating, daily newspapers and the Websters are "interwoven in the annals of Port Angeles and the Olympic Peninsula."[12] The Websters were active in a variety of worthwhile civic activities as well.

From 1916 to March 1969, the **Evening News** was produced in a building at 114 South Lincoln Street which was specially designed by G. M. Lauridsen for a newspaper operation.[13]

In Volume Two of this history of Port Angeles, we will see how the **Evening News** becomes a vital force in Pacific Northwest news reporting, and later became **The Daily News**. We shall also witness the birth of **The Peninsula Herald** and Del Price's **Chronicle**.

Along with other Americans, Port Angelens in the early '20s had been startled by the "Teapot Dome" scandal which struck President Warren Harding's administration, and were properly awed by the riches of King Tutankhamen's tomb just revealed to the world. And living on the fringe of earthquake country, a collective shiver could be felt throughout the community when news arrived of a 1923 Japan quake which killed a half-million people and revamped that country's entire east coast. Meanwhile, nobody gave much notice to an arrogant little fellow who that year staged something he called a "Beer-Hall Putsch" in Munich, Germany. It was the first of many such rallies Adolf Hitler would conduct, leading ultimately to the horror known as World War Two.

Port Angelens witnessed a few other important changes in their town during the mid-'20s. The sparkling new Washington School on East First Street — replacing the Cooperative Colony's venerable Old Central School — opened with a community housewarming on January 20, 1923, thus completing the School Board's ambitious building program begun two years earlier.[14] That same year, the old Opera House on Front Street was demolished, to be replaced by the 50-room Olympus Hotel just one year later.[15] And City Park at Cooke's Prairie west of town was rechristened in honor of Abrahan Lincoln. Federal funds rolled into town in the form of a permanent U.S. Immigration Office and a U.S. Coast Guard Section Base, specially-designed to operate small patrol vessels in the area, was established.[16]

1925: The Town, The Fleet . . . The Problem

From 1895 to the mid-Thirties, the U.S. Pacific Fleet made regular trips to the deep, sheltered Port Angeles harbor to conduct summer maneuvers. It was a regular sight, spectacular, and one keenly anticipated by most Port Angeles residents, for with the arrival of thousands of sailors, the town throbbed with social activity. Picnics, baseball games, band concerts, and ships tours — all were a welcome respite for the somewhat isolated community. Parents with marriageable daughters vied with one another for the attention of ships officers. Many marriages took place, too.

It's a well-known fact that sailors like to be entertained after long tours at sea. By 1925 most churchgoing Port Angelens were certain they knew what

kind of entertainment the gobs were getting and how and where it was being provided.

Newspaper accounts declare that a mass meeting was called "for the purpose of expressing indignation over certain conditions" in Port Angeles. One thousand people crammed into the Masonic Temple, demanding that a Grand Jury be convened to "investigate alleged immoral conditions in the city." (Ironically, there is little doubt that many of these same indignant citizens had cheerfully participated in the enthusiastic KKK rallies there just two years earlier!) At the climax of the "sizzling" February 3rd session,

SUPPOSE!

One of your family, or one that was very dear to you, was in serious need of the best service and equipment that a hospital could furnish. Suppose the case meant life or death, as cases sometimes do.

How grateful you would feel; how glad you would be to know that a modern well equipped hospital was at hand in your time of need. These are the things to think

about NOW; not some time in the future. November 2 is the day when you can make it possible to have a splendid new hospital in Clallam County.

Tuesday November 2nd.

Tuesday November 2nd.

VOTE for the HOSPITAL

ADVERTISING A BOND ISSUE. Typical of the sort of emotional advertising often used in the 1920s and 1930s, was this November, 1926 plea for voter approval of a hospital bond issue. Such appeals often were effective, but not always. This particular ad, complemented by several heart-wrenching letters to local newspapers, was not quite enough to carry the hospital bond by the needed 60% majority. It came excruciatingly close, however. With 3,283 total votes cast, 1,966 "yes" votes — 59.999% — were counted, so the levy failed! PHOTO SOURCE: *Port Angeles Evening News*

PORT ANGELES BAY

U.S. NAVY'S PACIFIC FLEET IN PORT ANGELES. For about 40 years, from 1895 well into the 1930s, the U.S. Navy's Pacific Fleet visited Port Angeles to conduct summer maneuvers. Because such maneuvers often featured the firing of huge guns and torpedoes, night attacks and land assaults, the fleet's annual visit was keenly anticipated by local residents, and its impact on Port Angeles was enormous. While the fleet was anchored here in 1896, the Elks Lodge was formed, and ten senior officers became charter members — the reason that organization still is called Elks Naval Lodge #353. This photo was taken in the mid-1920s. PHOTO SOURCE: Bert Kellogg

AMERICAN LA FRANCE FIRETRUCK, 1926 MODEL. The huge 120-horsepower vehicle in this photo was a top-of-the-line model, capable of speeds up to 60 miles per hour, and able to pump 1,000 gallons of water a minute. Total cost: $13,500. This picture was taken in front of the Port Angeles Railroad Depot at Cherry and Valley Streets. Chauncey McNay is behind the wheel, Fire Chief Clay Wolverton is seated beside him, Larry Rayton (in civilian clothes) poses in front and fireman Bob Puryear sits in the back of the La France. Restored to nearly original condition, the powerful old rig is presently owned by Dr. Harlan McNutt. PHOTO SOURCE: Bert Kellogg

MOOSE TEMPLE, at the northeast corner of Lincoln and Sixth Streets, was dedicated by the Port Angeles Lodge # 991 on November 3, 1927. It served as Lodge headquarters until 1934 when it was purchased by Don and Ivor Smith to house the Smith Ice and Bottling Works. The Smith "sody pop factory" as it was affectionately known, manufactured banana soda, ginger ale and birch beer. The 50-year landmark later housed the Port Angeles Business College and several other businesses before being razed in 1973 to make way for a service station. PHOTO SOURCE: Don and Ivor Smith

during which many stirring speeches were delivered praising a recent vice raid on East Fifth Street, the irate residents formed something called the "Port Angeles Welfare and Law Enforcement League" to "root out and eliminate the bottom of the evil."[17] It must have been "rooted" more deeply than anticipated, though, for despite strenuous efforts of this sort, the fleet's customary onshore maneuvers persisted unhampered. A few houses of ill repute would, in fact, flourish in Port Angeles through the latter days of World War Two!

Good Times Definitely Arrive . . . Or Have They?

Two more years of national prosperity ensued, and by 1927 a heady, euphoric atmosphere seemed to blanket the whole country, thoroughly penetrating the public consciousness. Jobs were easy to find. Cash was plentiful. Debts were few. There was ample time for fun. Then, too, this was the Golden Age of Sports, when one couldn't read a newspaper that didn't headline the exploits of Babe Ruth, Bill Tilden, Willie Hoppe and Jack Dempsey. It was a time when anything seemed possible. Why, there might even be some use for that unlikely device called "television," which made its formal bow in April, 1927.

Good times were definitely here. But . . . we now know the financial burner was turned up too high.

Economic crisis was inevitable.

Precious few observers bothered to analyze this marvelous prosperity, but those who did quickly spotted its deceptive character. In a word, it was superficial. The country's capacity to produce had run ahead of its capacity to consume. Easy-money policies had for years triggered fantastic over-speculation in the stock market, yet simultaneously the government's tariff and war debt policies were destroying foreign markets. If proof were needed that hard times lay just ahead, one only had to compare this unprecedented affluence with the plight of the nation's farmers and unskilled workers: They were dirt-poor. But nobody *wanted* to listen. The "boom" psychology had taken firm root, seeping into Americans' lifestyle, dazzling them and obscuring the Tomorrow that had to come. So they disregarded what few warnings there were.

Port Angeles, too, was caught up in the maelstrom. Architects, engineers and builders were toiling furiously all over town. A new City Hall, a new federal building and a second, larger Elks Lodge were all on the drawing board, primed to follow the recently built J. C. Penney structure downtown and the Moose Hall at Sixth and Lincoln. Three physicians, D. E. McGillivray and Walter and Will Taylor, remodeled the three-story brick, 50-room Hotel Olympic at Third and Francis (later it would be the YMCA) into a medical clinic known as the Port Angeles Hospital and Sanitarium. Three weeks later, on December 19, 1927, two of those same men, McGillivray and Walter Taylor, officially threw open the doors of the huge (four stories, 60 rooms) Lee Hotel on First Street.[18] The optimism, contagious, even radiated to City Council: After taking a hard look at the disgraceful condition of Port Angeles' walkways, Council ordered First Street property owners from Lincoln to Race Streets to build new sidewalks "Forthwith!"[19]

And so it continued. Like a marathon runner's last-gasp sprint toward a finish line he can't quite see, the pace of life in Port Angeles over the next few years of the decade intensified. Both the town and nation raced toward their inevitable date with Black Tuesday and The Great Depression.

Nineteen-twenty-eight closed with Herbert C. Hoover's election as President, and the new year dawned on unsuspecting Americans as one that seemed to promise even more affluence than they had already experienced. Nobody foresaw calamity because the financial house of cards had not yet begun to tremble noticeably. It was due to start rumbling and the bubble was about to burst.. . .

ELKS LODGE GROUNDBREAKING, February 26, 1927. Groundbreaking committee for this second Elks Lodge at the northwest corner of First and Lincoln were as follows: S.S. Mullen, general contractor; Ed Taylor, plumbing contractor; Joe Paris, Dr. D.E. McGillivray, Herman Swanson, Ray L. Haynes, secretary; K.O. Erickson, chairman; Senator W.J. Taylor, Exalted Ruler; and Mayor W.D.Hedrick, superintendent of the work. PHOTO SOURCE: Bert Kellogg

GLINES CANYON HYDROELECTRIC DAM on the Elwha River, just west of Port Angeles, was placed in operation in 1927. Construction of this 216-foot dam by the Washington Pulp and Paper Corporation was the largest hydroelectric project ever completed on the North Olympic Peninsula. Lake Mills (named for Edward M. Mills, who was instrumental in the project's financing) is formed behind the Glines Dam. PHOTO SOURCE: Jerry Laurance

Chapter Eight: 1929 — December 7, 1941

The Depression, a "New Deal" and . . . December 7th

"Sure, the Depression was rough, but, you know, the thing is . . . we had fun!"
— Ivor Smith

Trouble loomed on August 8, 1929, when the stock market broke and prices tumbled, creating a tinge of panic. Again, it was a warning few heeded. Less than three months later, October 29th (Black Tuesday), a record 16,410,000 shares changed hands on the New York Stock Exchange and the bottom fell out. Even as President Hoover endeavored to reassure a nervous nation that it was still "financially sound" (he expected a $120 million surplus), the truth was that a terrible economic blight had begun settling over the nation like a rotten rag.

Till the crash, life in Port Angeles had been especially upbeat. Old businesses prospered, new ones caught on with the public, curb lighting was installed on downtown streets, and the never-used U.S. Spruce Division building had been dismantled to make room for Olympic Forest Products' new plant. This demolition job, in fact, and subsequent construction of the new mill on Ennis Creek, resulted in Port Angeles not immediately feeling a job pinch. Construction of the Olympic Forest Products mill required many people, and economic fallout from it postponed most ill effects of the Depression for nearly a year after it had slammed into other parts of the country.

The crunch, however, finally arrived in town in mid-1930.

President Hoover was given a standing ovation in May of that year when he told the nation's business leaders that the worst effects of the stock market crash had passed and that recovery lay "just ahead." He was probably still beaming from the applause when, just six days later, 500 employees of Port Angeles' Crescent Logging Company were laid off because of poor market conditions.[1] The cold, hard facts of the Depression finally began drifting into Port Angeles like a clammy morning fog.

Bad news poured down in a relentless stream after that. Cash was scarce. Crown Zellerbach cut back its work week midway through 1931, and Mayor Ralph Davis set up a city relief committee for the unemployed. Appeals were made to farmers to share their excess produce with the needy. Public officials devised plans for a "winter campaign against cold and hunger." A large group of mill workers even offered to take a 10 percent cut in salary just to keep their jobs. Finally, in November, 1931, the ultimate symbol of the Depression arrived with the opening of what was incorrectly – but appropriately – called the "Unemployment Offfice." According to reports of that day, "scores of men" registered for work at the office located at 111 North Oak (formerly occupied by The Strait Tobacco Company).[2] Newspapers issued stern warnings to outsiders that "unemployed and needy" of other communities should give Port Angeles a wide berth, since 400 deserving citizens "had already listed their names with the City Employment Office as out of work." Going one step further, salesmen were told they would do Port Angeles a favor by criticizing, rather than praising, the town. Such praise, it was noted, merely "attracts the broken-down merchants of other towns and sends hopeful workers from other fields. . ."[3]

Beacon Bill . . . Bad Times . . . A New President

Local businesses donated great quantities of food to the needy that bleak 1931 Christmas season: 165 homes were aided. Many donations, then as in so many other years, were solicited by the well-known newspaper columnist William D. Welsh. Welsh, who during the year was known to the reading public via his newsy column "Welsh Rarebits," became at Christmas the popular "Beacon Bill." Under that byline he gleefully extorted generous contributions from businessmen — always in a gentle, good-natured fashion — by simply publishing "blackmail" stories about them in his special Holiday column.

Things were so bad in 1931 that it would have been easy to believe Mother Nature herself was frowning upon the hapless little town: The day after Christmas, a vicious storm swept in from the Pacific and tremendous waves smashed into Ediz Hook, obliterating 1,000 feet of roadway near the little Indian village then located there.

A smattering of good news was registered during 1931, though, when regular air passenger service com-

J.P. CHRISTENSEN. Colorful Jens Peter Christensen, Port Angeles banker and businessman. During more than 50 years in Port Angeles, the energetic Christensen was associated with Michael Earles, G.M. Lauridsen and others in business deals ranging from the Manhatten Packing Company to the Port Angeles Telephone and Telegraph Company; and from the Citizens National Bank to the Washington State Bank.

menced between Port Angeles and Seattle (two trips daily, starting April 1st), the Port Angeles Chapter of the Business and Professional Women was formed (May) and the Port Angeles Symphony Orchestra unofficially organized, with a "small group of players meeting in homes just to play for the fun of it."[4]

By 1932 the crippled economy had further deteriorated, and genuine hunger was a way of life for some residents. St. Andrew's Episcopal Church at Second and Peabody, began offering one meal per day to those in need, and at one point served up to 150 people. In May of that year, some help arrived from the United States Farm Board in the form of one thousand sacks of surplus flour; all were dis-

"BEACON BILL" WELSH. This 1927 photograph features "Beacon Bill" Welsh standing before Welsh's Christmas Lighthouse, near the Olympus Hotel on East Front Street. Welsh, a newspaper reporter, had a knack for wheedling money from local residents for various charities. Here, he poses with a number of his fund-raising assistants. Those shown are, left to right: Art Shellberger, Clyde McDonnall, Ernest Harding, Clay Wolverton, Clair Fleming, Billy Welsh himself, Carl Jacobson, Harold Thompson, Ivor Smith, Byron Winters and Oscar "Ole" Ullstrom. PHOTO SOURCE: Clallam County Museum

THE *U.S.S. AKRON*, famous American dirigible, appeared in Port Angeles May 24, 1932. The huge helium-filled ship was 785 feet long, 133 feet across with an envelope that could hold 7.4 million cubic feet of helium. When fully inflated, it weighed nearly a quarter of a million pounds. On April 13, 1933, less than a year after its appearance over the Port Angeles skyline, the *Akron* caught fire and crashed over the Atlantic Ocean, killing 72 of the 76 men aboard.

tributed to needy families by the Red Cross. Clallam County's Commissioners were at their wits end, and desperately established a "Committee for the Relief of Unemployed," charging it with issuing food to those working on County or City Relief Projects. However, by this time things were so bad that banks refused to cash County Warrants! Taxpayers were simply not paying enough to meet expenditures.

Then, as if more were needed, another crushing blow landed. Disastrous news arrived from Washington, D.C. when City officials were notified that after almost eight years in town, the payroll-producing U.S. Coast Guard Base would be transferred from Ediz Hook to Port Townsend! Even though fickle bureaucrats would later return the base (within one year), timing of the news was especially demoralizing to the town's residents.

Things were getting serious. And they were no better at the state or national level, either. Americans everywhere found themselves careening down a dark road that seemed to have no end. Something drastic had to be done! And so it was . . . in November of 1932. Franklin Delano Roosevelt was elected to the Presidency of the United States.

CREAMERY TOKENS. From 1928 to 1955, the Port Angeles Cooperative Creamery cast thousands of tokens, and sold them to customers for cash. Each token was then redeemable for the item printed on it. At a time when home delivery of dairy products was commonplace, creamery officials found it to be a convenient way for customers to notify the milkman of dairy products needed daily. PHOTO SOURCE: Clallam County Museum

CREAMERY MONEY. Early in 1933, before President Roosevelt's inauguration, the Great Depression held Port Angeles and the rest of the country in an icy grip. Since there was little real cash available, the County Commissioners frequently issued warrants (similar to Promissory Notes) in lieu of checks, to pay bills. A warrant issued on a certain date could not be cashed until later, because County tax dollars had not yet been collected. In an effort to "thaw" outstanding warrants which had accumulated in buyers' hands, the Port Angeles Cooperative Creamery began issuing scrip certificates to customers in exchange for warrants. The scrip could be used to pay wages and to buy merchandise whenever practicable. As security for the scrip, the Creamery held warrants in trust until they were redeemed by the County. PHOTO SOURCE: Clallam County Museum

CITY FIRE DEPARTMENT. Posing before a new "Diamond T" fire truck — lengthened at the Fire Chief's insistence, to carry a ladder — is the entire crew of the Port Angeles Fire Department in 1933. The photo was taken in the new firehall at Second and Lincoln Streets (site of the Senior Citizens Center when this book went to press in 1982). Identification of firemen made possible with help of Tony Masi. Front Row, left to right: Louie Howser, Ernie "Hacksaw" Harding, Chief Clay Wolverton, F. Van Scoyoc and Walter Madsen. Middle Row: Don Smith, Hugo Olson, Bob Staeger, Irving "Rip" Hansen, Ken Nichols, Carl Jacobson, Oscar "Ole" Ullstrom, Ivor Smith and C.W. "Dutch" Headrick. Back Row: William Watts, Charles "Punch" Goodwin, Harold Thompson, Tony Masi, Don "Red" Jacobson, Clay Stewart, Virgil Johnson and Frank Hickok. PHOTO SOURCE: Clallam County Museum

"OLD IRONSIDES" IN PORT ANGELES HARBOR. For four days in May, 1933, the famous United States frigate *Constitution* visited Port Angeles harbor. Launched October 21, 1779, the 204-foot-long vessel acquired the name "Old Ironsides" after British cannonballs failed to damage her hull during the War of 1812. During her stay in Port Angeles, 22,590 persons — a number exceeding the total population of Clallam County — visited her. PHOTO SOURCE: Bert Kellogg

OLYMPIC HOT SPRINGS LODGE, just a few miles west of Port Angeles, was a popular resort for more than 50 years. Billy Everett discovered the Hot Springs in 1906, and soon thereafter secured a lease from the United States Forest Service to develop the area around them. Following construction of a small sawmill (1909) and a dam on nearby Boulder Creek to supply power, the lodge was built in 1917. In 1925 the resort had a new owner, Harry Schoeffel. Schoeffel built several dozen cabins, and the resort became so popular that, five years later a road through the woods had to be constructed. This photo was taken in 1932, after a new addition provided the lodge with twenty new sleeping rooms. A fire destroyed the lodge in 1940 and a kitchen, store and dining room were built to replace it. Finally, the area was taken over by the Olympic National Park, and Schoeffel's lease ran out in 1966. Today, visitors can still hike in to the hot springs. There is a campground, but the area has been allowed to return to its natural state. PHOTO SOURCE: Bert Kellogg

FDR's "New Deal" and Port Angeles

Roosevelt's "New Deal" rolled across the country in 1933 like a balmy breeze from the South Pacific. Unlike his predecessor, FDR (the new President was fond of using initials) was armed with a firm belief that the federal government should directly stimulate a sluggish economy rather than merely react to unpredictable dynamics of the marketplace. Therefore, exuding confidence, the new chief executive instigated a broad spectrum of reforms and trial programs; certainly his drastic measures were not long in coming.

Roosevelt declared a Bank Holiday just two days after taking office. (The **Port Angeles Evening News** noted on March 3, 1933, that Port Angeles was without the service of a commercial bank for the first time in 32 years.) Many banks which closed their doors were never able to reopen, but those that did were at least guaranteed solvency by Uncle Sam. Moreover, and more important to the American workingman, the Government would thereafter protect individual depositors against bank failure via its newly-created Federal Deposit Insurance Corporation (FDIC).[5]

For the next several years, pump-priming, job-creating projects (referred to as make-work, pork-barrel nonsense by the President's critics) flowed from Washington, D.C., like honey from a jar, with dollars backing all of them. Reacting to Roosevelt's fondness for brevity, bureaucrats identified the programs (and they became widely known) by their initials: CCC for the Civilian Conservation Corps; PWA, the Public Works Administration;

and NRA, the National Recovery Administration. It is noteworthy that for the remainder of the decade, Port Angeles profited greatly from such federal largesse. And it started almost immediately; an extraordinary number of federal dollars were spent in this area during 1933.

Civilian Conservation Corps

The Civilian Conservation Corps, the recovery program's launching pad, announced in April, 1933, that 600-1,000 men would be employed in three Clallam County Forestry Camps to be established within a few months;[6] six other camps were to be installed the next summer. Clallam County's first CCC enlistee was Eugene Vannausdle of 118 West Seventh Street, Port Angeles.[7] By June, the "greatest single government venture these parts have glimpsed since Spruce Division days of World War I" was in full swing at an Elwha Canyon CCC Camp.[8] The Corps' goals — all accomplished — were to build 24 miles of standard-width automobile highway in the vicinity and widen six miles of the Olympic Hot Springs Road. Also, one crew was designated the important responsibility of producing sanitarily-constructed wooden outhouses, with seat covers, screened ventilators and doors with locks on them. (By November, 1933, the crew was reported to have 26.5 of the attractive toilets under construction![9])

More federal money ($60,000) was awarded to the city in July of 1933, for concrete paving of Lincoln and First Streets, and then State Relief programs — prodded by the federal money tree — leaped into the affair. A crew of men under the Civil Works Program began improving

NRA INSIGNIA. Bright red and blue, this colorful symbol of the National Recovery Administration was designed by President Roosevelt's strategists, and signified the kind of economic recovery sought by his Administration during the 1930s. Thousands of badges and flags were exhibited nationwide at the height of this promotion. PHOTO SOURCE: *Port Angeles Evening News*

Washington School in November, the first of 17 such Clallam County projects planned by the Welfare Board.

Under the withering gaze of Roosevelt's National Recovery Act, Clallam County loggers began making more money. With the NRA their avenging angel, 1,000 Bloedel-Donovan and Merrill-Ring workers received a series of pay increases totaling 40 percent over a two-month span during 1933, coercing businessmen to accept collective bargaining, minimum wage and maximum hour stipulations.

All in all, a striking beginning. By August of that year, the combination of CCC programs and slightly increased mill activity had forced the Port Angeles/Clallam County

unemployment relief caseload down to one-half its previous high.[10] Nationwide, the President's "New Deal" appeared to be working. The crippled, stagnant economy was stirring and Americans tingled with optimism once again, their faith in the democratic process much restored. Problems still dangled overhead, to be sure, but a tiny beam of light was winking at the end of that economic tunnel.

Works Progress Administration

For the remainder of the '30s, Roosevelt presided over the astounding growth of the national government. His Administration emphasized both business recovery programs and social reforms. As a result, Americans observed the

THE "NEW DEAL" IN PORT ANGELES. This picture of the Eighth Street bridge over Valley Street was taken shortly after construction was completed in 1936. A federal PWA grant of $53,600 was made available in September, 1935, and the bridge opened to automobile traffic July 10, 1936. PHOTO SOURCE: Clallam County Museum

FDR's "New Deal" Continued

birth of another make-work program, the Works Progress Administration (WPA), the far-reaching Social Security Act and the Wage and Hour Act — all of which had lasting impact on Port Angeles and Clallam County. Under the WPA, for example, libraries and cemeteries were refurbished, mile after mile of streets and highways repaved, several new bridges erected (others repaved) and many public parks improved and beautified. Moreover, in a cooperative venture utilizing County staff and equipment and WPA labor, the Clallam County Airport was enlarged and modernized.[11]

By 1938, the National Debt, not surprisingly, had swollen to a whopping $40 billion, and Port Angeles was but one of many American cities engulfed in the tidal wave of federal projects. One out of every eight wage earners in town was on WPA or some other kind of state or federal relief![12]

America's abrupt entry into World War Two in 1941 ended Franklin Roosevelt's New Deal experiments. From that time until his death four years later, he would be a wartime president. The preceding nine years, however, had been a period during which the federal government had expanded at an astonishing rate — a fact of great importance to this day. Moreover, legislation introduced during the Roosevelt era was destined to affect every man, woman and child in this country for five more decades.

FIRST NATIONAL BANK SCRIP. When President Roosevelt declared a bank holiday in March, 1933, local financial institutions, and others throughout the nation, were informed by U.S. Treasury Secretary William H. Woodin that they might be permitted to open for business on the condition that each bank carefully prepare and distribute "personalized" scrip backed by that institution's own assets. Local banker B.N. Phillips printed thousands of dollars worth of currency — only to have the Treasurer change his mind at the last minute! The entire batch of scrip was destroyed immediately. PHOTO SOURCE: *Port Angeles Evening News*

A mood of change impelled the nation in 1933. Not only was there a vigorous gadfly in the White House, lighting fires of hope and promise from coast to coast, but a populace "dry" for more than 12 long years was in full rebellion. The Twenty-First Amendment to the Constitution, designed to kill Prohibition and up for ratification, was welcome news to thirsty Americans. In rapid succession that year, thirty-six states voted to repeal the Eighteenth Amendment, and on December 5, 1933, Prohibition ended officially. In the midst of the unprecedented "wet" wave sweeping the U.S.A., Washingtonians streamed to the polls on August 29th to vote Prohibition out as a law of the land. (Freedom-loving, hard-drinking Clallam Countians voted for repeal by the hefty score of 9,573 to 2,201.)

By the end of 1933, even though the Federal Government was demonstrating some degree of progress at most levels of the economic spectrum, the New Deal was still too new to have aided everybody. Many families were still saving, scrounging, and, as the saying went, "eating out of the sock." Yet the Depression, if hardy Port Angelens thought much about it at all, had been relegated to "a way of life" and something "we didn't get depressed about," according to long-time Port Angeles resident Ann Gehrke, who lived through it. Others, like the well-known former Mayor Ivor Smith, readily concede that times were rough, but insist that despite hardships, Port Angelens accepted their lot uncomplainingly. "Sure, the Depression was rough," he smilingly recalls, "but, you know, the thing is . . . we had fun!" However, had they and other Americans been able to foresee what misery lay ahead, they surely would

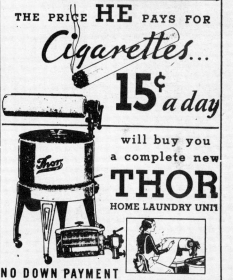
ADVERTISEMENTS FROM THE '30s (this page and next). Advertisements which appeared in the *Port Angeles Evening News* in the mid-1930s. These ads feature businesses, some of which are no longer on the scene, and many products no longer manufactured. Moreover, they emphasize the quantum leap in prices for everyday products that has occurred during the past five decades. PHOTO SOURCE: *Port Angeles Evening News*

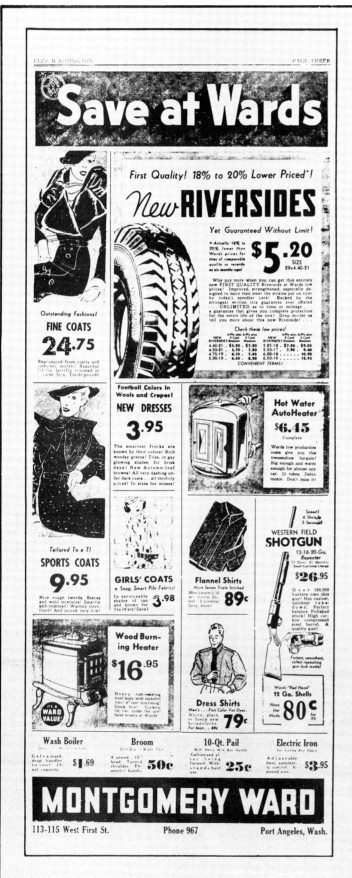

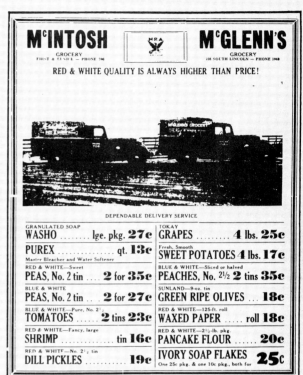

HUGHTO WINS SALMON DERBY CAR

HEADLINE TELLS STORY of the first Port Angeles Salmon Derby, won by Wilbur Hughto on September 2, 1934. The winner and his young son Donald, left, hold the 27-pound, 6-ounce prize-winning salmon that Hughto hooked just off the lighthouse dock, less than 200 yards from the Ediz Hook Clubhouse. Hughto's victory earned him the first prize, a 1934 six-cylinder Studebaker sedan, pictured above. Below, all the happy winners in this, the first-ever Derby, pose outside the Clubhouse. PHOTO SOURCE: Donald Hughto

THE NOTORIOUS
HIASCHUCKALUCK. During the
1930s, in conjunction with the annual
Derby, the Port Angeles Salmon Club
collected dozens of bizarre stories from
its members about sea serpents and
other marine monsters lurking in Juan
de Fuca Strait. The sketch shown here
was drawn "from memory" by an
Olympic Forest Products Company
employee, who vowed that he and
14 of his fellow workers had seen
this fellow swimming near the company wharf at the mouth of Ennis
Creek! PHOTO SOURCE: *Port Angeles
Evening News*

have been distressed upon reading that Adolf
Hitler had officially taken over the reins of power in
Germany.

The First Salmon Derby . . . And a Stag Party

Following on the heels of sensational news such
as the Dionne Quintuplets' birth and the FBI's
killing of Public-Enemy-Number-One, John Dillinger,
the big local story of 1934 was that 190 salmon fishermen entered the qualifying round of the First Annual Port Angeles Salmon Derby. Forty-four men
made it, and later in the year (September) the big
winner was Wilbur Hughto, with a 27-pound, 6-ounce
fish; his prize was a $1,000 Studebaker automobile.

The fact is, 1934 was a good year for fishermen.
As if to demonstrate how good it was, many who
were members of the Port Angeles Salmon Club
decided their annual Jamboree at the Ediz Hook
Clubhouse would be a raucous stag party. Announcement of the "Men Only" affair, however, generated
white-hot criticism from the fair sex. Embarrassed,
the anglers hastily pointed out the real reason why it
had to be a stag event: Fishermen, they anxiously
explained, truly loved their spouses and eagerly
anticipated the ladies' attendance at most ordinary
get-togethers; but this year's all-male party was to
be an extraordinary one, and the delicate creatures,
if in attendance, might actually be *endangered.*

TAX TOKENS. Aluminum Sales
tokens, worth one-fifth of a cent,
issued by the State of Washington
in 1935. Two million such tokens,
about the size of a quarter and with
a hole in the center, were purchased
by the State Tax Commission as a convenient means of collecting the new 2% Retail Sales
Tax. Merchants would buy a quantity of tokens from
the State (available locally at the First National Bank),
sell them to consumers, then remit actual cash to the
State in the amount of all the taxes collected. Aluminum tokens were recalled in 1941 and replaced by
dark, green fibre disks weighing, as one news account
described it, not much more "than a flea in a famine."
PHOTO SOURCE: Pete Capos

With a straight face, spokesmen insisted that it was
old-fashioned chivalry (thank Heaven it was still
alive and well within the ranks of the Salmon Club!)
which prompted the "stag" decision, for "a big
crowd was expected and some (of the ladies) . . .
might get trampled in the excitement!"[13]

In September, the U.S. Coast Guard approved
plans to establish a seaplane base on Ediz Hook and/
or construction of a new and larger cutter to replace
the old *Snohomish* at this port.

For at least a couple of years in the mid-1930s,

PRESIDENT FRANKLIN D. ROOSEVELT IN PORT ANGELES. On September 30, 1937, Franklin D. Roosevelt became the first American President to visit Port Angeles while in office. Arriving aboard the Destroyer *Phelps*, FDR gave a short speech in front of the Clallam County Courthouse during which he pledged his support for creation of the Olympic National Park. A huge sign over the doorway of the courthouse implored, "Please Mr. President, we children need your help. Give us our Olympic National Park." PHOTO SOURCE: Bert Kellogg

FDR GREETS PORT ANGELENS. This fascinating portrait of Roosevelt was snapped as he greeted well-wishers in front of the Clallam County Courthouse on Lincoln Street during his September 30, 1937 visit. PHOTO SOURCE: Clallam County Museum

Port Angelens were content to just sit back and react (predictably, it might be added) to events taking place on the county, state and national level . . . and to knit their brows in alarm as Adolf Hitler, gearing Germany for another war, whipped his people into a frenzy of nationalistic pride.

Clallam Countians grumbled a little when slot machines and punch boards were banned throughout the county (February 1935), howled in anguish two months later when ordered by the state to use the 1/5-cent tax tokens for all purchases, and mourned the passing of America's foremost humorist Will Rogers, who, with noted aviator Wiley Post, was killed in an August 1935 plane crash near Point Barrow, Alaska.[14] The old, flimsy Eighth Street bridges were replaced by sturdy, new ones in 1936; an unknown 34-year-old named Warren Magnuson was first elected to Congress in Seattle; and an employee of Olympic Forest Products, Frank A. Feeley, was assigned the very first Social Security

number to be issued in Port Angeles.

Roosevelt in town

Genuine progress was demonstrated on another front in 1937, aided considerably by a September 30th visit from none other than President Franklin D. Roosevelt. During the popular FDR's visit — the only one a President has ever made to Port Angeles while in office — he promised his considerable help in establishing Olympic National Park. That one pledge alone guaranteed him a warm welcome, and his tour through town was a festive, happy one. It was also significant to Peninsula residents, 10,000 of whom lined flag-draped streets to greet him. Upon returning to the nation's capital he kept his promise to help by urging Congressional passage of a bill setting boundaries for what is now the spectacular 860,000-acre Olympic National Park.[15] Roosevelt then signed the bill into law on June 28, 1938.

ITT Rayonier, Inc.

Long-term military plans by Uncle Sam and the abrupt ending of the First World War in 1918 combined to provide Port Angeles in 1929 with one of its leading industries, today's ITT Rayonier, Inc.

The U.S. Spruce Division in 1918 had just finished laying a standard gauge railroad along the north shore of Lake Crescent from a point west of Joyce, Washington (at a place called Tyee, or Lake Pleasant) all the way into Port Angeles, to its newly constructed spruce sawmill at the mouth of Ennis Creek.[16] The mill was virtually finished and ready for operations, when World War One suddenly ended — and the war-induced need for spruce lumber dissolved. The Port Angeles Western tracks rusted and the Ennis Creek sawmill sat idle for 11 years until Olympic Forest Products was organized in 1929 by Edward M. Mills and his associates.[17] Mills' affiliated plants at Shelton and Grays Harbor were already producing chemical cellulose for subsequent manufacture elsewhere (into rayon, cellophane and photographic paper), and he saw a plant at Port Angeles — with its essential rail connections to hemlock forests already completed — as a necessary adjunct to his marketing plans. The Port Angeles mill was designed to produce both lumber and pulp from hemlock logs and enabled Olympic Forest Products to make full use of all logs —

even the bark, which was burned as hog fuel and converted into steam and power. In a gesture of support for the new venture, city residents voted overwhelming approval (2,819 to 11!) for construction of a 7½-mile water line — all costs paid by Olympic Forest Products — from the Elwha River.

Demolition of the old spruce mill and construction of the new one provided a real boost to the town in 1929, coinciding with the final closing of Port Angeles' largest industrial plant, the Charles Nelson Lumber and Shingle Mill (formerly Michael Earles' "Big Mill") — and with the start of the Great Depression. As noted earlier in this chapter, the project — which included building the water line, pulp mill, chipping plant, dock, warehouses, filter plant, railroad spurs and log booming grounds — delayed any significant impact of the Depression in Port Angeles for almost a year after it had struck the rest of the country.

Though well-planned and administered, Olympic Forest Products inevitably was pinched by the economic stress of that day; by 1932, while continuing to operate, it went into receivership. Owner E. M. Mills kept the company limping along until November 1, 1937, at which time he merged it with Rainier Pulp and Paper Company and the Grays

Harbor Pulp and Paper Company to form Rayonier, Incorporated. He was elected the corporation's president and coined the name "Rayonier" by combining the term "Rayon" — trade name for the kind of pulp produced by the firm — with the last three letters of his now defunct Rainier Pulp and Paper Company.

From the time of that 1937 merger, Rayonier proceeded to grow vigorously. Gradually, lumber manufacturing at the Port Angeles mill was discontinued and as pulp production increased, the entire capacity of the woodmill was switched to chip production.

In Volume Two of this work we will discuss Rayonier's corporate realignment when it became a subsidiary of International Telephone and Telegraph Company.

FIRST JUNIOR SALMON DERBY in Port Angeles was held September 12, 1936 and was won by young Glen Rudolph, age nine, and Sally Price, age eleven, shown here holding their prize winners. Glen's fish weighed 11 pounds, 1 ounce, and Sally's 11 pounds, 4 ounces. Both youngsters won a bicycle for their efforts. PHOTO SOURCE: *Port Angeles Evening News*

LITTLE SYMPHONY ORCHESTRA, predecessor to today's Port Angeles Symphony, shown here, with its first Conductor, Charles Thompson after a 1937 concert in the Elks Lodge Room. The Little Symphony started a few years earlier when a small group of players began meeting in the home of Dr. Will Taylor to play orchestra music for their own enjoyment. The players are: At rear, left: Marie Willson Read and Price Harriman, bass viols, and Bertha Dunning, piano. Seated, from left: Margot Aal, Don Smock, Gene Pearson and Lillian Day, violins; Homer Dunning, oboe; Leslie Day, violin; Dr. Will Taylor, flute; Andrew Ward, cello; Spencer Adams, percussion, and Neil Thomas, clarinet. Behind the podium is conductor, Charles Thompson. Then, from left: Less Rodda, percussion; Bessie Brown, cello; Ralph Davis, clarinet; Helen Tradewell, viola; Donald Bailey, French horn; Erma Smith, violin; Roger Bailey, trombone; Oliver Guy, violin; Guy Montgomery, horn; Charles (Pop) Warner, trombone; Phillip Redford, horn; E.R. (Biz) Gehrke, trombone; Eleanor Champion, violin; Oscar Fogde, trumpet; Lewis Iverson, violin; and Gerald Sullivan, trumpet. PHOTO SOURCE: Mrs. Robert Allman

KLAHHANE GARDENS at Lake Dawn, near the Heart o' the Hills, south of Port Angeles. Established by E.B. Webster around 1932, (they were later named for their founder), the Gardens featured waterfalls, rock structures, pools and hundreds of plants and flowers, and were the showplace of the Olympic Peninsula for several years until they were abandoned during the Second World War. PHOTO SOURCE: John and June Nelson

Germany girds for War

By 1938, the entire world was beginning to wonder where Hitler's Nazidom was headed. Some reports from Germany were favorable, describing the economy as sound, and unemployment nonexistent. Other accounts, however, depicted incredible Nazi brutality toward Jews and intellectuals, told of goose-stepping children being molded into automatons and of enormous rallies where thousands passionately roared allegiance to their Fuhrer. To "protect" Germans from the "Bolshevik Terror" he claimed now resided there, Hitler sent his Divisions to over-run neighboring Austria in March 1938, then bluffed and bullied England's weak Prime Minister Neville Chamberlain into "giving" him Czechoslovakia's Sudentenland. Encouraged by the fact that the League of Nations did nothing to stop him, he then launched a spine-tingling war of nerves against Poland.

Meanwhile, Port Angelens worked at the task of stabilizing their little community. They wrestled with local ordinances, bought one another's products, and, in the fashion of people in remote areas, created their own happy times. Occasionally, those happy times arrived in the person of a world-famous personality. John Philip Sousa (twice), band leader Phil Harris, fiction writer Erle Stanley Gardner, movie and singing star Roy Rogers, and heavyweight champion James Braddock — all stopped in town for varying lengths of time. None, however, generated as much excitement — especially among youngsters — as the visit from Jim Thorpe, generally conceded to

JIM THORPE, one of the greatest all-around athletes in
history, visited Port Angeles in
1938. Thorpe, winner of both
the Pentathlon and the Decath-
lon events in the 1912 Olympic
Games, appeared in native garb
before the students of Roosevelt High School on October
24th of that year. PHOTO
SOURCE: Cumberland County
Historical Society, Carlisle,
Pennsylvania

be the greatest athlete of his era. Thorpe, a native
American (Souk-Fox) who brought fame to the small
Indian college of Carlisle in Pennsylvania, was truly
a legend in his own time. He appeared in native garb
as he addressed the students at Roosevelt High School
in 1938.

Courthouse Scandal

Unquestionably the most electrifying news item
to hit Port Angeles during 1939 was the scandal exposed within the hallowed halls of the Clallam
County Courthouse. Police investigation of an alleged
burglary in the Treasurer's Office revealed that
$117,000 had been stolen over a period of years
(some embezzled, some physically looted from the
safe) by none other than the County Treasurer and
accomplices! The Treasurer and ten others were convicted on a number of charges, some of which were
Misappropriation of Funds, Forgery, Nonfeasance in
Office, Perjury and Grand Larceny. Most of those
convicted in the tawdry affair (carried out, as one of
them said " . . . in an attempt to stem the tide of
personal business reverses") served time in jail;
County Treasurer Walter Baar received the stiffest
sentence and ultimately served five years (of a maximum 155) at Walla Walla State Prison.[18] Upon his
release from prison, the popular Baar moved to

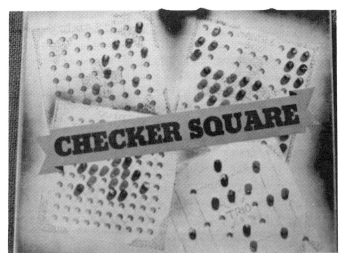

LOCAL MANUFACTURING EFFORT — the
"Checker Square" game. This parlor game, consisting
of a 9" x 9" plywood board and 25 marbles, was
originated by Melvin J. Senz in 1939. His M.J.S.
Company manufactured and distributed 10,000
sets out of their Front Street plant. PHOTO
SOURCE: Pen Print, Inc.

Joyce, Washington, west of Port Angeles where he
lived an exemplary life until his death on July 30,
1980.

PRIVY PLANT. Located on the old city dock, the Epperson and Sons Community Sanitation Privies Plant mass-produced an improved rural outhouse in 1938. With a staff of WPA workmen under the direction of the Washington State Department of Health, privies were made of wood, with two coats of paint on the exterior and one coat on the interior; both the seat and cover were varnished. Numerous ventilation and other construction improvements gave a certain flair to the "back lot telephone booths," which sold for $25.00 per unit. PHOTO SOURCE: Clallam County Museum

PORT ANGELES GUARDSMEN. Shown here are officers and men of Battery A, 248 Coast Artillery (H.D.). In September of 1940, they moved to Fort Worden for a full year's active duty in the regular army. Note the two kinds of uniforms used at that time: the barracks uniform shown at top, and the field uniform worn by men in the lower photograph. Identification of the guardsmen was made possible with the help of local residents Harvey Hussey and Charles "Chuck" Beam. In the top photo, kneeling: Gifford Tiller, Norman Cahill, Albert Schell, Gordon Johnson, Harvey Hussey, William Faires, Richard Jones, T. Richard "Dick" Thompson, Russell Heuhslein; In the top photo, standing: Joe Faires, Charles Beam. Augustine Del Guzzi, Neal Franklin, Eldon Drake, Joseph Harley, Jack Hayne, Albert Marsura, Donald Short, Douglas Bailey, Captain Walter F. Winters, commanding officer, John Eldridge, Dan McGrew, Charles Boyd, Keith Cleland, Stan Gallagher, William B. Gellor, Arthur Stetson, Charles Thompson, Vernon Hahn, Norman Sather. In the bottom photo, kneeling: Gilbert Gallagher, William Morrish, Donald Arnold, Felix Church, Raymond Gastman, Larry Layton, Brian McDonald, Orin Burgman, Joe Hart, Richard Bennett, Eugene Waldron, Richard Goin, Howard Rittenhouse. In the bottom photo, standing: Richard Cummings, James Taylor, Mike Reed, Aaron Gebhardt, Paul Poulsen, Ted Hutchinson, Walter Lafeman, Delbert Daugaard, George Burdick, Allen Forrest, Roy Sage, First Lieutenant H.W. Pollock, Robert Johnson, Albert Levesque, Leroy Jaggers, Ralph Ward, Underwood, Arthur Waldron, Max Johnson, Alvin Paulstick, Frank Fountain, Robert "Tank" Taylor, Max Egli, Joel K. Pickering. PHOTO SOURCE: *Port Angeles Evening News*

BUILT IN 1915 by G.M. Lauridsen, this building on south Lincoln Street was originally the home of Smith and Webster Printers and their weekly newspapers. Long the home of the *Evening News* (since April 19, 1941), the sturdy old structure was still in use as a commercial printery when this book went to press in 1982. PHOTO SOURCE: *Port Angeles Evening News*

The War Nears — Roosevelt's Third Term

Throughout the country war talk was in the air during the early months of 1940, for Hitler had undeniably embarked on his tragic, tortuous journey. Having already smashed Poland, he was by now bombarding Great Britain with 1,000 Third Reich planes and continued snarling defiantly at the rest of Europe. World War Two had unofficially begun.

Nevertheless, many miles of ocean separated the two continents, and what most Americans referred to as "Europe's War" would remain distant for two years. Roosevelt solemnly pledged that this nation would stay out of the conflict, but acknowledged he hadn't the right to "ask that every American remain neutral in thought as well."[19] Neutrality began to dissolve in certain quarters, and American military strategists began speculating openly on this nation's contingency plans if it were drawn into the conflict. One talkative War Department expert even revealed that five million dollars worth of fuel would soon be stored underground at a little-known spot in the Pacific called Pearl Harbor. The prognosis for world peace was indeed gloomy.[20]

Near the end of 1940, nationwide registration of aliens was in full swing, and Draft Boards were formed all over the country. Franklin D. Roosevelt, riding a wave of popularity that only a war-conscious electorate could set in motion, was elected to an unprecedented third term as United States President.

Americans collectively shook their heads, reeling from the surge of world unrest; most struggled just to retain a sense of proportion. After all, they said, the U.S. wasn't at war yet and the continent of Europe *was* a long way off. Japan, despite its obvious military strength and its recent invasion of China, still showed no inclination to enter the European Theatre — the only war Americans were really concerned about. Something, a miracle perhaps, would happen to stop the carnage and we wouldn't have to get involved. . . .

Things were still normal around Port Angeles. Aftershocks from the Depression were diminishing and 1940 actually saw the little town take healthy strides toward stability. A sparkling, new Civic Stadium on Race Street was finished and dedicated that year. And in one of the more spectacular events, the old Nelson Mill near the head of the bay was deliberately torched to make room for another plant on that site.

As 1941 dawned, Roosevelt had successfully recast the die: His countrymen were mentally primed for war. Draft Boards reached out and began tapping the nation's youth, with 20 Port Angeles area men among the first to be mustered into the U.S. Army.[21] Petrus Pearson bought the first of many defense bonds to be sold in Port Angeles and word reached town that a large fleet of British war ships and planes had combined to destroy the notorious Nazi war ship *Bismarck* in the North Atlantic.

The Lady of the Lake

Late in 1941, a story of intense local interest broke, all but completely diverting Port Angelens' attention from the depressing war news.

More than a year earlier, on July 6, 1940, the hog-tied, fully clothed body of a woman had popped to the surface from the icy depths of Lake Crescent, just a few miles west of Port Angeles. Two fishermen, Louis and Joe Roff[22] had pulled the corpse ashore just off "Rocky Point," near the Olympic Highway. They immediately reported their grisly discovery to A. F. "Fred" Immenroth, Superintendent of the State Fish Hatchery then located at Lake Crescent. Immenroth phoned Clallam County Sheriff Charles W. Kemp, who, accompanied by Deputy Karl Kirk and Prosecuting Attorney Ralph Smythe, went to the lake and recovered the body . . . and the stage was set for one of the most bizarre tales in the annals of this nation's criminal justice system.

The unidentified corpse — wrapped in two blankets and bound with rope from neck to calves when found — was taken to the Christman Mortuary, where it was examined by County Medical Officer, Dr. Irving E. Kaveney. Kemp, Kirk, Smythe, Kaveney, Mortician Frank Christman and Harlan McNutt, Jr., (then a pre-med student) spent several hours trying to find some clue to the woman's identity, but to no avail. Dr. Kaveney then performed an autopsy on the remains five days later, and ruled that the woman had been strangled.

But there was something else about the body. Something strange. Though the face was unrecognizable, the corpse, was, eerily, far from decomposed. It was not bloated, and emitted no odor; its total weight was estimated by the coroner at 125-130 pounds. But the flesh was not flesh at all. It was soft and pulpy — "like putty with the oil dried out," said Sheriff Kemp.

Medical analysis revealed that a rare combination of the cadaver's original fatty tissue, bacillus in the water, and near-freezing Lake Crescent temperatures

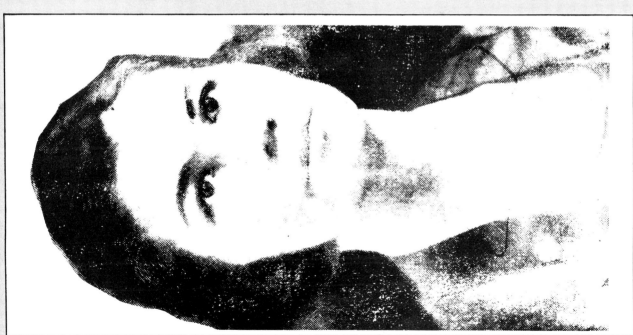

HALLIE LATHAM SPRAKER STRICKMAN ILLINGWORTH, the murder victim known as "The Lady of the Lake," as shown in a newspaper photo of the trial coverage. Testimony revealed that she had been killed and thrown in Lake Crescent in December, 1937. PHOTO SOURCE: Bert Kellogg

"THE LADY OF THE LAKE." On July 6, 1940, the hog-tied body of a woman floated to the surface of Lake Crescent, west of Port Angeles. An autopsy on the unknown woman, shown here shortly after she was pulled ashore, revealed that she had been strangled — and that her flesh had saponified, or turned to soap (like "putty . . . with the oil dried out," according to Clallam County Sheriff Charles Kemp). Identifying "The Lady of the Lake" — so named by newsmen — and bringing her killer to justice resulted in a spectacular murder trial in Port Angeles early in 1942. PHOTO SOURCE: Bert Kellogg

(at the great depths where it had hovered — for almost three years, authorities would later discover), had caused the body to undergo a radical chemical transformation. It had saponified, or *turned almost completely to soap.*[23]

The remains of the woman — by this time, dubbed "The Lady Of The Lake" by newsmen — then lay in the Port Angeles morgue for two months, while Sheriff Kemp and his staff made strenuous efforts to establish identification. During that time, hundreds of local residents viewed the corpse, but nobody recognized it. "The Lady" was then taken to the county cemetery and buried without a name.

With the woman's dental work his only tangible clue, Sheriff Kemp and the other investigators began sending circulars to individual dentists and to law enforcement officers all over the country, asking that the information be circulated among dental personnel in their respective areas. The circular focused on a photograph of partial plates taken from the mouth of the victim. It paid off. More than six months later, in Faulkton, South Dakota, Dr. Albert J. McDowell received a letter from the new Clallam County Prosecutor Max Church (Ralph Smythe was by this time Judge Ralph Smythe), in which the circular was enclosed. The picture of the gold bridge work caught his eye: He had performed that work on a woman then known to him as Mrs. Hallie Spraker. He contacted Clallam County authorities . . . and "The Lady Of The Lake" was identified.

Hallie Latham Spraker Strickman married Monty Illingworth in Port Angeles in 1936, and had lived with him in this community until dropping from sight in December, 1937. Monty Illingworth, who had since moved out of State, would later testify that during their two-year marriage, his wife had frequently threatened to leave him; therefore, when she disappeared, he figured she had finally deserted him.

Intensive investigation by authorities — with able assistance from Hollis B. Fultz, special investigator for the State Attorney General's office — conclusively linked Monty Illingworth to the murder, and he was

$100 REWARD

for the positive identification of this partial plate

or for identification of the body on which it was found

DESCRIPTION OF PLATE: Partial upper denture swung from upper right bicuspid and upper left cupid. Right side has two true-bite teeth; left side has four teeth, two molars, and being a close bite, it has been necessary to replace the two bicuspids without occlusal surfaces. Lower cuspid teeth were used instead of bicuspids in the replacements. Palate of case is cast gold; saddles put on with brown vulcanite, and pink facing. Upper left first bicuspid been knocked out and replaced. Saddles worn by scrubbing: retention of gold on inside of plate worn down and exposed: ten years or more old from the surface wear. Casts are of cast clasp: one on bicuspid is a very heavily constructed clasp with occlusal stop on distal. Clasp on lingual of cuspid clasp covers at least third of tooth structure and has no occlusal stops or rests. Casting of the palate of the gold section extends only up to beginning of rugae and back as far as soft palatal area, making a palate approximately inch in width with the center section open. It is not an Akers design case.

DESCRIPTION OF BODY: Found floating in Lake Crescent, Wash., 17 miles from Port Angeles, July 6, 1940. In water from 5 to 12 months, possibly longer. Wrapped in gray-black and lighter gray striped camp style blankets. Bound with weather-stained heavy rope. Five feet, five to six inches in stocking feet; weight 135 to 150; dark brown hair which may have been dyed. Between 35 and 45 years old. Prominent bust. Wore silk stockings, green wool dress decorated with white petticoat braid; snaps on side; 18 PRINCESS stamped inside belt; waist measurement about 29 inches. Dress value probably around $9.00; likely manufactured in Los Angeles; size 38. Rayon braissiere; no shoes, hat or coat. Probably been strangled. Not likely ever had children.

Please Show this Circular to All Dentists in Your County. If Identified

NOTIFY (Telephone 24)

SHERIFF CHAS. W. KEMP, Port Angeles, Wash.

THIS CIRCULAR offering a $100 reward for identification of "The Lady of the Lake" dental plate, was circulated in dentistry journals and among law enforcement agencies throughout the United States. It was a key leading to the identification of Hallie Illingworth, living in Port Angeles with husband Monty J. Illingworth at the time of her death. PHOTO SOURCE: Bert Kellogg

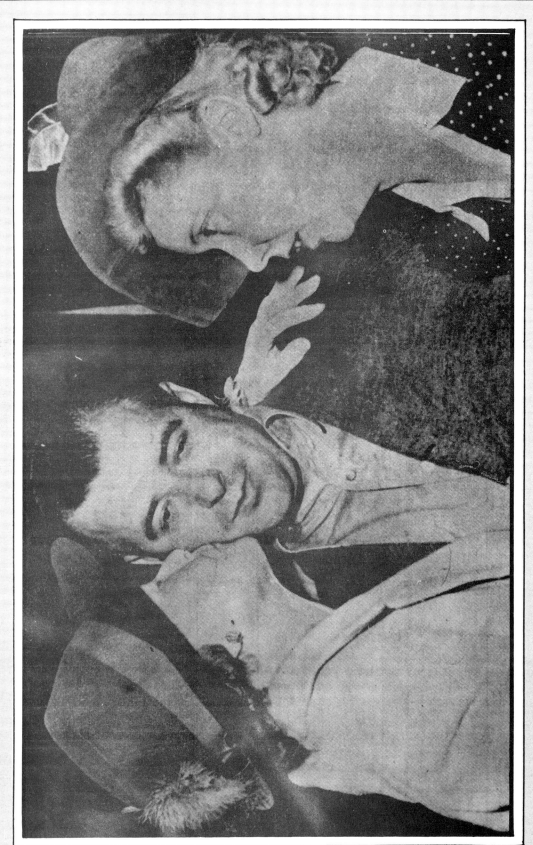

MONTY ILLINGWORTH, shown here being kissed by his mother, Mrs. Flossie E. Illingworth, after being extradited from California to face trial for the murder of his wife, "The Lady of the Lake." At his trial, Monty Illingworth was convicted of beating and strangling his wife Hallie to death, tying her in a blanket with heavy weather-stained rope, and, after weighting it down, dropping it into the icy depths of Lake Crescent. PHOTO SOURCE: *Port Angeles Evening News.*

traced to Long Beach, California, where, since 1938, he had been living with his (self-described) common-law wife, Eleanor Pearson. California Governor Culbert L. Olson signed extradition papers on November 19, 1941, and the spectacular trial that followed overshadowed virtually all other news for several weeks.

Numerous witnesses testified at the trial that Monty and Hallie fought incessantly during their brief marriage; physical violence between them was commonplace. Hallie Illingworth, it seemed, was "insanely jealous" of Monty. She thought he paid too much attention to other women. On the heels of such damning testimony, jurors heard Harry Brooks, owner/operator of a resort on the west end of Lake Crescent testify that in December, 1937, Monty Illingworth had entered his store to borrow a length of rope. Monty, he said, told him the rope was needed to tow a beer truck that was disabled nearby. Dr. Charles P. Larson, Tacoma Pathologist, then testified that he had taken laboratory tests of pieces of rope found wound around the victim's body, and of rope still in Brooks' possession. Larson declared that in his opinion, they were exactly the same fibre and size.

Illingworth's defense attorney, Joseph H. Johnston, was unable to overcome such a skillful presentation by Prosecutor Max Church; all clues found on the soap-like body of "The Lady of the Lake" pointed accusingly at her killer.[24] On March 5, 1942, Monty Illingworth was convicted of second degree murder, and on March 20th, visiting Judge H. G. Sutton of Kitsap County sentenced him to life imprisonment at Walla Walla. Paroled on January 10, 1951, Illingworth dropped out of sight.[25]

Hallie Illingworth's body was exhumed during the trial, so that positive identification could be made by relatives. She was laid to rest at Vancouver, Washington, January 23, 1942.

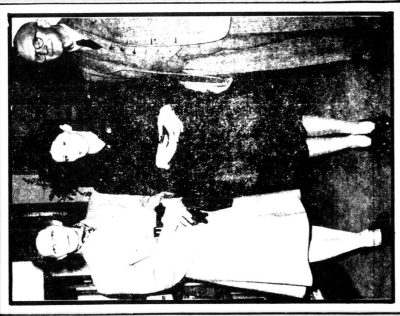

SISTERS OF "THE LADY." Shown here are Mrs. James Johnson (left) and Mrs. Emory Bailie, sisters of Hallie Illingworth, the murdered "Lady of the Lake," with the prosecuting attorney, Max Church. Both women gave vital testimony in the trial which brought Monty Illingworth to justice. PHOTO SOURCE: *Port Angeles Evening News*

THIS IS THE JURY which convicted Monty Illingworth of second degree murder and sentenced him to life in federal prison. Front row, left to right: Bailiff William B. Smith, Thomas J. Barton, Ralph Edgington, Ed Rushford, David Warnock, Mrs. Jessie McCourt, and Matron, Mrs. Edith Bayton. Top row, left to right: T.T. Carlson, E.W. Kreaman, Foreman A.A. Evans, A.A. Schmith, Kenneth Reid (partially hidden), Ray Goss and Ivan Mesford. PHOTO SOURCE: *Port Angeles Evening News.*

"HOLLYWOOD BEACH" at the north end of Lincoln Street, is shown in these two August, 1941 newspaper photographs. For centuries the scene of Indian gatherings, the entire area had, by the 1930s, deteriorated into a slum — and County Health Department officials considered it both a health and fire hazard. All the shacks were burned down in 1942. As this book went to press in 1982, the site was occupied by a restaurant, and was also a small beach facility adjacent to the Port Angeles City Pier. PHOTO SOURCE: *Port Angeles Evening News*

Many years ago, a wry, unknown philosopher defined Time as "Mother Nature's way of making certain that everything doesn't happen at once." Sure enough, even as these fascinating events unfolded in Port Angeles during the early '40s, a story equally important had begun taking shape in the little western Washington town of Hoquiam. It was a story destined to have great impact on Victor Smith's Second National City.

PENINSULA PLYWOOD CORPORATION was formed April 15, 1941. Founders Oscar Groth and Carl Stromberg based the corporate organization of this firm on the cooperative groups so prevalent in Scandinavian countries. The first carload of plywood was shipped from Port Angeles in November, 1941. PHOTO SOURCE: Itt Rayonier, Inc., Peninsula Plywood Division

KRON "K.O." ERICKSON, native of Sweden and early homesteader (1888) near La Push in Clallam County's west end. For over two decades, Erickson operated a successful trading venture out of Mora — named for his birthplace in Sweden — and later, on March 1, 1923, he founded the Port Angeles Savings and Loan Association, and headed that organization for 20 years. In 1945, he built and equipped Erickson Playfield, donating it to the City of Port Angeles for use by the town's young people. K.O. Erickson died in 1954. PHOTO SOURCE: Clallam County Museum

Peninsula Plywood

In Hoquiam during the 1930s, two hard-working woodsmen, Oscar Groth and Carl Stromberg, dreamed of building a plywood plant modeled after cooperative groups which functioned so well in their native Sweden. In a cooperative, a firm's owners are also its workers. Stock is issued but no dividends are paid; worker-owners receive profits by means of a fluctuating wage scale that absorbs net income.

As they were still travel-ing about inspecting potential sites in Washington and Oregon, Groth and Stromberg formally organized their cooperative. Only 150 original shareholders had been envisioned by the planners, but response to their idea was greater than anticipated. When the corporation was registered April 15, 1941, a grand total of 282 people bought one share of common stock for $1,000 each.[26] Peninsula Plywood was born.

The Port of Port Angeles fill offered them was not exactly ideal, and there was no log pond available; nevertheless, Groth and Stromberg were wooed successfully by several aggressive promoters in the town. Fred Epperson, Emory Moore and the ever-present Thomas Aldwell helped the men negotiate a satisfactory lease on Port property, and by means of a joint agreement among "PenPly," the Port of Port Angeles and the Milwaukee Railroad, a log pond was constructed.

Ground was broken for the new plant on May 20, 1941, and PenPly began oper-ations making sanded fir plywood on November 23rd of that year.

Though it would there-after grow and prosper to become one of Port Angeles' great industries, soon after the groundbreaking, PenPly and all other local news subsided to a whisper of secondary importance by the Japanese sneak attack on Pearl Harbor, 7:55 a.m. (Hawaii time), December 7, 1941.

Chapter Nine: December 7, 1941 — 1945

World War Two and Port Angeles

"Sweet is War to those who have never experienced it."

— Latin Proverb

Japan's first successful attack on naval fortifications at Pearl Harbor December 7, 1941 had a particularly stunning effect on the west coast cities of the United States and Canada, for it seemed patently obvious to military observers that Japan would follow up her advantage and immediately invade America's shores. President Roosevelt's Declaration of War on Japan on December 8th — just a few days later on Italy and Germany (both had already taken such action against the United States) — only heightened fears of Port Angeles residents that marauding Japanese ships would come steaming around Ediz Hook any moment. Dim-out and black-out orders were issued immediately. Dim-out hours, sunrise to sunset, required that motorists use only parking lights when driving, shielded street lights, and severely restricted home lighting. Total black-out hours extended from 1:30

a.m. to 7:30 a.m. Port Angelens and all other west coast residents began hanging blankets and quilts over windows so that not a single beam of light escaped. More than 150 Air Raid Wardens swung into action in 25 precincts, and the town's Civil and Military Defense Units were placed on 24-hour alert. And it was just starting. . . .

An underlying, but repressed, sense of near-panic and hysteria bubbled through the city; fears, doubts and wild stories caromed from one end of town to the other — embellished with each telling — in such numbers that officials found them impossible to counteract.

Japanese subs were in the harbor!

A battalion of Japanese soldiers had landed at Neah Bay!

TORPEDO SURVIVORS. Shown here on a Port Angeles beach are 34 survivors of the 3,286-ton steamship-freighter, *S.S. Coast Trader*, torpedoed by Japanese submarine *I-26* on Sunday, June 7, 1942, 43 miles west of Cape Flattery. The *S.S. Coast Trader* was carrying rolls of newsprint from Port Angeles to San Francisco. Survivors were rescued in a joint effort of United States and Canadian Coast Guard personnel. Destruction of the *S.S. Coast Trader*, resulting in the loss of one life, was the only such loss to enemy subs on the west coast during World War Two. PHOTO SOURCE: *Port Angeles Evening News*

The entire Japanese fleet was enroute to the North Olympic Peninsula!

Japanese bombers were primed to destroy Seattle's Boeing Company and lay waste all towns in Puget Sound![1]

As weeks sped by, at least some of the stories seemingly were corroborated by dozens of bustling military units in the area, soldiers digging foxholes for a camouflaged camp on the West Fifth Street bluff, while others erected a tent city at the mouth of Ennis Creek. The army's takeover of some downtown buildings — not to mention its full-scale occupation of City-owned Lincoln Park — seemed to be tangible proof of the danger nearby. Trucks rumbling along city streets in the black of night carried military personnel to Neah Bay, where they were shipped to

Alaska and Pacific war areas. Local boys, members of the National Guard Unit of Port Angeles were sent to man the beaches near Jamestown and what is now the Three Crabs Restaurant. The Coast Guard Station on Ediz Hook was a frenzy of activity, with plane patrols making dawn and dusk sweeps clear out to Cape Flattery, Guardsmen boarding and examining all inbound vessels, and anti-submarine patrols combing the Strait day and night.

Installation of an elaborate string of fortifications and military bases began along Juan de Fuca Strait under the command of Brigadier General James H. Cunningham; this necessitated trainloads of ordnance and soldiers moving to and fro, their destinations shrouded in secrecy. (Port Angeles businessmen were quick to note that construction of fortifi-

FORT HAYDEN GUNS. As part of defense installations deployed along America's west coast and the Strait of Juan de Fuca after Pearl Harbor, two massive cannons were installed near the east end of Crescent Bay at Tongue Point. The two guns were among the largest ever manufactured in the United States. Each barrel was 45 feet long, 16 inches in diameter; both had the capacity to fire a one-ton-plus projectile nearly 28 miles! Official reports indicate that gun No. 1 was fired a number of times in practice, while No. 2 never was fired. PHOTO SOURCE: Bert Kellogg

FORT HAYDEN BUNKER. It required the controlled efforts of a full crew of 20 men to maneuver the mammoth 16-inch cannons into position before firing. Here, some of the crew are shown in the hollowed-out bunker, which still stands at what is now the Salt Creek Recreation Area. PHOTO SOURCE: Bert Kellogg

FORT HAYDEN. Here one of the 16-inch guns is in vertical position after firing a test round in 1945. The one-ton projectiles often rattled windows in Victoria, B.C. when they landed in the Strait of Juan de Fuca. PHOTO SOURCE: Bert Kellogg

A FULL CREW of two officers and eighteen enlisted men standing before one of the forty-five-foot cannons at Fort Hayden during World War Two. None of the men in the photograph have been identified. The sixteen-inch guns, which cost a million dollars apiece, were declared obsolete after the war and were cut up for scrap, each yielding 500 tons of metal. The tunneled coast defense military reservation which housed these and other five-inch guns overlooking the Strait, is now part of the Salt Creek Recreation Area owned by Clallam County. PHOTO SOURCE: Bert Kellogg

cations — especially the massive Fort Hayden ordnance — gave a real boost to the local economy!) Grim stories of incendiary bomb-carrying balloons and reports of two real (albeit harmless) sub attacks on the California coast further reinforced the anxiety.

Nevertheless, for a brief while, Port Angeles residents tried to cling to the remnants of their pre-War, day-to-day, civilian activities. Roosevelt's confident, almost fatherly leadership alleviated some of the tension, and folks learned to keep their ears glued to the radio. There, however, they heard not only the reassuring Roosevelt, but bad news about the war. Numerous Japanese conquests throughout the South Pacific, especially at Guam and Bataan, saddened them, and signaled a long, bloody conflict.

Within a few months, startling events close to home altered their thinking permanently. As each occurred, conventional "civilian" thought began receding within Port Angelens' consciousness, soon to

be replaced by a definite wartime mentality and the more primitive, urgent need to defend, the need to survive. . . .

Aliens, Arrests, and Official Controls

Early in March 1942, headlines in the **Evening News** shrieked of a series of lightning-like raids on "enemy aliens" right in little old Port Angeles! Local officials and FBI agents confiscated a "veritable arsenal" and great quantities of short wave radio equipment when they swooped down on 12 local homes, arresting two Germans and one Italian for possession of contraband. One of those arrested, a World War One German U-Boat Commander named Rudy Lauchner, owned a radio shop at 110 East First Street (which accounted for the large amount of "contraband" short wave radio equipment confiscated). Whether Lauchner and the others were actually guilty of collaborating with the enemy was a story never publicly told. That, however, was of secondary importance at the time. Authorities felt compelled to demonstrate action on the home front. Defend . . . survive. . . .

War Gardens — Waterfront Defense and Air-Raid Wardens

Heeding official warnings of incendiary bombs, many in Port Angeles began washing beach sand in fresh water; after drying, it was reputed to be an excellent defense measure against the dreaded fireballs.[2]

All Clallam County men aged 20-45 not previously registered for military service were ordered to sign up by mid-February and public officials strenuously urged cultivation of War Gardens for Victory.

Seeking to protect what was considered the town's most vulnerable flank, a Waterfront Defense Committee teamed up with the U.S. Coast Guard to watch over Port Angeles beaches 24 hours a day.

Caught in a web not of their making, nine Japanese families throughout Clallam County (22 in Jefferson County) were quickly rounded up, registered, and evacuated to detention camps, where they were incarcerated for the rest of the war.[3] Those evacuated included Port Angeles' only Japanese family, the popular Osasas — owners of the Angeles Noodle and Chop Suey Restaurant on West Front Street. Mrs. Chiyono Osasa and her two children, Tommy and Betty, expressed appreciation to their many friends and patrons before closing the doors of their 15-year-old business for the last time on May, 26, 1942.

Gas masks arrived at Civilian Defense Headquarters on June 1st, and were immediately distributed to Air Raid Wardens and other officials.

In the midst of such excitement, it seems impossible to imagine that the war could have come any closer to these shores. But it did.

Word reached Port Angeles that for the first time since the Civil War, enemy shells had actually fallen in the proximity of a U.S. Military Reservation. On June 21st a Japanese submarine, the *"I-25,"* fired 17 rounds at Fort Stevens (Astoria, Oregon) area over a 15-minute span. As with previous random sub attacks in non-military areas, the projectiles did minimal damage. However, the *"I-25"* deeply underscored the west coast's vulnerability to such assault.[4]

Officials were unnerved, and began tightening controls to the point of suffocation.

The 1942 Port Angeles Salmon Derby was immediately canceled.

Possession of cameras and binoculars was prohibited to all passengers and crew members of ferries and commercial boats throughout the Pacific Northwest.

WARTIME TAGGING OF CHILDREN. As just one more security precaution taken during the war, registration and tagging of preschool children was considered necessary. Two copies of each child's registration were completed, one filed in Olympia, the other filed with the local Civilian Defense Director. Each child was then given an aluminum identification tag corresponding to his registration number. PHOTO SOURCE: Robert McMahan

Then Clallam County fell under a massive coast-wide dim-out order "designed to remove a glow which might silhouette coastwise ships and thus place them in a vulnerable position for submarine attack."[5] The order also effectively canceled night baseball, darkened theatre marquees and prevented night driving, for if headlights had to be used, automobiles were forbidden to travel on country roads.[6]

Rationing

Before the end of 1942, the city would experience its first air raid alarm, and . . . rationing was already a familiar nuisance.

All World War Two rationing procedures were controlled by the Federal Office of Price Administration (OPA). In Port Angeles, that agency was administered by insurance man Graham Ralston, who set up headquarters in the basement of the Post Office Building (southeast corner, Oak and First) and began selecting volunteers for the thankless job of apportioning scarce materials to residents. W. C. (Babe) Adams, a well-known Crown Zellerbach millworker and union leader, headed the Ration Board under Ralston, and found it to be a genuine challenge. In fact, before the war ended, Adams grew accustomed to threatening phone calls, anonymous letters and pressure tactics from groups or individuals demanding larger quantities of rationed materials than they were entitled to. There were even a few times, Adams recalled, when the glass door to his office was disintegrated by departing, frustrated favor-seekers!

Port Angelens had begun lining up for their first ration books of the war in May of 1942, and were soon exasperated by the whole thing. Why, it seemed that new products were being regulated with each passing week! The gasoline quota (most difficult of

RATION STAMPS. Shown here is a sampling of ration stamps available to local residents during World War II: Gasoline, shoes, canned fruits, meat, vegetables — and numerous other products — all fell under the purview of the ration board and were in short supply throughout World War Two. PHOTO SOURCE: Pete Capos

all to dole out) was fixed at four gallons weekly per person. Then butter-users were penalized, with strict upper limits being set for individual purchases; stores and restaurants saw their supplies slashed 50 percent! (This latter cut back seemed to spur the imagination of Port Angeles citizens, for they proceeded to concoct myriad recipes for low-sugar desserts, including one popular, ingenious delicacy known far and wide as Economy Fruitcake.[7])

The U.S.O., Entertainment . . . and more Rationing

Toward the end of summer in 1943, women were beginning to replace men in most local industries, including the Post Office; Laurine Wait became Port Angeles' first woman mail carrier.[8] "Rosie the Riveter" became a term familiar to Americans; she certainly was a familiar face at the shipyard owned by Olympic Shipbuilders, Inc., on the site of the former Earles/Charles Nelson Mill.[9] At the Olympic shipyard, construction had begun on the first of eight wooden barges officials hoped would aid the war effort.[10]

At year's end, however, with Uncle Sam still frantically gearing up a war machine, news from the

LAUNCHING OF THE FIRST *RED ALDER*. First of eight ships ordered by the U.S. Maritime Commission from the Port Angeles-based Olympic Shipbuilders during World War Two, the *Red Alder* is shown being launched on August 2, 1943. The 284-foot, ship-type wooden barge was christened that day by Mrs. Anna Roosevelt Boettiger of Seattle, daughter of President and Mrs. Franklin Delano Roosevelt, who was accompanied to Port Angeles by her mother. The *Red Alder* and its sister ships had no power of their own, and were supposedly designed so they could be towed in groups of three or four, by ocean-going tugs. After completion of three such barges, it was discovered that they were impossible to steer — and none ever saw service. PHOTO SOURCE: *Port Angeles Evening News*

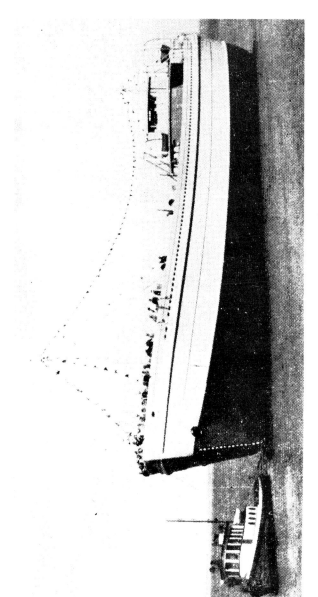

THE CUTTER *CAMPBELL*. Shown here during World War Two, bedecked with camouflage, is the proud U.S. Coast Guard Cutter *Campbell*. Named for a former Secretary of the Treasury, George W. Campbell, the 327-foot vessel — one of an original group of four — was built and commissioned in the Philadelphia Navy Yard in June, 1936. During World War Two, few ships saw more continuous service than the *Campbell*, and, during one epic voyage — on February 22, 1943 — she rammed and sank a German submarine as it surfaced. In 1974, the *Campbell* was assigned to her station at Ediz Hook where she remained until being decommissioned April 1, 1982. PHOTO SOURCE: United States Coast Guard

battlefront remained distressing. During 1942, thousands of American boys had given their lives in countless battles, and literally hundreds of naval vessels had been destroyed by torpedoes — including one merchant ship, the *S.S. Coast Trader*, just 40 miles off Cape Flattery.

Frazzled Port Angelens yearned for something to cheer about. They were delighted to help operate a United Service Organization (USO) Club in the basement of the Elks Building, and many smiled wearily when a large, county-wide Victory Garden Contest at the 4-H Fair was won by Mrs. Mary Wallace of Eighteenth and C Streets. Then too, professional entertainment was a welcome diversion. Throughout the war, a number of top flight bands traveled to Port Angeles' Blue Danube Dance Hall on the east end of town where today a "McDonald's" fast-food restaurant is located. The Blue Danube (formerly the popular "Clyde's" and later known as "Chubby's") hosted stars such as Louis Armstrong, Louis Prima, Noble ("Shoeshine Boy") Sissole and others, helping to make the realities of wartime just a little more tolerable for folks in this part of the world.

The town's first Federal Housing Project units on Lauridsen Boulevard, known as "Mt. Pleasant View," were built and ready for occupancy early in 1943 . . . and still more rationing was on the horizon. By February practically everything in cans came under the Ration Board's pitiless mandate: Fruit, soups, baby foods and vegetables topped the list. The allotment noose constricted even more when a rigid quota of three pairs of shoes per person per year was imposed. Coffee, sugar, fuel and meat were next, stimulating the creation of more toothsome delights, such as Meatless Spaghetti (soybean added), Peanut and Cheese Casserole, Victory Meatloaf (easy on the meat), and several unnamed delectables featuring proper utilization of salvaged kitchen fats!

Rationing, though, wasn't the only wartime irritation.

Along with many others, Port Angelens were confused by the Treasury Department's newly-minted zinc pennies, shiny as dimes — and frequently mistaken for that coin.

Housing was scarce.

Homeowners cultivating Victory Gardens and

ON CONVOY DUTY in the North Atlantic. This handsome painting of the U.S. Coast Guard Cutter *Campbell* was done by *LIFE Magazine* artist (and Lieutenant Commander) Anton Otto Fischer, early in the war. The *Campbell* was wearing a British camouflage scheme at the time — one of several different designs utilized during World War Two. Because his works were to be published while the war still raged Fischer was not permitted to include in this painting the top-secret High Frequency Range Finder mounted on the *Campbell's* decks. PHOTO SOURCE: Coast Guard Museum/Northwest

OLYMPIC SHIPBUILDERS, INC., shown in this previously unpublished photograph, circa 1943, on the site of the old Michael Earles/Charles Nelson Mill. During the Second World War, when this photo was taken, the Port Angeles shipyard was responsible for construction of the "Red Alder" wooden barges discussed elsewhere in this chapter. PHOTO SOURCE: Fred and Beth Sands

owning pressure cookers were ordered to register their homes as possible Civil Defense Shelters.[11]

A few citizens unlucky enough to own less-than-perfect pedigrees had to contend with even more vexing predicaments. For example, a short distance down the Olympic Highway in Carlsborg, one Vincent Noga was infuriated by official denial of his citizenship papers. Following damaging testimony from several prominent citizens and petitions of protest about Noga from the Sequim Veterans of Foreign Wars, the U.S. Immigration Office declared that he had not established that he was "attached to the Constitution of the United States sufficiently to make him a desirable citizen." Noga and his supporters, however, complained bitterly that the real reason for denial of the coveted papers was because some years earlier (1927), he had gained a questionable reputation as proprietor of a sedate Chicago night spot called the "Indolent Society of the Bootless, for

the Promotion of Modesty and Sobriety, Monogamy and Kindred Homely Virtues." Immigration officials (probably because they couldn't immediately recognize the singular merits of the "Indolent Society"!) considered Noga's charges groundless.[12]

As news arrived in town that Allied troops had successfully landed in Sicily and that Generals Montgomery and Patton were both racing toward Messina, Mrs. Franklin Delano Roosevelt journeyed to Port Angeles (in July 1943). She was in town to witness the launching of Port Angeles' first wartime ship, the unusual wooden barge *Red Alder I.* Christened by her daughter Anna Roosevelt Boettiger, the *Red Alder* was the first of five such ships started at the local shipyard (of eight originally scheduled for construction). Later that year the Maritime Commission, citing delays in construction and an already improved shipping situation, canceled its contract with Olympic Ship-

MEDAL OF HONOR WINNER Marine Corps Private First Class Richard Beatty Anderson, son of Mr. and Mrs. Oscar A. Anderson of Port Angeles, as he appeared shortly after his enlistment in World War Two. Anderson died during a battle for Roi Island in the Kwajalein Atoll, when he hurled his body upon a live grenade, saving the lives of several nearby companions. He was awarded the Congressional Medal of Honor posthumously. PHOTO SOURCE: Naval History Division, Washington Navy Yard, Washington, D.C.

RICHARD B. ANDERSON. Named for Port Angeles Medal of Honor winner Richard B. Anderson, the destroyer shown here was launched at the Todd Pacific Shipyard in Seattle on July 7, 1945, and commissioned on October 26th of that year. A much-decorated vessel — four battle stars during the Korean War, eleven during tours of Viet Nam — the *U.S.S. Richard B. Anderson* was sold to the Taiwan Government June 10, 1977. There she was rechristened the *Kai Yang* (No. 915), and still served in the Taiwanese Navy when this book went to press. PHOTO SOURCE: Naval History Division, Washington, D.C.

LOCKHEED P-38 LIGHTNING. During World War Two, a squadron of twin-engine P-38s similar to the one shown here was stationed in Port Angeles, at what is now the Fairchild International Airport. The P-38 was considered to be the first American fighter which could match the performance of Germany's Messerschmidt ME-109. PHOTO SOURCE: U.S. Air Force

builders for three of the Red Alders, thus closing the only major war industry on the Olympic Peninsula. Though never confirmed officially, several news accounts since that time have stated that the real reason the contract was cancelled was because of a design flaw, which made them "fishtail." Thus, they were useless for war *or* peacetime use.[13]

The War Turns

By mid-summer 1943, the pendulum of battle had begun a definite swing in favor of the Allies. Berlin was devastated by heavy bombing in August, and on the Russian Front, Soviet troops were slicing German supply lines, relentlessly driving the Nazis from their homeland. Over 1,000 American planes then leveled the Nazis' Nuremberg Industrial Center, and on September 8th, Italy surrendered.

Early in 1944, as the Port Angeles Chamber of Commerce listened to Rayonier chemist Henry Charnell describe modern methods of producing alcohol from waste wood and waste pulp liquor, thousands of American soldiers were wading ashore

in the Marshall Islands, the first invasion of strategic Japanese strongholds. Simultaneously, Supreme Allied Commander Dwight D. Eisenhower had received approval for a stupendous invasion of Europe and in a short time had amassed incredible military strength to carry it out.

June 6, 1944 – D-Day!

Allied Forces landed at key locations all the way up the French Coast, from Cherbourg to LeHavre. It was without question the largest and most daring such undertaking in the history of warfare and was the culmination of intensive, secretive planning. It was also the beginning of the end of the war in Europe.

At home in Port Angeles, the army ended its use of city property in and around Lincoln Park, and specific plans were formulated to establish a rural Library District for Clallam County. The big news, though, was that, after seven years effort, The Evening News Press, Inc., had received official notice from the Federal Communications Commission that it had been granted a license to operate a radio station in

WAR EXTRA! WAR EXTRA!

Port Angeles Evening News

U.S. DECLARES WAR ON JAPAN

All Local Civil Mess

WAR EXTRA! WAR EXTRA!

Seattle Post-Intelligencer

SEATTLE, THURSDAY, DECEMBER 18, 1941

SUBMARINE ATTACKED BY PLANE OFF COAST

ANTI-AIRCRAFT *Evacuees From Sitka*

Port Angeles Evening News

PRESIDENT DIES!

Stroke Ends Roosevelt's Life Late Today At Warm Springs, Ga.

Local Stores Closing Friday

American Planes Raid Many Areas In Great Strength

Complete Report on Club Parker's Wide For City Commission

U.S. NINTH HAS CROSSED ELBE IN DASH TO BERLIN

Juvenile's Father Testifies His Son Not in Right Mind

WAR EXTRA! WAR EXTRA!

Seattle Post-Intelligencer

SEATTLE, MONDAY, DECEMBER 8, 1941   TWENTY PAGES   DAILY 5c SUNDAY 10c

JAPAN, U.S. AT WAR

BOMB HAWAII, SINGAPORE;

Port Angeles Evening News

TUESDAY, MAY 1, 1945

ADOLF HITLER IS DEAD

Hamburg Radio Declares Nazi Leader Killed This Afternoon

Organization of Conference Has Been Completed

Six Yanks Enlist In Navy During April

World May Not Know If Hitler Is Actually Dead

Fred Smith Missing Since Leyte Battle

Aleuts Return to Their Alaska Home

ADOLF HITLER
Allies Invading

WAR EXTRA! WAR EXTRA!

Seattle Post-Intelligencer

SEATTLE, WEDNESDAY, DECEMBER 17, 1941   TWENTY-EIGHT PAGES   DAILY 5c SUNDAY 10c

JAPS RAID HAWAII AGAIN; WARSHIPS SHELL BASES

MIFFLIN FIRED BY WARNER IN SURPRISE ACT

Navy Orders Magnuson To Duty

SENATE GROUP APPROVES NEW DRAFT PLANS

Hawaii Ruins WHERE BOMB STRUCK In Island City

Sub Bombards Shipping Center

Warship Blast Johnston Isle

HISTORY IN HEADLINES. This montage of headlines from the *Port Angeles Evening News* and *Seattle Post-Intelligencer* illustrates the intensity with which news was reported to Port Angeles residents during World War II. PHOTO SOURCES: *Port Angeles Evening News* and *Seattle Post-Intelligencer*

WAR HERO IN PORT ANGELES. Shown here in October, 1945 during an appearance in Port Angeles, is the famous Lt. Colonel Gregory "Pappy" Boyington. The United States Marine 28-plane "Ace" addressed several Port Angeles groups while on a Victory Loan tour. "Pappy" Boyington was shot down in January, 1944, and was held prisoner in a Japanese POW camp near Yokahama until August, 1945, when he was released. His wartime exploits were later made into a popular television series entitled "Baa Baa Black Sheep." PHOTO SOURCE: *Port Angeles Evening News*

Port Angeles. KONP (**K** - **O**lympic National Park),[14] authorized to operate at 250 watts and broadcasting on a frequency of 1450 kilocycles, (the term has since been changed to "kilohertz") would go on the air in February of 1945 with a 190-foot Douglas Fir pole supporting its vertical wire antenna at First and Cherry Streets.[15]

As the "Big Three" leaders, Roosevelt, Stalin and Churchill, conferred at Yalta in February, 1945, devising plans which would shorten the war in Europe (and divide the continent afterwards!), United States forces in the Pacific were preparing for successful landings on Corregidor and Iwo Jima. Even though the horrible conflict was by this time weighted heavily in favor of the Allies, fanatical German and Japanese leaders refused to acknowledge defeat.

The Port Angeles Transit Company's new city buses began rolling in March,[16] and a scant one month later (April 12th) townspeople and the world were stunned by the death of President Franklin Delano Roosevelt at Warm Springs, Georgia. Vice-President Harry S Truman's assumption of the Presidency would signal the end of the Second World War.

Olympic Peninsula residents, somewhat surprisingly, accepted the reported deaths of Benito Mussolini (April 28th) and Adolf Hitler (April 30th) without undue emotion, and even reacted "very calmly, with scarcely a ripple of excitement" to news of Germany's surrender on May 7th.[17] There was, in fact, considerably more passion generated locally when eight faculty members at Port Angeles High School, blamed in a case of mass truancy, were told by the school board they showed a "lack of leadership and supervision." All eight promptly resigned their positions.[18]

Meanwhile, the war with Japan continued unabated. An especially bitter reminder of that fact invaded the consciousness of Port Angelens late in May, when the U.S. War Department announced that Mrs. Elsye Winters Mitchell, 26, well-known Port Angeles native, had been one of six victims of a Japanese balloon-bomb which exploded near Lake View, Oregon on May 5th. Mrs. Mitchell and her youthful companions on a church outing were the first and only recorded civilian fatalities on the United States mainland caused by enemy attack during World War Two.

The summer of 1945 served merely as prelude to America's ultimate answer to 20th Century warfare. Even as local residents welcomed news that the county library's first "Bookmobile" would soon be inaugurated, and that their city electricity would be free for one whole month (!), Japanese leaders, intractable to the end, refused Allied demands that they surrender. Finally, on August 6th, the decisive Harry Truman ordered an atomic bomb dropped on the city of Hiroshima. By throwing the dice in this manner, Truman took the greatest scientific and military gamble in mankind's history . . . and won the war. Following the utter destruction of Nagasaki one week later with a similar device, Japan surrendered unconditionally.

Peace

World War Two was history . . . and so was the lifestyle which existed in the United States before Pearl Harbor. The war had cost America 405,399 dead and over 650,000 wounded; 58 Clallam Countians lost their lives in the conflict.[19] More than just grim statistics, however, the war disrupted millions of lives, sparked a technological drive destined to last through the 1970s, and transformed the federal government's role in the economy. "Rosie the Riveter" and her friends, lured into the work force in large numbers for the first time, laid the groundwork for a social revolution, the effects of which are still being felt today.

Port Angeles certainly felt the impact of these

DURING WORLD WAR TWO, in an effort to demoralize the American people, Japan secretly launched 9,000 hydrogen-filled balloons, to which were attached both anti-personnel and incendiary bombs. Japanese military men hoped the bizarre weapons — each balloon was 32.8 feet in diameter and consisted of 600 pieces of paper glued together by hand — would be carried by thermal winds over the United States mainland. There, a control device would, they thought, automatically drop the bomb.

As a psychological weapon, the project would have to be termed a failure. Nevertheless, one isolated tragedy did occur. Six Americans died in the fiery explosion of a balloon-bomb on May 5, 1945 near the town of Lake View, Oregon. Mrs. Elsye (Winters) Mitchell, Port Angeles native, and five Sunday School children she was chaperoning on a Sunday afternoon picnic were killed instantly when one of the youngsters jostled a downed balloon. Elsye's husband, the Reverend Archie Mitchell, was far enough away from the explosion that he was uninjured; he was the only survivor. Others killed besides Mrs. Mitchell were: Jay Gifford, Edward Engen, Richard Patzke, Joan Patzke and Sherman Shoemaker.

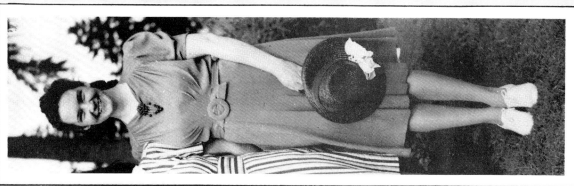

ELSYE MITCHELL Port Angeles native, shown here on an outing with her family prior to her marriage to the Reverend Archie Mitchell. PHOTO SOURCE: Laura Whipple

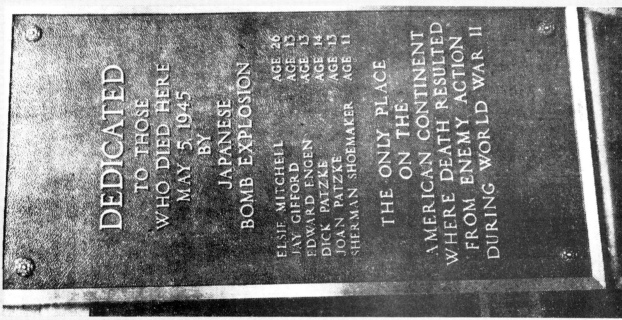

DEDICATED
TO THOSE
WHO DIED HERE
MAY 5, 1945
BY
JAPANESE
BOMB EXPLOSION

ELSIE MITCHELL   AGE 26
JAY GIFFORD   AGE 13
EDWARD ENGEN   AGE 13
DICK PATZKE   AGE 14
JOAN PATZKE   AGE 13
SHERMAN SHOEMAKER   AGE 11

THE ONLY PLACE
ON THE
AMERICAN CONTINENT
WHERE DEATH RESULTED
FROM ENEMY ACTION
DURING WORLD WAR II

PLAQUE dedicated to the six persons killed in the explosion of the Japanese balloon-bomb. PHOTO SOURCE: Laura Whipple

REVEREND ARCHIE MITCHELL AND ELSYE, shortly after their marriage, August 28, 1943. PHOTO SOURCE: Laura Whipple

THE MITCHELL RECREATION AREA AND MONUMENT, erected by the Weyerhaeuser Timber Company on August 20, 1950 at the site of the bomb explosion. PHOTO SOURCE: Laura Whipple

THE *U.S.S. TAMBOR* SS-198. Unknown to most local residents, the *Tambor* was based at Ediz Hook during most of World War II — the only submarine actually stationed in the entire Pacific Northwest. A 300-foot long vessel, displacing 1,475 tons and with a surface speed of 21 knots, the *Tambor* was manned by seven officers and sixty-five enlisted men. She was apparently quite active in the war in the Pacific, all the while under a veil of secrecy in Port Angeles. Only after the war, on August 15, 1945, did the U.S. Navy acknowledge that the sub was stationed in the local harbor. PHOTO SOURCE: U.S. Naval Institute

economic and social developments. Here, as every-where, the automobile would no longer be looked upon as a convenience item, but rather an obsession. (Local car salesmen found themselves recipients of bribe offers if they would only juggle names on waiting lists!) Over 2,000 people had to be re-absorbed into the local job market; women workers in large numbers — many of them reluctant to do so — drifted back into full-time housewife status, tem-porarily. The GI Bill afforded hundreds of local vet-erans the opportunity to attend college, thus giving them a chance at better-paying, white-collar jobs they could not have otherwise attained.

Many Port Angeles citizens were pleasantly sur-prised by the Navy's announcement in September 1945, that a large, Navy-gray, fully-armed submarine (*U.S.S. Tambor*) had been stationed at Ediz Hook for much of the war — the only such vessel based in the entire Pacific Northwest during hostilities. Enjoying "secrecy of the highest order," the sub's presence was not publicly revealed during its tour of duty, even though crew members and their wives had blended well into the community and had struck up many friendships with Peninsula residents.[20]

Thus did Victor Smith's Second National City witness the end of the war . . . and of yet another era.

Not a shot had been fired in anger along Peninsula shores during the conflict. Probably *because* of that fact, townspeople would for years recall with some degree of fondness, World War Two's impact upon their city. Gone but not forgotten were the two eight-inch railway guns that stood guard over the Strait from their vantage point on the West Fifth Street bluff — and the Army's camouflaged camp nearby. And who could forget the USO dances in the base-ment of the Elks Lodge, bus rides from downtown "way out to The Blue Danube" for a dance, or the "Red Devil Squadron" of P-38's stationed at what is now Fairchild International Airport. And what about the stories they told of the legendary cannons guard-ing Juan de Fuca Strait from the Camp Hayden hillside — fired only in practice (and whistling one-ton projectiles across the water near enough to Canada to frighten Victoria residents!).

The war was really over. And Port Angeles — indeed, all America — would never be the same again.

Notes

CHAPTER ONE (Pages 1-11)

1. Long-established scientific thought indeed holds that man came to the Americas from Asia via the Bering Land Bridge. However, in the interest of fairness, it should be noted that quite recently, a well-researched book by Archaeologist Jeffrey Goodman presents several opposite theories, namely that: Indians were the first human beings on earth; that they are the species of Homo sapiens known as Cro Magnon; they were indigenous to the Americas; and that *they* traveled to Asia, ultimately populating that continent. See Jeffrey Goodman, **American Genesis: The American Indian and the Origins of Modern Man** (New York, 1981).

2. Carl Johannessen, et. al., **Annals of the Association of American Geographers** (June, 1971), pp. 286-302.

3. Ruby El Hult, **The Untamed Olympics** (Portland, Oregon, 1971), p.2.

4. This is the same Captain Barclay after whom Barkley Sound (note change in spelling) on Vancouver Island was named. See G.M. Lauridsen, **The Story of Port Angeles and Clallam County, Washington** (Seattle, 1937), p. 2.

5. E.W. Wright, **Lewis and Dryden's Marine History of the Pacific Northwest** (New York, 1961), p.2.

6. Original records of Captain Vancouver indeed present no mention of Ediz Hook or the harbor area later to be settled. However, later additions to his charts — by persons unknown — "shows a bay named Pto. de Los Angelos, apparently the site of the present city of Port Angelos." See James S. Marshall, **Adventure in Two Hemispheres including Captain Vancouver's Voyage** (Vancouver, Canada, 1955), p. 27.

7. Lloyd Spencer and Lancaster Pollard, **A History of the State of Washington** (New York, 1937), Volume I, p. 21. The Michael T. Simmons family and five others and two unmarried men, settled near Tumwater, thus becoming the first American settlement on Puget Sound — and the first American settlement not missionary or fur trading, in what is now the State of Washington.

    Also, see Joseph Schafer, **A History of the Pacific Northwest** (New York, 1935), p. 211.

8. Charles J. Kappler, **Indian Affairs: Laws and Treaties** (Washington and New York, 1971), II, pp. 674-677.

9. Patricia Campbell, **A History of the North Olympic Peninsula**, Second Edition (Port Angeles, Washington, 1979), p. 13.

10. Also spelled "Reilly" by some. See Seattle *Times*, January 5, 1958.

11. Major Granville O. Haller was a well-known military man and pioneer, as well as an acquaintance of Isaac Stevens. See Hazard Stevens, **The Life of Isaac Ingalls Stevens by his Son**, (Boston, 1900), II, p. 28.

    Records conflict as to how many people actually lived in "Cherbourg" during these first few years. Most either imply or state flatly that only a dozen or more lived there through 1861. See Patricia Campbell, **A History of the North Olympic Peninsula**, Second Edition (Port Angeles, Washington, 1979), p. 22. However, an official territorial census two years earlier listed the names of 38 people claiming Cherbourg as their official residence. See Ronald Vern Jackson, **Washington 1860 Territorial Census Index** (Salt Lake City, 1979).

CHAPTER TWO (Pages 13-31)

1. *Port Angeles Evening News* (Port Angeles, Washington), July 15, 1950, p. 8. "In 1852 when Jay Cook (sic) had his great plan to build a railroad from Duluth . . . it was young Victor Smith who was sent . . . to locate the eastern terminal . . . When Victor went to Puget Sound in 1861, he located Port Angeles to be the western terminal of that great project. . ."

2. Early in 1861, on behalf of the Lincoln Administration, Smith had successfully performed the job of transporting materials to Harper's Ferry, Virginia. Confederate troops had burned the bridge there, posing a real threat to the Capital, and hampering the troop movement. See Herbert Hunt, **Washington West of the Cascades** (Chicago, 1917), I, pp. 226-227.

    Perhaps as a foretaste of things to come, Smith's quarrelsome nature manifested itself at Harper's Ferry. He got into an argument with a Union soldier and was run through with a bayonet, though the wound was not serious. See Seattle *Post-Intelligencer,* November 9, 1975.

3. Ex-Governor Stevens had been advocating a strong military base at Ediz Hook for several years, a strategy which had strong backing from the eminent General Winfield Scott and others who had been to the Pacific Northwest. Reaction to such an idea ranged the spectrum from the fiery enthusiasm of Victor Smith to a skeptical, even antagonistic response from nearby Canadian folk. "What has Puget Sound got to build up a city with at Edez (sic) Hook? If there is anything that will do it, it has not been discovered yet," declared the editor of the *British Colonist.* Then, assuming a somewhat biased view of Victoria's own importance, it ridiculed the idea of "founding a Tangier opposite the Vancouver Island Gibralter." See *British Colonist,* December 28, 1861.

4. According to Victor Smith, many prominent people — both in the Pacific Northwest and in the nation's capital — favored removal of the Customs House to Port Angeles. This is one of those rare Smith statements which appears to be true.

A Treasury agent, J. Ross Browne, traveling through the Territory sometime before Smith arrived had indeed drafted numerous witty descriptions of Port Townsend. They were critical — even tongue-in-cheek — satires which some readers have chosen to interpret as nothing more than exercises in creative writing. Other than Browne, though, if just a portion of what Smith said is true, the likelihood of a scheme hatched in Washington, D.C. is further enhanced. In a blockbuster of a letter by the customs collector, published in the *Overland Press,* he claimed that "his predecessors" Ross Browne and General Whalen had lamented the "unfortunate temporary location of the port of entry in the Roadstead of Port Townsend." See *Overland Press,* December 23, 1861. Then he proceeded to name General Winfield Scott, Isaac Stevens, Dr. George Sukely and Commander Boggs as several who "had warmly commended Port Angeles." Definite rumors of the proposed Customs House transfer were heard in Puget Sound for a long, long time before Smith's arrival on the west coast. Nobody, however, was able to determine their sources. In letters he wrote to his father a year-and-one-half before Smith assumed his post, Captain Alexander Sampson, Port Angeles settler, described his "fear" that the Custom House would be moved to Cherbourg. See *Seattle Times,* January 5, 1958. Certainly *The North-West* heard the stories before Smith debarked in Port Townsend. One edition suggested that there "is nothing in the (current) report . . . that the (Treasury) Department has contemplated any change in the location of the Custom House." See *The North-West,* (Port Townsend, Washington) August 1, 1861.

5.   This 1860 land purchase by Victor Smith is mentioned prominently in two different works by the distinguished author Patricia Campbell. In one she says "The first recorded contract between Victor Smith and (Dr. P.M.) O'Brien (land speculator from Port Townsend) was the 1860 ceding by the six land speculators of a half interest in their Cherbourg property to Victor Smith." See Patricia Campbell, "The Victor Smith Saga" in **With Pride in Heritage**: **History of Jefferson County,** ed. Jefferson County Historical Society (Portland, Oregon, 1966), p. 115. In another, Mrs. Campbell states that "He (Victor Smith) immediately bought the rights to the as-yet-unproved homestead next to the Riley claim, giving William Taylor $500 for this relinquishment, and in that same year (1860) he bought into the Cherbourg Land Company." See Patricia Campbell, **A History of the North Olympic Peninsula,** Second Edition(Port Angeles, Washington, 1979), p. 18.

To the author there seems to be little doubt that a transaction of some sort took place in 1860. It is quite apparent, however, that serious delays often occurred between the taking up of claims, exchange of rights and the granting of title to property not yet proven. There is even evidence that certain transactions, duly recognized by public officials everywhere, were *never* recorded; if they were, no trace of them could be found. A painstaking, frustrating search of available records — indeed, of Mrs. Campbells's own somewhat contradictory notes at the University of Washington — revealed no primary documentation of the land transfer which she mentioned as taking place in 1860. Clallam County's records list the earliest property exchange involving Victor Smith as April 29, 1862, when he purchased from J.W. White 7/40ths of the land claimed by the Cherbourg Townsite Company (a proceeding, incidentally, which was not recorded until *November* of that year!). *That date – April 29, 1862 – cannot be accepted as the first purchase made by Smith,* for in a letter he wrote to Salmon Chase October 5, 1861, almost seven months before, he told the Treasury Secretary that he, Smith, had already "purchased 25 acres of land at Port Angeles." As with a few other incidents related within these pages, corroborating records for this land transfer range all the way from scarce to non-existent. Mrs. Campbell's two separate statements in this regard, combined with her splended reputation as a researcher, have persuaded the author that when she wrote about the 1860 purchase, she had in her possession personal letters from Smith or some other evidence which authenticated it.

6.   A formal, almost priggish man, Chase at first wrote prim congratulatory notes to the new President, but later warmed somewhat, and praised Lincoln in much of his correspondence. In a letter to George Fogg on November 10, 1860, he said "No man . . . better deserves the confidence of the true friends of the cause which has just triumphed so gloriously through the election of Mr. Lincoln." Later, in a January 9, 1861 note to Pennsylvania Representative Thaddeus Stevens, he emphasized his admiration for the newly-elected President, when he said that Lincoln ". . . *is a man to be depended upon."* See Salmon P. Chase, **Diary and Correspondence of Salmon P. Chase** (New York, 1971), pp. 290-295.

For his part, Lincoln's fondness for Chase was an established fact in Civil War Washington. He only infrequently meddled in Chase's vast patronage empire and was later to say "Chase is about one-and-a-half times bigger than any man I ever knew." See Salmon Portland Chase, **Inside Lincoln's Cabinet** (New York, 1954), p. 24.

The mutual respect was seemingly genuine, but there were also practical, political reasons why Chase received a position in the Lincoln Administration. Lincoln's nomination as the compromise candidate of the Republican Party did not exactly weld together the diverse elements of the Party in 1860. After his election, the new President saw a Cabinet post for Chase as one possible way to heal some wounds and unite his badly-fragmented party. The attempt worked, but only partially, for Chase — who badly wanted the top spot of Secretary of State — was not overly thrilled to discover he was Lincoln's second choice for a Cabinet seat, behind the powerful New Yorker William Seward. He later resigned several times, but was usually persuaded by Lincoln to reconsider.

All this is significant because it helps to explain why Chase remained so long a member of Lincoln's Cabinet. *His* longevity, in turn, combined with blind loyalty toward friends, explains why Victor Smith was retained as a federal officer in the face of enormous pressure for his permanent removal.

7. *The North-West,* January 25, 1862. It seems to be commonly accepted by most historians that Smith was officially appointed by Chase to two different Treasury posts. An exhaustive search, however, failed to turn up any records verifying two actual appointments — but did reveal several items suggesting that two different positions were apparently filled by Smith for awhile. Victor Smith said in a letter written to Mr. J.R. Meeker on January 27, 1862 that he had been Special Agent as of August 16, 1861, but that he "resigned some months since." An actual letter of resignation from the job of Special Agent was mailed by Smith to Washington, D.C. on October 5th to take effect on September 30, 1861 and is still on file in the Treasury Department archives. People living in the Pacific Northwest at that time seemed to regard Smith as only the Customs Collector — and just *possibly* as a secret agent. The Victoria, B.C. *British Colonist* said as much when it editorialized "It is whispered that (Collector of Customs) Mr. Smith . . . has been acting as a secret agent of the Treasury Department." See *British Colonist,* July 19, 1861. The *Washington Standard* expressed bewilderment at Smith's varied titles: "One week he is a plain Collector, another the Special Agent of the Treasury . . . and again a special agent on postal affairs . . ." See the *Washington Standard,* August 16, 1862.

   In light of later events, and because of its inherent logic, the author leans toward a description put forth by Clinton A. Snowden, who said that Smith was named Collector of Customs, but before leaving Washington, D.C. for Puget Sound, he ". . . received some general instructions, or suggestions, from Chase . . . in regard to observing the general management of affairs in the territory, particularly as to the expenditures of public funds, that impressed him (Smith) with the idea that he was to be a confidential agent of the government in the territory, as well as Collector of Customs for the Puget Sound District, and that as such he was an official of unusual authority and importance." See Clinton A. Snowden, **History of Washington** (New York, 1909), IV, p. 166.

8. Ruby El Hult, **The Untamed Olympics** (Portland, Oregon, 1954), p. 95.

9. *The North-West* (Port Townsend, Washington), August 1, 1861.

10. There seems to be little question that Victor Smith and his family traveled *together* from the East Coast to Port Townsend. However, two accounts have been published in recent years suggesting that Smith sent for his family *after* arriving to begin his official duties as Customs Collector. It is the author's belief that these accounts are inaccurate. Two newspapers published at that time made very specific reference to Smith's family accompanying him on the journey. The *Washington Standard* (Olympia, Washington), in its August 3, 1861 edition noted that "Victor Smith, esq., the lately-appointed Collector for the Puget Sound District, called upon us one day last week. Mr. Smith *and* family left (the town of Olympia) on the last trip of the *Anderson* for Port Townsend."
   The August 1, 1861 edition of *The North-West* (Port Townsend) notes that ". . . the new Collector Victor Smith, esq., the Collector of Customs for Puget Sound District, arrived on the steamer *Eliza Anderson* Tuesday morning *with his wife and family.*"

   As further corroboration for this point, Victor's son, Norman Smith, in his memoirs, **Victory**, makes numerous references to the family's voyage to Port Townsend *with his parents* so that Victor could accept the post of Collector. See *Port Angeles Evening News,* June 13, 1950, p. 3 and June 14, 1950, p. 9.

11. Patricia Campbell, "The Victor Smith Saga" in **With Pride in Heritage: History of Jefferson County**, ed. Jefferson County Historical Society (Portland, Oregon, 1966), p. 114.

12. Alonzo Rothschild, **Lincoln, Master of Men** (Boston, 1906), p. 198.

13. Ruby El Hult, **The Untamed Olympics** (Portland, Oregon, 1954), p. 67.

14. Thomas H. Bradley, **O'Toole's Mallet**, Second Edition (1894), p. 7.

15. *Washington Standard* (Olympia, Washington), January 25, 1862.

16. *Washington Historical Quarterly*, 16 (1925), p. 268.

17. Thomas H. Bradley, **O'Toole's Mallet**, Second Edition (1894), pp. 7-8.

   To be perfectly fair, it must be said that some conflicting reports have been written as to why Victor Smith disliked Port Townsend and why he was so detested by residents there. Seemingly no amount of research will satisfactorily resolve the matter. For example, one account paints an especially ugly picture of Port Townsend as Smith found it upon his arrival there: Government funds being misappropriated, black marketeers illegally selling liquor to the red man, a poorly-administered Marine Hospital practically next-door to rowdy taverns, and, in general, corruption at all levels. See Herbert Hunt, **Washington West of the Cascades** (Chicago, 1917), I. p. 227.

18. Frequently during his tenure as Customs Collector, Victor Smith alluded to his great friendship with Treasury Secretary Salmon P. Chase, and hinted broadly that he (Smith) could not, or would not, be dismissed from his post. Rumors ricocheted around Puget Sound that he had been assigned to the job in the first place — and retained it — because Chase was heavily indebted to him. There may have been a real estate transaction between the two men; one account says that Smith sold his Cincinnati home to Chase, receiving $1,000 cash and carrying a $5,000 mortgage for his prominent friend. See Patricia Campbell, **A History of the North Olympic Peninsula**, Second Edition (Port Angeles, Washington, 1979), p. 18. However, in two letters he wrote to Chase, Smith made brief, vague references to a "note payable"

at the Valley Bank in Cincinnati, Ohio, and a house "on Broadway," asking Chase to arrange payment of the note via drafts on his (Smith's) salary. Both references are poorly-worded, but seem to imply that *Smith owed Chase money*, though this point could not be clarified. See *Washington Historical Quarterly*, 16 (1925), pp. 268-271. Yet another source points out that Smith, in September, 1863 sent a message to Chase in Washington, D.C. via an emissary, Mr. P.D. Moore. The gist of the message was that Smith "denied positively" that he had publicly asserted that Chase was indebted to him. See Salmon P. Chase, **Inside Lincoln's Cabinet** (New York, 1954), p. 197. Such a quote, taken directly from Salmon Chase's own notes, seems to suggest that — at least in 1863 — Chase owed nothing to the Puget Sound Collector.

To further muddy the water, however, it is certainly true that Chase "lived beyond his means . . . and had gone deeply in debt over the years." See Thomas G. Belden, **So Fell the Angels** (New York, 1956), p. 27. Moreover, although it is a known fact that his personal integrity was never publicly questioned, he was capable of great self-delusion much of the time, and always chafed under the impoverishment he felt was forced upon him by the trappings of high public office. Because his ambitions were more political than financial, his principal regret about lack of funds was that it hampered his effectiveness as he sought higher office. He and his family did accept small gratuities from financier Jay Cooke, and there were rumors of "quiet sales of prize Treasury posts" by the Cabinet official, but nothing of this nature ever flushed to the surface. *Ibid.*, p. 28. For a variety of reasons, history records that "many . . . incompetent and corrupt won their way into Chase's department." See Salmon P. Chase, **Inside Lincoln's Cabinet** (New York, 1954), p. 32.

19.   The *British Colonist* (Victoria, British Columbia), December 28, 1861.

20.   Victor Smith's weird sense of humor often manifested itself in the names he used when signing his letters to newspapers. "A. Scalpel" and "A Friend" were used a couple of times. See Patricia Campbell, **A History of the North Olympic Peninsula**, Second Edition (Port Angeles, Washington, 1979), p. 20. From 1862 to 1864, certain informative notes were published in the (Victoria, B.C.) *British Colonist* — the editor attributed them to a person "from Port Angelos" — which definitely bear the stamp of his strange brand of wit. The letters were sprinkled with praise for Victor Smith, outright lies and grossly exaggerated claims of Port Angeles' rapid progress; to wit: a Lyceum "prospering finely" and a Library Association "with a well-selected library of books!" All the notes were authorized by such suspicious characters as "Nero" (Victor Smith's father had a dog named Nero!), "Mingo Park," "Zerumbabel" and "G. Gnatross." Nowhere in the accounts of Port Angeles' early settlers do such peculiar appellations appear, and the strong suspicion is voiced here that Smith penned all such letters. See *The British Colonist* (Victoria, B.C.), November 26, 1862, April 1, 1863, April 6, 1863, April 29, 1863 and April 23, 1864.

21.   *The North-West* (Port Townsend, Washington), January 25, 1862. The reader will recall the letter Smith wrote to Treasury Secretary Salmon Chase on October 5, 1861, in which he resigned his "position" as Special Agent. See *Washington Historical Quarterly*, 16 (1925), p. 268. In that same letter, he also told the Secretary that he had "purchased in open market and at the full market price, for cash, 25 acres of land at Port Angeles," intending to make it his permanent home.

22.   O'Brien, it should be recalled, was one of Smith's fellow investors in the Cherbourg Land Company, and had apparently started off on good terms with the new treasury man. O'Brien was an influential man in Port Townsend, being not only a physician, but also owner of a drug store, a couple of taverns and the Marine Hospital. Victor Smith's ascerbic personality must have quickly alienated him, however, and when the agent (who was a teetotaller) began criticizing the hospital's proximity to some of O'Brien's "gin-mills" the doctor must have known his days of federal contracts were over. Cancellation of the contract was the final indignity, and O'Brien became a fierce enemy indeed. See Patricia Campbell, "The Victor Smith Saga" in **With Pride in Heritage: History of Jefferson County**, ed. Jefferson County Historical Society (Portland, Oregon, 1966), pp. 114-115.

23.   At least, those were the charges brought against Victor Smith by the new hospital director. Allyn too, had begun his career in Puget Sound as a close friend of Victor Smith's. However, he soon became disenchanted with the financial shenanigans of the Customs Collector, and later charged Smith with embezzling $4,354.98 in public funds. Specifically, he said that Smith rented the buildings to a private hospital (Marine Hospitals were usually privately-owned institutions in those days), that the hospital charged the government $1.50 per day for each sailor who was housed there, and that Smith pocketed $218 per month. Moreover, Allyn swore under oath — to a Grand Jury in Olympia — that a pre-condition of his job was that he mail $100 monthly to the *New York Herald of Progress*, a paper dealing exclusively with spiritualism. He claimed to have sent a total of $400 to the paper under this arrangement. The charges he leveled quite naturally caused a serious erosion of their friendship, and the two men nearly came to blows on the streets of Olympia. See Clinton A. Snowden, **History of Washington** (New York, 1909) IV, pp. 168-169 and Patricia Campbell, "The Victor Smith Saga" in **With Pride in Heritage: History of Jefferson County**, ed. Jefferson County Historical Society (Portland, Oregon, 1966), p. 117.

24.   Patricia Campbell, "The Victor Smith Saga" in **With Pride in Heritage: History of Jefferson County** ed. Jefferson County Historical Society (Portland, Oregon, 1966), p. 114.

25. The *British Colonist* (Victoria, British Columbia), January 16, 1862. "Hung in Effigy – Collector Smith of Port Townsend who has rendered himself obnoxious to the citizens of that place by his efforts to remove the custom house to Cherburg, was hung in effigy on Saturday last."

26. Also spelled "Cherburg." See R.L. Landis, **Post Offices of Oregon, Washington and Idaho** (Portland, Oregon, 1969), p. 15. See also *Port Angeles Evening News,* November 20, 1963, p. 14.

27. NOTE: It is reasonable to believe – even probable – that Smith saw Port Angeles before December, 1861, but no records could be uncovered to prove this.

28. Patricia Campbell, "The Victor Smith Saga" in **With Pride in Heritage: History of Jefferson County**, ed. Jefferson County Historical Society (Portland, Oregon, 1966), p. 115.

29. Thomas H. Bradley, **O'Toole's Mallet**, Second Edition (1894), p. 8.

30. *The North-West* (Port Townsend, Washington), January 18, 1862.

31. The *British Colonist* (Victoria, British Columbia), July 19, 1862.

32. Thomas H. Bradley, **O'Toole's Mallet**, Second Edition (1894), p. 9.

33. *Ibid.,* p. 9.

34. U.S. Congress. House. *Change of Location of Port of Entry for Puget Sound Collection District from Port Townsend to Port Angelos,* 37th Congress, Second Session, House Report 119 to accompany S. 241. (Washington, D.C.: U.S. Government Printing Office, 1864)

    Chase's letter effectively sounded the death knell for Port Townsend's Port of Entry status – at least, for the time being – because just two months later, on June 16, 1862, the Commerce Committee officially forwarded to the full Senate its own recommendation that the law be enacted. ". . . your committee, referring to the . . . letter of the Secretary of the Treasury . . . think the public interest would be promoted by such a change." This, despite Territorial Delegate Colonel William H. Wallace's personal appearance before the Committee urging "that the change should not be made."

35. Caroline Smith may or may not have been the first white woman in Port Angeles; the matter could not be determined with certainty. The 1860 Washington Territorial Census names, among the 38 people listed as residents (of "Cherbourg"), Lotty Winthrop, Elizabeth Bell and Mary Bell (the latter two of whom, it is believed, really lived in Dungeness, 15 miles away). The official count, according to a recent publication, included whites, blacks and mulattoes, but not Indians, so the three women named above probably were not Indian. Could one of them have been the first white woman in town?

    The entire population of Cherbourg/False Dungeness, according to that 1860 Census is as follows: Atkinson, George; Bagley, J.W.; Bell, Elizabeth; Bell, James; Bell, John; Bell, Mary; Boswell, George L.; Brackett, Thomas; Burster, W.H.; Chambers, M.T.; Croswell, Fred; Culver, Edward; Dunn, John; Fitzgerald, G.H.; Frazer, J.R.; Hand, George; Harwood, G.; Holmes, R.; House, George; Huntoon, John; Huntoon, M.; Jewet, S.; Johnson, George; Johnson, George B.; Mason, John; O'Brien, P.M.; Perry, E.; Sampson, A.; Scott, S.F.; Sisson, Levi; Stanchfield, J.H.; Taylor, William H.; White, J. M.; Windsor, W ; Winthrop, Lotty; Fisher, Jacob; Robinson, John; Johnson, A. See Ronald Vern Jackson, **Washington 1860 Territorial Census Index** (Salt Lake City, 1979).

36. Patricia Campbell, "The Victor Smith Saga" in **With Pride in Heritage: History of Jefferson County**, ed. Jefferson County Historical Society (Portland, Oregon, 1966), p. 115.

    Numerous accounts of these "family" appointments have been found. None, however, is more revealing of the enmity Smith engendered, than John Damon's allegation in *The North-West* on June 14, 1862, that Victor Smith charged his father George, $500 to secure the Tatoosh Lighthouse position. Later in the same article, he ridiculed the entire matter even further by stating that the senior Mr. Smith was so unqualified for the job that he was unable even to make the light work.

37. *The North-West* (Port Townsend, Washington), June 14, 1862.

38. According to writer Patricia Campbell, six of the land speculators, in 1860, gave Smith a half-interest in their Cherbourg property, in return for his "firm commitment that revenue cutters would use this jointly-owned property." See Patricia Campbell, "The Victor Smith Saga" in **With Pride in Heritage: History of Jefferson County**, ed. Jefferson County Historical Society (Portland, Oregon, 1966), p. 115.

39. In Dr. P.M. O'Brien's letter to Governor William Pickering, O'Brien told the Governor that Victor Smith, in October, 1861, drew up "a plan of operations" for his Cherbourg Land Company colleagues. His plan spelled out the broad powers he, Smith, had and intended to exercise in behalf of the company; these, he assured the speculators, would culminate in the transfer of the Customs House, and thus bring great financial return to all of them. It is interesting to note that, anticipating a profit-making venture, none of these gentlemen saw fit to question the propriety of Smith's actions at that time – yet later, when it appeared Smith alone would benefit, they joined the chorus of detractors! See *Washington Standard* (Olympia, Washington), April 16, 1864.

40.   *Ibid.*

41.   Thomas H. Bradley, **O'Toole's Mallet**, Second Edition (1894), p. 9.

42.   *Washington Standard* (Olympia, Washington), April 16, 1864. Letter from Dr. P.M. O'Brien to Governor William Pickering.

43.   Copy of official charges against Victor Smith, submitted to President Abraham Lincoln by Surveyor-General Anson G. Henry (fourth charge against Smith). See *Washington Standard* (Olympia, Washington), February 6, 1864.

44.   Some historians have speculated that Smith made this trip primarily to defend himself against the charges of his Puget Sound enemies. At this juncture, however, it seems much more likely that his main reason for going to Washington was to bind together loose ends of the land development scheme. Certainly, in light of what occurred in the nation's capital during his visit, it would seem that lobbying the Port of Entry transfer and the Port Angeles Military Reservation were his most vital concerns.

45.   *The North-West* (Port Townsend, Washington), June 14, 1862.

46.   Later, on March 3, 1863, following up on the Presidential order, an Act of Congress was passed for the purpose of "increasing the revenue by reservations and sale of town sites on public lands." It was based on the premise that Americans would buy property sold by Uncle Sam. In retrospect, it is truly astonishing that such a law could even be considered, for huge tracts of land throughout the west could be obtained *free* if one agreed to homestead. (The 1850 Donation Land Claim Act encouraged settlement by allowing homesteaders to take up "Donation Claims" of 160 acres.)

47.   Author Patricia Campbell says in her account that Lt. J.H. Merryman and William Chalmers were appointed by Smith. See Patricia Campbell, **A History of the North Olympic Peninsula**, Second Edition (Port Angeles, Washington, 1979), p. 20. Other writers, notably Lucile McDonald and Ruby El Hult, state that Victor Smith asked Captain J.S.S. Chaddock of the Revenue Cutter *Joe Lane*, to detail an officer to run the Customs House during his, Smith's, absence, and that Chaddock appointed Lt. Merryman. However it actually happened, Merryman did take charge, with William Chalmers on the payroll as his assistant. See *Seattle Times*, July 2, 1961, p. 4 and Ruby El Hult, **The Untamed Olympics** (Portland, Oregon, 1971), p. 70.

48.   The *British Colonist* (Victoria, British Columbia), August 1, 1862.

49.   Messrs. Loren Hastings and J.J. van Bokkelen. See Patricia Campbell, **A History of the North Olympic Peninsula**, Second Edition (Port Angeles, Washington, 1979), p. 21.

50.   Letter of Governor William Pickering to General George Wright, Commander of Military Department of the Pacific, dated August 16, 1862 (from archives of Adjutant General's office, Camp Murray, Washington). In this letter, Governor Pickering made a couple of fascinating veiled references to Victor Smith's past, and stated that the Collector was living in Puget Sound under an assumed name. The Governor said Victor Smith's real name was *Joseph Vials* Smith, but regretfully did not elaborate on the point, nor give any clear idea as to why Smith might have changed his first name. See W.F. Field, **Index to Washington Territorial Records** (Tacoma, Washington, 1960), p. 6.

51.   *Seattle Times*, July 2, 1961, p. 4.

52.   The *British Colonist* (Victoria, British Columbia), August 6, 1862.

53.   Victor Smith probably had good reason to be nervous about Lieutenant Merryman. The man not only had a good reputation, but he had a friend or two in high places. One of these friends, Abraham Lincoln, wrote to Salmon Chase on May 13, 1863, that Merryman's father had been "a very intimate acquaintance and friend of mine" and that the young officer had been "raised from childhood in the town where I lived, and I remember nothing against him as boy or man." See Roy P. Basler, editor, **Collected Works of Abraham Lincoln** (New Brunswick, New Jersey, 1953), IV, p 214.

54.   The *British Colonist* (Victoria, British Columbia), September 2, 1862.

55.   *Ibid.*, August 8, 1862.

56.   *Ibid.*, August 14, 1862.

57.   *The North-West* (Port Townsend, Washington), November 20, 1862.

58.   W.F. Field, **Index to Washington Territorial Records** (Tacoma, Washington, 1960), p. 6 and *Seattle Times*, July 2, 1961, p. 4.

59.   The *British Colonist* (Victoria, British Columbia), December 18, 1862.

60.   *Seattle Times*, July 2, 1961, p. 4.

61.   Ruby El Hult, **The Untamed Olympics** (Portland, Oregon, 1954), p. 72.

62.   Stanton actually filed suit against Smith, charging trespass, but records are fuzzy as to whether he won or was awarded any compensation. *Ibid.*, p. 98.

63.   12 Stat. 754

64. *Washington Standard* (Olympia, Washington), May 9, 1863.

65. *Ibid.*, February 6, 1864.

66. Carl Sandburg, **Abraham Lincoln, The War Years** (New York, 1939), II, p. 626.

67. Clinton A. Snowden, **History of Washington** (New York, 1909), IV, p. 174.

68. Alonzo Rothschild, **Lincoln, Master of Men** (Boston, 1906), pp. 198-199. It is worth noting that the *Washington Standard* and several other sources describe Lincoln's actions during the days of the Smith firing. When he dismissed Victor Smith, Lincoln actually appointed Henry Clay Wilson to replace him. However, upon discovering that the man was dead, he then made it known he wanted to appoint a Mr. Frederick A. Wilson. Salmon Chase, during the personal interview with Lincoln in which the President convinced him to stay on the job, asked that the new appointee be Dr. Lewis C. Gunn. That gentleman was officially named Collector of Customs on May 16, 1863. See *Washington Standard* (Olympia, Washington), May 23, 1863 and Carl Sandburg , **Abraham Lincoln, The War Years** (New York, 1939), II, p. 627.

69. Salmon Portland Chase, **Inside Lincoln's Cabinet** (New York, 1954), p. 30.

70. Herbert Hunt, **Washington West of the Cascades** (Chicago, 1917), I, p. 228.

71. Some writers have said that Smith was in Washington, D.C. to answer more charges from the *Shubrick*-Lieutenant Merryman affair. Nothing could be found to disprove this claim. *Ibid.*, p. 28.

72. Newspaper accounts of the day attributed the ghastly flood to a warm wind which melted much of the snow in the mountains, creating a heavy flow down the gully to the village. Most historians, however, now agree that the landslide and resulting dams far up the valley were actually responsible for the deluge.

73. G.M. Lauridsen, **The Story of Port Angeles and Clallam County, Washington** (Seattle, 1937), p. 25.

74. *Port Angeles Evening News*, June 26, 1950, p. 2.

75. *Ibid.*, June 24, 1950, p. 2.

76. The *British Colonist* (Victoria, British Columbia), December 30, 1863.

77. The entire plat consisted of 803 units of land, urban and suburban lots, and a few acreage tracts. Small urban lots were platted between Laurel and Tumwater Streets, Sixth Street and the Waterfront. The suburban lots were set out east of Laurel Street. All other land was considered government reserve. See Thomas H. Bradley, **O'Toole's Mallet**, Second Edition (1894), p. 15.

78. *Ibid.*, p. 16. The buyers were: John H. Taylor, Joseph M. Asher, James D. Laman, James Delgardno, David Evans, Nicholas Meagher, Thomas Stratton, J.W. Redfield, Henry Smith, Jardel Brown, Thomas Abernethy, Donald McJames, George Bates, John G. Sparks, Caroline E. Lightner, Owen O'Connell, William J. King, Simon Elbrecht, Thomas Gawley, Hiram McNear, Frederick W. Austin, William G. Conklin.

79. Patricia Campbell, **A History of the North Olympic Peninsula**, Second Edition (Port Angeles, Washington, 1979), p. 22.

80. 14 Stat. 252

81. There had already been (August 6, 1861) a temporary light established on Ediz Hook, according to newspaper reports. It consisted of "an upright pole, supported by struts and armed between its top and centre with three sets of different shapes, these later determining its characteristic distinction, the surface of each being presented to a separate point of the compass: the color of the entire beacon will be white. It will be fifty feet in height, the platform upon which it is erected being only a few feet above the mean level of the water. The Beacon should be visible, in a favorable state (of weather) at eight or nine and one-half statute miles. Latitude of Beacon, 48°, 08'; Longitude of Beacon, 123°, 25'; In time of beacon, 8h, 13' 40''. Newspaper accounts say only that driftwood was burned to provide light. It is not known who the keeper was during this early period. See The *British Colonist* (Victoria, British Columbia), September 7, 1861.

82. As mentioned earlier, a search of the records revealed nothing relative to decisions made in the Stanton and White cases.

83. G.M. Lauridsen, **The Story of Port Angeles and Clallam County, Washington** (Seattle, 1937), pp. 39-44.

84. As noted earlier, Lincoln and Chase admired one another. However, the tolerant Lincoln, recognizing his Treasury Secretary's tremendous ambition, stated on one occasion that Chase was "a little insane on the subject of Presidency." See Ishbel Ross, **Proud Kate: Portrait of an Ambitious Woman** (New York, 1953), p. 158. It came as no great surprise, therefore, when on June 30, 1864, Lincoln informed Chase in a letter that the two of them had "reached a point of mutual embarrassment" in their relationship, which "cannot be overcome, or longer sustained." See Salmon Portland Chase, **Inside Lincoln's Cabinet** (New York, 1954), p. 223.

85. 14 Stat. 25

86. The Smith family — which boarded separately from Victor because he was suspicious of a plot to rob him — was accompanied by Mrs. Silas Goodwin and two children, Hartley, 9 and Clara, 7 of Bangor, Maine. The Goodwins would survive

the wreck of the *Golden Rule*, join Mr. Goodwin in Port Angeles and become one of the true pioneer families of Clallam County, living first at White's Creek, then on a farm near the Lower Elwha. See *Port Angeles Evening News* (Port Angeles, Washington), April 12, 1944, p. 1.

87.   The *British Colonist* (Victoria, British Columbia), July 1, 1865.

88.   Patricia Campbell, "The Victor Smith Saga" in **With Pride in Heritage: History of Jefferson County**, ed. Jefferson County Historical Society (Portland, Oregon, 1966), p. 114.

89.   It was reported that Gibbs fled to Canada and later to England, where he surfaced briefly to defraud a ship owner of $25,000. See *Port Angeles Evening News*, July 10, 1950, p. 3 and July 11, 1950, p. 10. Captain Denny lost his commission and retired in Seven Hills, New York, a wealthy recluse. See Herbert Hunt, **Washington West of the Cascades** (Chicago, 1917), I, pp. 228-229.

90.   The number of people who died in the wreck of the *Brother Jonathan* is another of those puzzling discrepancies found so often while researching this book. Several eminent historians state that over 200 people met their deaths. The respected **Lewis and Dryden** claim only 166 died; even in their well-documented work, however, there is an apparent mistake. Their registered list of passengers and crew is presented to verify the 166 figure — yet a name-by-name head count reveals that there were only 172 persons aboard the *Jonathan* when it left San Francisco. See E.W. Wright, **Lewis and Dryden's Marine History of the Pacific Northwest** (New York, 1961), pp. 132-134. Since nobody disputes the fact that 19 survivors made it safely to shore, this would mean that only 153 were actually killed in the shipwreck. The difference in the death toll may be explained, though, if one considers the fact that some nameless Chinese were aboard. Norman Smith says that a story reached Port Angeles of two Chinese who made it to the surviving lifeboat — but that the white crew threw both orientals overboard to make room for two white nurses whom they found floating in life jackets. See *Port Angeles Evening News*, July 14, 1950, p. 12.

91.   School opened in Port Angeles for the first time on April 17, 1865, in a one-room building "with boards upright and visibility through every crack" located in the alley back of the R.D. Willson building. Miss Abbie Smith was the teacher, and E.G. Morse was the School Superintendent. Students in that first classroom were one Redfield, two Delgardnos, three Pilchers, two Conklins, Anna Whitacre, Laura McInnis and Imogene Whitacre, for a total of eleven. G.M. Lauridsen, **A Story of Port Angeles and Clallam County, Washington** (Seattle, 1937), p. 155.

92.   Patricia Campbell, **A History of the North Olympic Peninsula**, Second Edition (Port Angeles, Washington, 1979), p. 23 and 14 Stat. 252.

93.   Looking backward 120 years through the haze of political intrigue, obvious lies and personal animosities, the weight of accumulated evidence makes it rather clear that a small group of prominent Americans in Washington, D.C. and Puget Sound made a decision to move the Port of Entry to the sparsely-populated beach at Port Angeles even before Victor Smith moved to Puget Sound. A brief summation of the "coincidences" mentioned in the text seems to lend credence to the theory that a handshake deal had been effected and that Victor Smith was the clique's "man-on-the-scene." The "coincidences" are as follows:

      1. Isaac Stevens "discovers" Port Angeles. Bestows name "Cherbourg."

      2. Stevens describes area to other prominent people in Washington, D.C., and seeks money to study military potential of region.

      3. Strong rumors of change in location of Customs House to Puget Sound as much as full year-and-one-half before Lincoln (and Salmon Chase) take office.

      4. Smith hears about "Cherbourg" and ostensibly buys land there — while still in Washington, D.C.

      5. Smith begins making plans to move to Puget Sound even before the job is offered to him.

      6. Smith conveniently receives appointment to Treasury job in Puget Sound just 40 miles from "Cherbourg."

      7. Smith immediately is critical of Port Townsend as Port of Entry.

      8. Smith immediately begins promoting Port Angeles as Port of Entry.

      9. Smith names many prominent people whom he said "warmly recommended" Port Angeles as site of new Customs House.

    10. Smith, having once helped to locate eastern terminus of a proposed railroad, now recommends Port Angeles as western terminus.

    11. Smith resigns job as Treasury Agent, but . . .

    12. does not even leave Puget Sound. Resignation accepted by Treasury Department, but Smith retained in Port Townsend in another post.

    13. Smith buys much land in Port Angeles, some of it in name of H.G. Plantz of Treasury Department — a resident of Washington, D.C. Records fuzzy concerning involvement of Salmon Chase, but correspondence from

responsible office-holders hint some involvement.

14. Smith fired from position by President Abraham Lincoln. Chase, with special OK from Lincoln, re-appoints Smith to post similar to that which he'd earlier resigned, but with even greater powers!

15. Smith easily — with Chase's help — persuades Lincoln to declare Port Angeles Lighthouse and Military Reservation, an action never before carried out by Federal Government.

94. Ronald Vern Jackson, **Washington 1870 Territorial Census Index** (Salt Lake City, 1979).

The generally accepted population total for Port Angeles during this 18-20 year time span is ten. School records, however, indicate that between 1865 and 1883, several families must have settled in the town temporarily, then moved on, causing the count to fluctuate. For example, in March, 1868, a school in Port Angeles (part of what was then Clallam County School District # 2) noted that 20 students were to be found within the District's boundaries, McDonnel Creek on the east, and Elwha Heads on the west. Seven years later, in 1875, when Anna Whitacre was the teacher in a school affectionately known as the "Chicken House" (referring to its former function), seven pupils graced the premises. A slight population increase is noted then, for in 1878 there were 11 students in the Port Angeles School District (by this time changed to District # 7). See G.M. Lauridsen, **The Story of Port Angeles and Clallam County, Washington** (Seattle, 1937), pp. 150-155.

CHAPTER THREE (Pages 33-51)

1. Weather research was in its infancy, and when scientists discovered that barometric "highs" and "lows" entered the continental United States near Tatoosh Island, the Signal Corps decided to monitor them. Establishing an office in Port Angeles, the Corps ran a telegraph line from there to Neah Bay (stringing lines on trees the entire length of the Strait of Juan de Fuca!), then laid cable from Neah Bay to Tatoosh Island. The plan failed badly. Cables draped over rocks snapped and frayed beneath frothy seas, and high winds broke the telegraph line with monotonous regularity. In 1891, the Weather Bureau was formed and took over the system. See **Jimmy Come Lately: History of Clallam County**, ed. Clallam County Historical Society (Port Orchard, 1971), p. 53.

2. *Port Angeles Evening News*, April 2, 1953.

3. *Ibid.* Hotels were a definite sign of a town's progress in the 1880s and 1890s, as restless Americans became increasingly mobile. In 1886, Charles and Samuel Morse, along with Albert and Charles Draper, built the Merchants Hotel at Front and Laurel Streets. The structure was placed on property leased from C.W. (Wint) Thompson and in 1888 was transferred to the Puget Sound Cooperative Colony. The Merchants was razed in 1953.

4. Official estimates in 1880 placed the number of Chinese in Washington Territory at 3,186. The 1885 Census later counted 3,276 persons of Chinese extraction in the Territory, most living in Seattle, Tacoma and Olympia. See Art Chin, **Golden Tassels, A History of the Chinese in Washington, 1857-1977** (Seattle, 1977), p. 80.

5. On February 6 and 7, 1886, Seattle mobs, aroused by agitators, drove 350 Chinese from their homes and tried to expel them from the city aboard the steamer *Queen of the Pacific*. Firemen and The Home Guard, under the direction of Sheriff John H. McGraw (later the second Governor of Washington State) secured help from the Militia and dispelled one mob. However, the next day, 197 Chinese actually were shipped out. Those remaining were being escorted back to their homes by The Home Guard when they were confronted by an immense crowd on what is now First Avenue South, near the train depot. Direct contact was made and five rioters were shot, one of whom died the next day. See Lorraine Barker Hildebrand, **Straw Hats, Sandals and Steel: The Chinese in Washington State** (Tacoma, 1977), pp. 69-74.

6. The "General Officers" elected were: John J. Knoff, President; Lyman Wood, Recording Secretary; Mrs. Laura E. Hall, Corresponding Secretary; Mrs. Lyman Wood, Treasurer; and George Venable Smith, General Managing Agent.

7. An ambitious 32-page document, this descriptive booklet entitled "Puget Sound Co-Operative Colony" outlined in great detail all goals of the proposed utopia. A facsimile reproduction of the book was published in 1965 by the Shorey Book Store, Seattle, Washington.

8. *The Model Commonwealth* (Port Angeles, Washington), November 23, 1888.

9. **New Columbia Encyclopedia** (1975), p. 1208.

10. *The Model Commonwealth* (Port Angeles, Washington), November 18, 1887.

11. The Colony's Declaration of Principles (specifically No. 24), in fact, asserted that marriage was sacred and "the mora and physical foundation of the home . . . the anchor of stable upright conduct." See *The Model Commonwealth* (Por Angeles, Washington), October 7, 1887.

12.   *The Model Commonwealth* (Port Angeles, Washington), October 28, 1887.

13.   *Port Angeles Evening News*, December 14, 1951.

14.   A unique achievement of Colonists, The *Angeles* was launched Monday, April 29, 1889; her first captain was August F. England. Costing $4,200 to build, the sturdy little steamer, according to one respected source, was 58' 5" in length, with a 17' 7" beam. See E.W. Wright, **Lewis and Dryden's Marine History of the Pacific Northwest** (New York, 1961), p. 364.

      It should be noted, however, that other sources dispute the ship's dimensions, claiming it was 65 feet long and had a 19-foot beam. See **Jimmy Come Lately: History of Clallam County**, ed. Clallam County Historical Society (Port Orchard, 1971), p. 53 and G.M. Lauridsen, **The Story of Port Angeles and Clallam County, Washington** (Seattle, 1937). After its christening, The *Angeles* was commissioned to carry general freight in the Puget Sound area and the Strait of Juan de Fuca. See *The Model Commonwealth* (Port Angeles, Washington), May 26, 1889.

15.   Charles Pierce LeWarne, **Utopias on Puget Sound, 1885-1915** (Seattle, 1975), pp. 2-5.

16.   The election was held in February, 1888. See *The Model Commonwealth* (Port Angeles, Washington), April 6, 1888.

17.   Charles Pierce LeWarne, **Utopias on Puget Sound, 1885-1915** (Seattle, 1975), p. 52.

18.   Assets of the Colony were liquidated in 1904. On December 2, 1904, Judge Hatch closed the Trust. *Ibid.*, p. 52.

19.   One marriage which sent shock waves reverberating about town had Norman Smith, son of the town's founder, wooing the wife of George Venable Smith. May Smith, after divorcing the Colony's most prominent citizen, promptly married Norman, a tall, stately promoter. Though much-talked-about, all parties involved evidently took a mature approach to the uproar, and merely went about their business. Later, the two men even joined forces as Trustees in a firm trying to land the biggest fish in the promotional pond . . . the railroad.

20.   Other Colonists who "joined" the town and became assets therein, were: Madge Haynes Nailor, who was an active community worker and was City Treasurer from 1918-1948; Dr. Freeborn S. Lewis, whose daughter Minerva Troy became well-known as an artist, musician and politician; Charles Stakemiller, City Assessor and clothing store owner (his wife, the last known original colony member, died in October, 1958); William J. Ware, civil engineer and surveyor, became County Engineer; Hans (Henry) Westphal donated land and funds for the "poor farm" or County Home; and John Henson, whose son Jack later became a distinguished local reporter ("The Wandering Scribe") for the *Port Angeles Evening News.*

21.   The reader will recall that the Colony idea sprang originally from anti-Oriental roots, a fact which certainly belies their supposed recognition of individual rights. Acknowledging such bigoted behavior at the outset, however, one cannot dispute the Colonists' splendid record on womens' rights and in other areas of human endeavor. For example, The Puget Sound Cooperative Colony afforded women the right to vote in Colony affairs (when such a privilege was not being given to ladies), assured them wages equal to men and in general saw that they fared well in comparison with their sisters elsewhere in 19th Century America.

CHAPTER FOUR (Pages 53-71)

1.   The history of the planned city of Port Crescent, west of Port Angeles, is both brief and fascinating. Convenient to Canada, Crescent Bay on the Strait of Juan de Fuca, was originally "discovered" by smugglers. It was visualized as an ideal townsite location by promoters Cyrus F. Clapp, John Lutz and A.R. Coleman, who bought the entire west end of the bay from homesteader James Frank. They surveyed, platted, built a dock, planned a huge breakwater to lure ocean-going vessels and even named streets for the grand city being planned. By 1890, when its population was greatest, Port Crescent featured a large sawmill, three general stores, three saloons, a livery stable, blacksmith shop, weather bureau, Chinese laundry, hardware store, a newspaper and two hotels, the Ahola and the Markham House (the latter perhaps the finest in Clallam County).

      Within three short years, though, Port Crescent lost the election to become the County Seat, was rejected as a railroad terminal point, found that it was financially impossible to build the breakwater — then was victimized along with everybody else by the Great Depression of 1893. Eventually, everybody left and the beach reverted to its original wild state. Today, it is a private recreation area and there is not even so much as a "ghost town" left behind; no remnants whatsoever are there to remind visitors of the flourishing little community that died before its time.

2.   *Pacific Northwest Quarterly*, Vol. XXVIII No. 3, July, 1937, pp. 312-315.

3.   *Port Angeles Evening News*, January 21, 1937.

4.   The Councilmen elected in this first regular election were: Willard Brumfield, Mayor; Donald McInnes; J.F. Meagher; D.P. Quinn (the latter three re-elected); R.R. Harding and Lewis Levy (the latter two replacing Foster and Craig).

5. The history of this first banking effort in Port Angeles is sad indeed. Founded in 1890 by two promoters, B.F. Schwartz and I.A. Sahlinger, the bulk of the capital of the First National Bank, $50,000, was pledged by seven prominent Port Angeles citizens. It was apparently mismanaged by the two founders, for in April, 1891, Schwartz was ousted; Sahlinger followed him shortly thereafter. See *The Weekly Herald* (Port Angeles, Washington), February 11, 1891 and April 15, 1891. W.W. Gray and C.P. Brown ran the bank till it was squeezed by the 1893 Depression and suspended payments to depositors (June 26, 1893). The First National Bank opened again on December 15, 1893, but after floundering badly for six months, it closed for good. Schwartz, meanwhile, had opened another such institution in town — the Bank of Port Angeles — January 2, 1892. It too, was shortlived, closing in six months. Schwartz was promptly jailed for embezzlement, escaped, and was later arrested in St. Louis. See G.M. Lauridsen, **The Story of Port Angeles and Clallam County, Washington** (Seattle, 1937), p. 142.

6. 26 Stat. 814, p. 363.

7. *The Weekly Herald* (Port Angeles, Washington), April 15, 1891.

8. "The Port Angeles townsite reservation has at last been declared open to final settlement." See The *Democrat-Leader* (Port Angeles, Washington), August 4, 1893.

9. The "Port Angeles Base Ball Club" was organized in May, 1891, with H.B. Crockett, Manager; A.E. Tatemen, catcher; H.D. Kirmsey, pitcher; Teddy Beahan, shortstop; W.J. Dyke, first base; W.W. Crockett, second base; Frank Beahan, third base; W.X. Russell, left field; Joe House, right field; H. O'Brien, change catcher; Cliff Crockett, mascot. See *Port Angeles Tribune*, May 14, 1891.

10. E.B. Wright, **Lewis and Dryden's Marine History of the Pacific Northwest** (New York, 1961), p. 398.

11. The Grand Army of the Republic (GAR) was a society of Civil War veterans formed April 6, 1866 by Benjamin F. Stephenson in Decatur, Illinois. Credited with initiating Memorial Day, the group was active in relief work and pension legislation.

12. E.B. Wright, **Lewis and Dryden's Marine History of the Pacific Northwest** (New York, 1961), p. 409. Eighteen hundred and ninety-three is said to be the year the *Lydia Thompson* was built, and that date is deemed by the author to be correct, despite information to the contrary listed in other historical works.

13. The *Democrat-Leader* (Port Angeles, Washington), September 8, 1893.

14. *Ibid.*, August 4, 1893.

15. *Ibid.*, June 23, 1893.

16. *Port Angeles Evening News*, June 16, 1962, p. G-4.

17. G.M. Lauridsen, **The Story of Port Angeles and Clallam County, Washington** (Seattle, 1937), pp. 196-198.

18. *Ibid.*, p. 86.

CHAPTER FIVE (Pages 73-103)

1. *The Model Commonwealth* (Port Angeles, Washington), July 25, 1888. Thomas Malony was listed as Treasurer of the PAWRR. The reader will recall that Malony was successor to George Venable Smith as President of the Puget Sound Cooperative Colony.

2. The fourteen different promotions and the year each occurred in Port Angeles were:

Port Angeles and West Shore Railroad Company (PAWRR)	1888
Port Crescent and Chehalis Railroad	1890
Port Angeles Central Railroad Company	1890
Union Pacific Railroad	1890
	(Promotion actually initiated 1889)
Tacoma and Northwestern Railroad	1891
Chicago, Burlington and Quincy Railroad	1892
Washington Southern Railroad and Western Washington Development Company	1893
Plummer Railroad	1893
Oregon Railroad and Navigation Company	1895
Lehman-Martell Railroad	1898
Port Angeles Pacific Railway	1902
Port Angeles and Eastern Railroad	1904
Port Angeles Railway and Terminal Company	1908
Milwaukee Railroad	1911

See G.M. Lauridsen, **The Story of Port Angeles and Clallam County, Washington** (Seattle, 1937), pp. 104-127.

3.   *Ibid.*, p. 106.

4.   Following the unsuccessful operation in Tumwater Valley, the diamond drill was moved to Dry Creek five miles west of Port Angeles. There the speculators drilled 400 feet through solid rock, came up empty and the coal boom ended once and for all. See G.M. Lauridsen, **The Story of Port Angeles and Clallam County, Washington** (Seattle, 1937), pp. 127-128.

5.   *Ibid.*, pp. 130-131.

6.   Newspapers of that day credit Mrs. Matilda "Auntie" Cooper with the establishment of Ocean View Cemetery. She circulated petitions, maintained contact with federal officials and was instrumental in having the bill passed by Congress which donated to the city nine blocks of land for a cemetery in August, 1894.

7.   Much to the delight of Port Angeles residents, the Pacific Fleet came to the harbor annually to conduct ocean maneuvers. They included gun firing, night attack and land assaults. During the fleet's annual visits, Rear Admiral Leslie Beardslee, an avid fisherman, traveled often to Lake Crescent west of town to try his hand at luring a unique, deep-water species of trout from its 600-foot depths. Later, the species was named in his honor and the large Beardslee Trout is still a highly-prized freshwater fish.

8.   The Elks Naval Lodge #353 was established in 1896 under special permission granted by Elks International Headquarters. Only towns with a population of 5,000 or more were to be granted permission to open a Lodge, and Port Angeles' count in 1896 was about 2,000. See Thomas T. Aldwell, **Conquering the Last Frontier** (Seattle, 1950), p. 35.

9.   The *Democrat-Leader* (Port Angeles, Washington), January 10, 1896.

10.   President William McKinley was shot on September 6, 1901 by Leon F. Czolgosz, while in Buffalo, New York. He lingered for a week, succumbing on September 14, 1901.

11.   The *Democrat-Leader* (Port Angeles, Washington), June 13, 1902.

12.   The first control board was located at First and Oak Streets.

13.   Donald McGillivray, **Autobiographical Anecdotes of Dr. Donald McGillivray** (Port Angeles, Washington, 1950), pp. 89-90.

14.   *Seattle Times*, September 30, 1962, pp. 4-5.

15.   The *Clallam* was considered so safe that its owners carried only $100,000 in fire and collision insurance on her. It is known that there were 31 crew members, but nobody knows exactly how many passengers were aboard when it sank, for children weren't listed and nobody paid attention to how many disembarked at Port Townsend. See *Seattle Times*, January 6, 1963, pp. 12-13.

16.   Primarily through the efforts of Matilda C. Cooper, Major F.S. Lewis, and two Congressmen, Wesley L. Jones and Francis E. Cushman, what was later known as "Lincoln Park" became a reality.

17.   There is no question *The Daily Tribune* was the first daily paper published in town. The precise months during which it functioned, however, are in doubt. G.M. Lauridsen, in his book, **The Story of Port Angeles**, says that Colonel R.H. Ballinger and a recently-acquired partner, C.D. Ulmer, founded it in 1892 as a five-column folio sheet, "ran it through the campaign months of that year and put it to sleep January 1, 1893." See G.M. Lauridsen, **The Story of Port Angeles and Clallam County, Washington** (Seattle, 1937), p. 230.

In a "Peninsula Profile" article featuring C.D. Ulmer, written by "The Wandering Scribe," Jack Henson, *The Daily Tribune's* debut and cutoff date are considerably different. Henson (and presumably Ulmer) says it was first published in the "summer of 1893" and "folded January 1, 1894." See *Port Angeles Evening News,* July 8, 1949.

Another article researched and written in April, 1976 by the *Port Angeles Daily News*, though, states that *The Daily Tribune* was published while the government townsite was being opened to settlement (which could be anytime early in the decade of the 1890s) then "folded in April, 1892 (when it was) merged with the *Times.*"

Lauridsen's version appears to be incorrect as to the cutoff date, but is closest to the mark. Researcher Peggy Brady discovered in the weekly *Tribune-Times* of January 14, 1892, reference to an article which had appeared in the daily *Tribune-Times* just three days earlier; we know therefore that it was alive during the first weeks of that year. The August 4, 1892 weekly paper later carried its sister publication's obituary in the form of a small article stating that "publication of *The Daily Tribune* has been suspended until October first, unless affairs should take a change at an earlier date which would warrant resumption sooner." No further trace of it could be found after that August 4, 1892 reference, so it is the author's belief that it never reopened.

18.   A brief listing of some of the papers which flourished for a short time in Port Angeles: *The People* (1891); *The* (first) *Herald* (1891); *The Port Angeles Simoon* (1894); *The Typhoon* (1894); *The Daily Pop* (published by The Populist Party - 1896); *The Bee* (1913); *The Peninsula Free Press* (1913); and *The* (second) *Herald* (1914).

19.   Westphal deeded 50 acres of land to the County for the express purpose of establishing "a poor farm, or infirmary."

After other bequests were carried out, another $5,910.39 cash was left over, and it, too, went into the County coffers for this purpose. In 1941, patients still there were removed to other, newer nursing homes.

20. The signal and dwelling were erected during 1908 and began operations soon thereafter. See *Olympic-Leader* (Port Angeles, Washington), December 22, 1905.

21. The Commerce Department order specified that all vessels incoming from the Pacific Ocean were now required to take a licensed pilot aboard at Port Angeles if they intended to traverse inland waters. The Commerce Department ruling is today enforced by the Board of Pilotage Commissioners of the State of Washington. See *Olympic-Leader* (Port Angeles, Washington), March 23, 1906.

22. *Olympic-Leader* (Port Angeles, Washington), May 21, 1909.

23. *Ibid.,* March 11, 1910.

24. *Ibid.,* June 24, 1910.

25. Aldwell's Elwha River Dam blew out on October 31, 1912. Just a little more than one year later, on November 5, 1913, it opened again, fully functional and generating more than enough electricity for Port Angeles. See Thomas T. Aldwell, **Conquering the Last Frontier** (Seattle, 1950), pp. 106-107.

26. Ellis Lucia, **The Big Woods: Logging and Lumbering – From Bull Teams to Helicopters in the Pacific Northwest.** (New York, 1975), pp. 70-71.

    In addition to the cynical nickname "Wobblies," some newspapers of that day considered the I.W.W.'s actions as downright un-American, and often referred to its members in other, more derogatory terms, such as "I Won't Work," "Imperial Wilhelm Warriors," and "I Want Wilhelm." See Ralph W. Hildy, **Timber and Men**; **The Weyerhaeuser Story** (New York, 1963), p. 341.

27. G.M. Lauridsen, **The Story of Port Angeles and Clallam County, Washington** (Seattle, 1937), pp. 122-123.

28. *Olympic-Leader* (Port Angeles, Washington), January 24, 1913. Prejudice against non-whites was prevalent and freely expressed in the early days of the 20th Century. And it was not couched in delicate terms. In this same year, 1913, just down the road in the town of Sequim, an incident occurred which was described in one local newspaper under the bold headline "No Time For Japs." The article noted that "Several stopped in Sequim for lunch and were told they were not wanted and they should lose no time in making their exodus from that section." See *Olympic-Leader* (Port Angeles, Washington), July 14, 1913.

29. *Port Angeles Olympic* (Port Angeles, Washington), March 11, 1913.

30. *Olympic-Leader* (Port Angeles, Washington), November 7, 1913 and November 28, 1913.

CHAPTER SIX (Pages 105-131)

1. *Olympic-Leader* (Port Angeles, Washington), July 17, 1914.

2. *Ibid.,* August 7, 1914 and October 16, 1914.

3. *Ibid.,* May 8, 1914.

4. G.M. Lauridsen, **The Story of Port Angeles and Clallam County, Washington** (Seattle, 1937), p. 123. "With Ordinance No. 457, granted by the City Council July 15, 1914, to the Seattle, Port Angeles and Lake Crescent Railway, the right was given to run along and across all the streets east and west, as required."

5. *The Weekly Herald* (Port Angeles, Washington), January 15, 1916 and February 10, 1916.

6. *Olympic-Leader* (Port Angeles, Washington), February 9, 1916.

7. *Democrat-Leader* (Port Angeles, Washington), April 26, 1895.

8. There is conflicting information as to the exact founding date of the Cain Bank. According to G.M. Lauridsen, John Cain "entered the field and obtained Charter" on August 12, 1901. See G.M. Lauridsen, **The Story of Port Angeles and Clallam County** (Seattle, 1937), p. 144. However, an October 16, 1969 letter from Kenneth W. Leaf, Regional Administrator of National Banks in Portland, Oregon, says "The Cain National Bank of Port Angeles was chartered by the Comptroller of the Currency on December 31, 1901."

9. *Port Angeles Evening News*, December 20, 1919.

10. There have been several "Lincoln" Schools in Port Angeles. One, a one-room log cabin built on Deer Park Road, circa 1900, was used for approximately eight to ten years, both as a schoolhouse and as a residence. (This is the building discovered under some bushes by Port Angeles High School teacher, Sandy Keys, in 1966. Keys and his students restored the building and donated it to the City of Port Angeles. Today, it can be found at Lincoln Park.) That building

is not to be confused with a much older, one-room school on Lincoln Heights (in the vicinity of today's Eighth and C Streets), known simply as "the old school house." Construction date on "the old school house" is unknown, and a search of the records failed to reveal its fate.

Then, in 1894, another Lincoln School opened on Lincoln Heights, this one near the corner of what is now West Ninth Street. It was a two-story, wooden structure, and (adding to the confusion), like its predecessor, also referred to as "the old school house." It was used for educational, religious and social functions until 1917, at which time it was moved to the southeast corner of the school grounds, where it was later torn down.

The large "red pressed brick" Lincoln School (as described at the time it was built) at the southeast corner of Eighth and C Streets opened January 8, 1917 and still was standing, though abandoned, when this book went to press in 1982. A $25,000 bond issue approved by Port Angeles voters in 1917 provided funds for this 320-pupil structure, which saw continuous service until 1978 when it was closed by action of the Port Angeles School Board.

11. *Olympic-Leader* (Port Angeles, Washington), April 10, 1917.

12. The first name drawn in that 1917 Draft was John Nylander, Alaska Hotel, #850. Second: Edwin C. McFarlane, Clallam Bay, #458. Third: Steve Curtis, Dungeness #854. Fourth: Carroll M. Blood, Snohomish #783. Fifth: William Swenn, Carlsborg, #837. Sixth: Edwin F. Eacret, City, #337. See *Olympic-Leader* (Port Angeles, Washington), July 24, 1917.

13. The federal government stated its requirements as one hundred million to one hundred seventy million board feet of acceptable spruce. This meant that *one billion board feet had to be cut*, for only 167 feet of every 1,000 would meet the rigid specifications for airplane manufacture.

14. *Olympic-Leader* (Port Angeles, Washington), December 4, 1917.

15. Robert L. Tyler, **Rebels of the Woods: The I.W.W. in the Pacific Northwest** (Eugene, Oregon, 1967), p. 102.

16. Ellis Lucia, **The Big Woods: Logging and Lumbering – From Bull Teams to Helicopters in the Pacific Northwest** (New York, 1975), p. 76.

17. James Rowan, **The I.W.W. in the Lumber Industry** (Seattle, 1969), p. 53.

18. Ellis Lucia, **The Big Woods: Logging and Lumbering – From Bull Teams to Helicopters in the Pacific Northwest** (New York, 1975), pp. 77-78.

19. *Port Angeles Evening News*, October 18, 1918.

20. A summary of official and private reports of Washington State's war dead published January 6, 1919, showed that 58,000 state residents had served in the war, and that 929 gave their lives. Clallam County contributed a total of 325 men through the Selective Service, and an estimated 175 others enlisted in other branches of the armed services. Seven Clallam County men died in The Great War. The list is as follows:

Walter E. Akeley, Port Angeles, Private, A.E.F. – killed August 22, 1918.
Donald E. Dorr, Port Angeles, Private, A.E.F., Co. H. 160th Infantry – killed October 25, 1918.
William H. Grayson, Port Angeles, Private, A.E.F., Co. G. 157th Infantry – died of disease September 26, 1918.
Earl C. Jenkins, Port Angeles, Naval gunner – died at Naval Hospital, Brooklyn, New York, October 31, 1918.
Clyde Rhodefer, Sequim, Sergeant, Battery B, 34th Field Artillery, A.E.F. – September 23, 1918.
Jacob Sunde, Port Angeles, Private, Co. B., 347th Machine Gun Battery, A.E.F. – died of wounds, October 11, 1918.
Gusstein Borgford, Clallam Bay, Private, Co. B., 162nd Infantry, A.E.F. – died of accident or other causes June 30, 1918.

See *Port Angeles Evening News*, January 6, 1919.

CHAPTER SEVEN (Pages 133-147)

1. Several discrepancies exist regarding the exact starting date of Crescent Boxboard. The *Port Angeles Olympic-Tribune* noted in a February 21, 1919 edition that the starting date was February 20, 1919.

The *Port Angeles Evening News* on April 8, 1919 (in an article stressing that the firm "employs no Japs, nor will they do so here") noted that the plant was "complete" and would be in operation "in a few days."

A later story in the *Port Angeles Evening News*, on September 9, 1926 stated flatly that Crescent Boxboard had "commenced operation June 1, 1919."

2. An article in the *Port Angeles Evening News* on November 9, 1927, described the merger thus: "The Crescent Boxboard mill, a Paraffine Company subsidiary, officially lost its identity as the "Crescent" mill and became the Port Angeles Division of Fibreboard Products, Incorporated, Monday, November 1."

3. *Port Angeles Evening News*, November 3, 1920 and December 21, 1920.

4. The Volstead Act defined an intoxicating beverage as one containing more than .5 percent of alcohol by volume. The Act was modified in 1933 to permit the sale of 3.2 percent beer and wine and became void after the repeal of the Eighteenth Amendment late in 1933. See **The Columbia Encyclopedia**, Third Edition, (New York and London, 1963), p. 2267.

5. Dedication of the Port Angeles Masonic Lodge was highlighted by a Lodge meeting November 22, 1921. At the grand occasion, W.H. Thompson, engineer at Crescent Boxboard Plant, presented to the Masons a solid ivory gavel from a walrus tusk. See *Port Angeles Evening News*, November 23, 1921.

6. Port Angeles Rotary Club founded . . . . February 23, 1921
    Knights of Columbus Council No. 2260 founded. . . . . May 18, 1921
    Kiwanis Club founded . . . . July 21, 1921
    Camp Fire Girls founded. . . . . .January 28, 1922
    Boy Scout Council founded. . . . . May 5, 1922
    Wolf Cubs founded 1923
                                                                                                  (No precise date available)

7. *Port Angeles Evening News*, November 24, 1922.

8. *Ibid.*, December 8, 1922.

9. *Ibid.*, December 12, 1922.

10. *Port Angeles Olympic-Tribune*, August 10, 1923 and September 4, 1923.

11. *Port Angeles Evening News*, September 7, 1926.

12. *The Daily News* (Port Angeles, Washington), April 8, 1976, p. 2A.

13. Coincidentally, the building at 114 South Lincoln Street designed by G.M. Lauridsen and which housed the *Port Angeles Evening News* for 53 years, is also the same plant where this book, **Port Angeles, Washington: A History**, Volume I was produced.

14. *Port Angeles Olympic-Tribune*, January 26, 1923.

15. In 1924, the Olympus Hotel was built on the site of the old Opera House, which had been torn down one year earlier. (The same plat, incidentally, was earlier the location of Samuel Stork's store.) Of the Olympus' 50 rooms, builders took pains to make certain that 20 faced the bay, 30 the mountains. See *Port Angeles Olympic-Tribune*, October 5, 1923 and March 29, 1924.

16. On March 29, 1924 the Olympus Hotel held its Grand Opening. See *Port Angeles Olympic-Tribune*, April 4, 1924. The U.S. Coast Guard Office and Section Base opened on January 15, 1925. See *Port Angeles Evening News*, January 15, 1925. Lincoln Park was named after our sixteenth President on May 13, 1925. See *Port Angeles Evening News*, May 13, 1925. And on July 1, 1925 the Immigration Office opened. See *Port Angeles Evening News*, July 1, 1925.

17. *Port Angeles Evening News*, February 4, 1925.

18. *Ibid.*, July 5, 1927 and December 19, 1927.

19. *Ibid.*, March 9, 1927.

CHAPTER EIGHT (Pages 149-181)

1. *Port Angeles Evening News*, May 8, 1930.

2. *Ibid.*, November 4, 1931 and November 11, 1931.

3. *Ibid.*, November 14, 1931.

4. *Ibid.*, June 16, 1962. There really is no way of determining exactly when the informal gatherings began which led ultimately to formation of the Port Angeles Symphony. The year 1931 was used in this text because James Van Horn, a conductor during the 1950s and 1960s, listed such a date in the 1962 article cited here. Van Horn, however, was not present at the outset, and obtained his information second-hand; presumably that information came from one of the musicians in the original group.

    It may be that the informal gatherings began in 1931 and carried over to the next year, when a more formal organization was established.

5. When the Bank Holiday was declared by President Roosevelt, the U.S. Treasury Department, hoping to offset any potentially disastrous consequences, authorized banks that re-opened to print scrip — temporary money backed by the assets and collateral of the bank. Port Angeles' First National Bank placed huge amounts of collateral on the line, then had

thousands of dollars worth of scrip printed. Treasury Secretary William H. Woodin changed his mind overnight, and the beautifully lithographed "money" was never used. See *Ibid.*, March 18, 1933.

6.   *Ibid.*, April 15, 1933.

7.   *Ibid.*, April 24, 1933. The spelling of the name of the first CCC enlistee was "VanAusdle" in the *Evening News* article. However, Robert Van Ausdle, Eugene's nephew was contacted just before this book went to press; he said the correct spelling in 1930 should have been with two "n's" and a lower-case "a" — Vannausdle.

8.   *Ibid.*, June 10, 1933.

9.   *Ibid.*, December 7, 1933.

10.   Lew Rockman, Employment Office Commissioner said in July, 1933 that "the aggregate" (total cases) would be cut "to about 660, or approximately one-half the number receiving direct relief in March (1,276 cases)."

11.   *Ibid.*, March 26, 1936.

12.   *Ibid.*, January 6, 1938.

13.   *Ibid.*, March 23, 1934.

14.   *Ibid.*, August 16, 1935.

15.   President Roosevelt's official remarks at the signing of the bill authorizing Olympic National Park:

> "I have taken great pleasure in signing the act to establish the Olympic National Park in the State of Washington. This is the logical development arising out of the establishment of the Mount Olympus National Monument during the Administration of President Theodore Roosevelt, together with the added section from the Olympic National Forest. In the future the new Olympic National Park may be extended in area by adding land acquired by gift or purchase or additional lands from the Olympic National Forest.

> "The establishment of this new national park will be of interest to everybody in the country. Its scenery and its remarkable tree growth are well worth addition to the splended national parks which have already been created in many parts of the country." See *Port Angeles Evening News*, June 29, 1938

16.   The Spruce Railroad, as it was called, ran along the north shore of Lake Crescent to the town of Disque — named after Colonel Bryce P. Disque — where it joined the Port Angeles Western Railroad (formerly the Milwaukee Railroad). It, in turn, went clear through to Port Angeles.

17.   ITT Rayonier's Port Angeles mill did indeed begin operations in 1929 as Olympic Forest Products. However, the firm marks its anniversary date as April 26, 1926, when E.M. Mills founded *its* predecessor, Rainier Pulp and Paper Company in Shelton, Washington. See *Port Angeles Daily News*, Monday, April 26, 1976.

18.   Following is a complete alphabetical breakdown of the participants in the Clallam County Courthouse scandal of 1939, charges filed against them and the outcome of their separate trials.

> BAAR, WALTER (File No. 941). Charges: Larceny, Misappropriation of money by a public officer and forgery. Sentenced to 155 years; released from prison May 13, 1944.

> BOWLES, ROLLIN E. (File No. 914). Charges: Nonfeasance in office. Fined $100; sentenced to ten years; released.

> BROWN, HUGH (File No. 916). Charges: Misappropriation of money by public officer. Sentenced to 15 years; ordered confined for 27 months. Released January 1, 1941.

> CLARK, ALFRED (File No. 886). Charges: Misappropriation of money by public officer. Sentenced to 15 years; ordered confined for 27 months. Released July 12, 1942.

> FOSTER, IVA (File No. 880). Charges: Accessory to the commission of crime of larceny. Sentenced to five years; ordered confined for one year. Paroled October 17, 1939.

> FOSTER, ROBERT (File No. 881). Charges: Forgery in the first degree. Sentenced to five years; ordered confined for three years. Paroled January 1, 1943.

> LEVY, ARNOLD (File No. 944). Charges: Misappropriation of money by public officer. (Change of venue — trial held in Snohomish County.) Sentenced to 15 years. Released February 6, 1943.

> RANEY, JUNE (aka J.E. Smith), (File No. 904). Charges: Forgery in the second degree and misappropriation of money by public officer. Sentenced to six months. Released on bond due to pregnancy; no time served.

> SULLIVAN, MABEL (File No. 913). Charges: Misappropriation of money by public officer. Released on bond October 17, 1939.

> WOOD, FAY E. (File No. 883). Charges: Accessory to a crime. Sentenced to five years; ordered confined for one year. Paroled May 26, 1940.

> YELLE, CLIFF (File No. 915). Charges: Nonfeasance in office. (Change of venue to Thurston County.) Sentenced to

pay prosecution costs. Charges dismissed.

19. *U.S. News and World Report*, September 10, 1979, p. 65.

20. *Port Angeles Evening News*, August 29, 1940.

21. The first number drawn by the Clallam County Selective Service Board was #158, belonging to Lowell Burditt, Joyce. The next five numbers selected and the men holding those numbers were: 192, Orvall Richardson; 105, Raymond Clary; 2441, Lester Gulseth; 2563, Frank Smith, Jr.; 188, Lloyd Munro, Port Angeles.

22. Exact spelling of the fishermen's name is hard to determine. Newspaper articles, Coroners Reports, official court records and other sources have identified the brothers' name as "Ross," "Roff," "Rolf," and "Rolfe."

23. *Ibid.*, March 3, 1942 and March 4, 1942.

24. Because there still are residents of Port Angeles who are familiar with the Illingworth trial – including some who testified at or attended it – the author believes that certain previously-published inaccuracies about the case should be corrected. Among the stories found to be most inaccurate is the tale of "The Lady of the Lake" as found in the book **Crime Doctor**.

    –Hallie Illingworth's body was found on July 6, 1940. (**Crime Doctor** says it was found in the "Summer, 1939.")

    –Trial transcripts reveal that Tacoma Pathologist Dr. Charles P. Larson testified that the body had probably remained between 100 and 250 feet for at least a year, and that water temperature at those depths was approximately 44.6 degrees. (**Crime Doctor** purports to quote Larson as saying that the body hovered at 5,000 feet, where the temperatures were "three degrees above freezing.")

    –"The Lady," Hallie Illingworth, was born January 8, 1901, and was 36 years old when she dropped from sight around Christmas, 1937. (**Crime Doctor** agrees that she was 36 years old when she disappeared, but claims that was in 1932. Hallie Spraker didn't even marry Monty Illingworth until 1936.)

    –The autopsy report on Hallie Illingworth stated that the body weighed "in the vicinity of 125 to130 pounds." (**Crime Doctor** claims its weight was exactly 43 pounds.)

    –The body of water mentioned prominently in **Crime Doctor** – twice – as the one into which Lake Crescent empties (via an underground stream) is not Lake Sullivan, but rather Lake *Sutherland*.

25. In a letter dated July 13, 1981 from T.G. Pappas, Supervisor of Case Management and Records for the Washington State Board of Prison Terms and Paroles, no clue could be found as to Monty Illingworth's whereabouts following completion of his five-year parole period in 1956.

26. *Port Angeles Evening News*, April 17, 1941.

CHAPTER NINE (Pages 183-203)

1. From published reports in Japanese Monograph No. 102, translated after the war, it would seem that Port Angelens – indeed, *all* west coast residents – had good reason to be concerned about attacks on their towns. Shortly after Pearl Harbor, a Japanese Sub Force Detachment – believed to be nine vessels – was dispersed to the United States' west coast. They were ordered to attack shipping *and* to shell coastal cities on Christmas Eve. However, the U.S. Army's strenuous anti-submarine measures "became very severe," and the Japanese plan was abandoned. See Bert Webber, **Retaliation: Japanese Attacks and Allied Countermeasures on the Pacific Coast in World War II** (Corvallis, Oregon, 1975), p. 15.

2. *Port Angeles Evening News,* January 27, 1942.

3. *Ibid.*, May 23, 1942.

4. *Ibid.*, June 22, 1942.

5. *Ibid.*, August 5, 1942.

6. *Ibid.*, August 5, 1942.

7. The recipe for Economy Fruitcake:
    1 cup dark brown sugar
    1/3 cup lard (or other fat)
    1 cup seeded raisins
    1 cup chopped dried prunes
    1 cup water
    2¼ cups, flour
    1 teaspoon soda

1 teaspoon baking powder
1 teaspoon cinnamon
¼ teaspoon cloves
¼ teaspoon mace
1 teaspoon vanilla
½ teaspoon salt

Simmer ten minutes, sugar, lard, raisins, prunes and water. Cool, add rest of ingredients. Mix thoroughly and pour into loaf pan lined with heavy waxed paper.

Bake 1¼ hours in moderately slow oven (325°).

8. *Port Angeles Evening News*, January 16, 1942.

9. *Ibid.*, August 1, 1942.

10. *Ibid.*, August 27, 1942 and September 16, 1943. Of the eight *Red Alders* planned, only five were started, and three completed, when Olympic Shipbuilders' contract was cancelled.

11. The availability of food and the cooking of canned food were deemed prerequisites for an adequate Civil Defense Shelter in those hectic early days of World War Two.

12. *Port Angeles Evening News*, June 26, 1943.

13. *Ibid.*, September 16, 1943, September 27, 1943 and June 30, 1962.

14. *Ibid.*, October 11, 1944.

15. *Ibid.*, February 3, 1945.

16. *Ibid.*, March 29, 1945.

17. Germany actually surrendered on May 7, 1945, but V-E Day was declared officially by the Allies as May 8, 1945. See *Port Angeles Evening News*, May 8, 1945.

18. *Ibid.*, May 12, 1945.

19. *Ibid.*, August 28, 1945. A list of those who gave their lives in the service of their country is as follows: L.B. Wimberley, USA; Henry C. Echternkamp, USN; Marshall Dompier, USN; Marlyn Wayne Nelson, USN; Henry Irons, USN; Irvin LeRoy Faulkner, USN; Hubert Hayter, USN; William Grayson, USA; Rudolph P. Weisel, Jr., USAAF; David Ritchie, USA; Thurlow Elmore Kesner, USCG; Earl Muyskens, USCG; Henry Huff, USMS; Welch, George, USA; Richard Anderson, USMC; Richard B. Traul, USAAF; Joseph A. Piszesek; Robert A. Gage, USAAF; William H. Woodcock, Jr., USA; Edwin B. Anderson, USCG; James W. Lee, USN; Arthur V. Shields, USN; Ralph Hess, USAAF; Fredrick W. Cramer, USMC; Billy Dean Purcell, USA; Bernard F. Baugh, USA; John M. Miller, USA; Eugene B. Fleming, USAAF; Robert Johnson, USA; Guy E. Coble, USA; Reginald Solway, USAAF; Andrew MacZinko, USA; Donald Harrison, USA; Gordon William Schlichting, USAAF; Robert Morris, USAAF; Jack Comstock, USAAF; John R. Uphouse, USAAF; William C. Nicholas, USA; Joseph J. Pearce, USN; Junior K. Egloff, USA; Charles Bornstein; John E. Shore, USA; Charles E. Bartels, USA; James M. Kilgore, USA; Joseph M. Harley, USA; Walter A. Fletcher, USA; Richard Wood, USA; Alfred A. Johnson, USA; Arthur Wittenborn, USA; Richard J. Cummings, USA; Ellis Robbins, USA; Marion F. Roup, USN; Maurice F. Dean, USN; Edward C. Webber, USN; Robert O'Bryant, USA; Jack Bergman, USAAF; Carl E. Pearson, USMCR; Clarence Merton Caskey, USN.

20. *Ibid.*, September, 15, 1945. The *U.S.S. Tambor* SS-198 was built at the Electric Boat Company, Groton, Connecticut in 1939, and Commissioned June 3, 1940, Lt. Commander J.W. Murphy, Jr., commanding.

Coming Attractions

In the next volume of **Port Angeles, Washington: A History**, we shall pick up our story at the end of World War Two.

The impact of post-war expansion upon Port Angeles will be explored in detail, and the town's steady growth will be chronicled — all the way from "Automobile Row" to the All-American City Award, and from Local Improvement Districts to the proposed Northern Tier Pipeline.

Following are a few sample photos from Volume Two, which illustrate the wide variety of subjects to be covered.

Bert Thomas becomes the first man to swim the frigid Strait of Juan de Fuca.

Howard Doherty (yes, that's Howard Doherty!) promoting the annual Port Angeles Salmon Derby.

Growth of the Olympic Peninsula Travel Association (OPTA), shown here at a meeting in the 1940s.

"Blithe Spirit" (1951), first major production by a group that would later become the Port Angeles Community Players.

The expansion of medical facilities at Olympic Memorial Hospital.

The popular Bill Fairchild and development of the airport named in his honor.

Long-time Port Commissioner and community leader Fred Strange.

225

THREE PROMINENT PORT ANGELENS, brought together in this 1948 picture. At left is Jack Henson, popular *Evening News* reporter for over 30 years and best known as the "Wandering Scribe." Henson came to Port Angeles as a youngster with his parents, who joined the Puget Sound Cooperative Colony. In the center is Clay Wolverton, long-time Fire Chief for the City of Port Angeles. An outstanding public official, Wolverton is generally conceded to be responsible for the low fire insurance rates Port Angelens enjoyed during his 36 years as Fire Chief. On the right is John Schweitzer, another newspaper man of many years standing. It is worth noting that one of Schweitzer's most important contributions to city and county residents was his donation to the North Olympic Library System of an extensive file of a variety of Port Angeles and Clallam County newspapers. Without such a collection, a thorough history of Port Angeles would be a virtual impossibility. PHOTO SOURCE: *Port Angeles Evening News*

BERT KELLOGG. Owner of one of the most comprehensive photograph collections in the entire Pacific Northwest, Bert Kellogg is responsible for many of the reproductions found in **Port Angeles, Washington: A History, Volume One.** A remarkable man who is nearly sightless, Mr. Kellogg became interested in collecting and reproducing historical photographs after a 1940 accident left him with very little vision. He grinds his own special lenses, enabling him to perform exceptionally delicate darkroom work. Mr. Kellogg has donated hundreds of negatives and photographs to the North Olympic Library System in Port Angeles, and in 1981 was one of the finalists for Port Angeles' "Citizen of the Year" award. PHOTO SOURCE: Bert Kellogg

Bibliography

Books, Articles

Aldwell, Thomas T. **Conquering the Last Frontier**. Seattle: Superior Publishing Company, 1950.

Andrews, Ralph W. **Glory Days of Logging**. Seattle: Superior Publishing Company, 1956.

Andrews, Ralph W. **Indian Primitive**. Seattle: Superior Publishing Company, 1960.

Andrews, Ralph W. **"This was Logging," Selected Photographs of Darius Kinsey**. Seattle: Superior Publishing Company, 1954.

Andrews, Ralph W. **This was Sawmilling**. Seattle: Superior Publishing Company, 1957.

Andrews, Ralph W. **This was Seafaring, A Sea Chest of Salty Memories**. Seattle: Superior Publishing Company, 1955.

Avery, Mary W. **Government of Washington State**. Revised Edition. Seattle: University of Washington Press, 1973.

Avery, Mary W. **History and Government of the State of Washington**. Seattle: University of Washington Press, 1961.

Bacon, George H. **Booming and Panicking on Puget Sound**. Bellingham, Whatcom Museum of History and Art, 1970.

Bancroft, Hubert Howe. **History of the Northwest Coast, 1543-1800**. Two volumes. San Francisco: Bancroft, 1884, 1866. Reprint, 1967.

Bancroft-Hunt, Norman. **People of the Totem: The Indians of the Pacific Northwest**. New York: G.P. Putnam's Sons, 1979.

Basler, Roy P., ed. **Collected Works of Abraham Lincoln**. Eight volumes. New Brunswick, N.J.: Rutgers, 1953.

Belden, Thomas Graham. **So Fell the Angels**. Boston: Little, Brown and Company, 1956.

Bradley, Thomas H. **O'Toole's Mallet or the Resurrection of the Second National City of the United States of America**. Second Edition. n. p., 1894.

Brown, Vinson. **People's of the Sea Wind: The Native Americans of the Pacific Coast**. New York: Macmillan, 1977.

Brown, William Compton. **The Indian Side of the Story**. Spokane: C.W. Hill Printing Company, 1961.

Browne, J. Ross. **Indian Affairs in the Territories of Oregon and Washington**. Fairfield, Washington: Ye Galleon Press, 1977. Reprint of the 1858 edition, which was issued as Ex. Doc. No. 39, 35th Congress, First Session,, House of Representatives.

Brumfield, William. "The Removal of the County Seat from Dungeness to Port Angeles, Washington." *Pacific Northwest Quarterly*, 28 (July 1937):312-315.

Campbell, Patricia. **A History of the North Olympic Peninsula**. Second Edition. Port Angeles: Peninsula Publishing, Inc., 1979.

Chase, Salmon P. **Diary and Correspondence of Salmon P. Chase**. New York: Da Capo Press, 1971. (Unabridged republication of the first edition published in Washington, D.C. in 1903 as Volume II of the Annual Report of the American Historical Association for the year 1902.)

Chase, Salmon Portland. **Inside Lincoln's Cabinet: The Civil War Diaries of Salmon P. Chase**. Edited by David Donald. New York: Longman, Green, 1954.

Chin, Art. **Golden Tassels: A History of the Chinese in Washington, 1957-1977**. Seattle: Author, 1977.

Clark, Ella E. **Indian Legends of the Pacific Northwest**. Berkeley: University of California Press, 1953.

Colson, E. **The Makah Indians**. Minneapolis: University of Minnesota Press, 1953.

Coman, Edwin T. Jr. **Time, Tide and Timber, A Century of Pope Talbot**. Palo Alto: Stanford University Press, 1949.

Doty, James. **Journal of Operations of Governor Isaac Ingalls Stevens of Washington Territory in 1855**. Fairfield, Washington: Ye Galleon Press, 1977.

Drucker, Philip. **Cultures of the North Pacific Coast**. San Francisco: Chandler Publishing Company, 1965.

Drucker, Philip. **Indians of the Northwest Coast**. New York: McGraw-Hill, 1955.

Dryden, Cecil. **Dryden's History of Washington**. Portland, Oregon: Binfords and Mort, 1968.

Eells, Myron. **The Twana, Chemakum and Klallam Indians of Washington Territory**. Seattle: Shorey Book Store, 1971. (Extract from: Smithsonian Annual Report, 1897.)

Ficken, Robert E. **Lumber and Politics: The Career of Mark E. Reed**. Seattle: University of Washington Press, 1979.

Field, W.F. **Index to Washington Territorial Records**. Tacoma: Washington State Office of the Adjutant General, 1960.

Gates, Charles Martin. **Readings in Pacific Northwest History: Washington, 1790-1895**. Seattle: University Bookstore, 1941.

Gibbs, George. **Indian Tribes of Washington Territory**. Fairfield, Washington: Ye Galleon Press, 1967.

Gibbs, George. **Tribes of Western Washington and Northwestern Oregon**. Seattle: Shorey Book Store, 1970. (Facsimile Reproduction.)

Gibbs, James A. **Shipwrecks of the Pacific Coast**. Second Edition. Portland, Oregon: Binfords and Mort, 1962.

Gibbs, Jim. **Pacific Squareriggers, Pictorial History of the Great Windships of Yesteryear**. Seattle: Superior Publishing Company, 1969.

Gibbs, Jim. **West Coast Lighthouses: A Pictorial History of the Guiding Lights of the Sea**. Seattle: Superior Publishing Company, 1974.

Gibbs, Jim. **West Coast Windjammers in Story and Pictures**. Seattle: Superior Publishing Company, 1968.

Goddard, Pliny. **Indians of the Northwest Coast**. New York: American Museum Press, 1934. (American Museum of Natural History Handbook. Series No. 10. Second Edition.)

Goodman, Jeffrey. **American Genesis: The American Indian and the Origins of Modern Man**. New York: Summit Books, 1981.

Gregory, V.J. **Keepers at the Gates**. Port Townsend: Port Townsend Publishing Company, 1976.

Gunther, Erna. **Klallam Ethnography**. Seattle: University of Washington Press, 1927. (Publications in Anthropology, Volume 1, No. 5, pp. 171-314.)

Haeberlin, Herman. **The Indians of Puget Sound**. Seattle: University of Washington Press, 1952. (Publications in Anthropology, Volume 4, No. 1, pp. 1-84, Sept. 1930.)

Hart, Albert Bushnell. **Salmon Portland Chase**. Boston: Houghton Mifflin, 1899.

Hays, Finley. **Crown Zellerbach Loggers**. Chehalis, Washington: Loggers World, Inc., 1970.

Hays, H.R. **Children of the Raven: The Seven Indian Nations of the Northwest Coast**. New York: McGraw-Hill, 1975.

Hazard, Joseph T. **Companion of Adventure: A Biography of Isaac Ingalls Stevens, First Governor of Washington Territory**. Portland, Oregon: Binfords and Mort, 1952.

Hilderbrand, Lorraine Barker. **Straw Hats, Sandals and Steel: The Chinese in Washington State**. Tacoma: Washington State American Revolution Bicentennial Commission, 1977.

Hildy, Ralph W. **Timber and Men: The Weyerhaeuser Story**. New York: Macmillan, 1963.

Hodge, Frederick Webb. **Handbook of American Indians North of Mexico**. New York: Pageant Books, 1959. (Smithsonian Institution Bureau of American Ethnology, Bulletin 30.)

Holbrook, Stewart. **Green Commonwealth, a Narrative of the Past and a Look at the Future of One Forest Product Company**. Shelton, Washington: Simpson Logging Company, 1945.

Howell, Patricia. **Dictionary of Indian Geographical Names**. Seattle: American Indian Yearbook, 1947.

Hult, Ruby El. **Untamed Olympics: The Story of a Peninsula**. Portland, Oregon: Binfords and Mort, 1954.

Hunt, Herbert. **Washington: West of the Cascades: Historical and Descriptive, the Explorers, the Indians, the Pioneers, the Modern**. Three volumes. Chicago: S.J. Clarke Publishing Company, 1917.

Jackson, Ronald Vern. **Washington 1860 Territorial Census Index**. Salt Lake City, Utah: Accelerated Indexing System, Inc., 1979

Jackson, Ronald Vern. **Washington 1870 Territorial Census Index**. Salt Lake City, Utah: Accelerated Indexing System, Inc., 1979

Jefferson County Historical Society, ed. **With Pride in Heritage**: History of Jefferson County. Port Townsend, Washington: Jefferson County Historical Society, 1966.

Johannessen, Carl. *Annals of the Association of American Geographers* (June 1971):286-302.

Johansen, Dorothy O. and Charles M. Gates. **Empire of the Columbia: A History of the Pacific Northwest**. New York: Harper and Brothers, 1957.

Kappler, Charles J. **Indian Affairs, Laws and Treaties**. Washington, D.C.: United States Government Printing Office, 1950.

Keller, C.W. **Life of Alanson Wesley Smith**. Seattle: *Seattle Times*, 1935.

Kellogg, Bert. **Early Days of the Olympic Peninsula in Photographs from the Bert Kellogg Collection**. Port Angeles: Peninsula Publishing, Inc., 1976.

Kirk, Ruth and Richard D. Daugherty. **Exploring Washington Archaeology**. Seattle: University of Washington Press, 1973.

Labbe, John T. and Vernon Goe. **Railroads in the Woods**. Berkeley, California: Howell-North, 1961.

Lambert, Mary Ann. **Dungeness Massacre and other Regional Tales**. n.p., 1961.

Landis, R.L. **Post Offices of Oregon, Washington and Idaho**. Portland, Oregon: Patrick Press, 1969.

Lauridsen, G.M. **The Story of Port Angeles, Clallam County, Washington: An Historical Symposium**. Seattle: Lowman and Hanford Company, 1937.

Leighton, Caroline C. **Life at Puget Sound with Sketches of Travel in Washington Territory, British Columbia, Oregon and California, 1865-1881**. Boston: Lee and Shepard, 1883.

LeWarne, Charles. **Utopias on Puget Sound, 1885-1915**. Seattle: University of Washington Press, 1975.

Lincoln, Abraham. **The Writings of Abraham Lincoln**. Arthur Brooks Lapsley, ed. New York: G.P. Putnam's Sons, 1888-1906.

Lincoln, Abraham. **The Lincoln Encyclopedia; the Spoken and Written Words of Abraham Lincoln Arranged for Ready Reference**. Archer H. Shaw, ed. New York: Macmillan, 1950.

Lofgren, Svante E. **Barth Ar-Kell (The White Bear)**. Seattle: Publications Press, 1949.

Lucia, Ellis. **The Big Woods: Logging and Lumbering – From Bull Teams to Helicopters in the Pacific Northwest**. Garden City, New York: Doubleday, 1975.

Maunder, Elwood. **Four Generations of Management: The Simpson-Reed Story**. Santa Cruz, California: Forest History Society, 1977.

Marshall, James Stirrat and Carrie Marshall. **Adventure in Two Hemispheres Including Captain Vancouver's Voyage**. Vancouver, British Columbia, Canada: Talex Printing Service, 1955.

McCallum, John and Lorraine Wilcox Ross. **Port Angeles, U.S.A.** Seattle: Wood and Reber, 1961.

McCurdy, James G. **By Juan de Fuca's Strait: Pioneering Along the Northwestern Edge of the Continent**. Portland, Oregon: Binfords and Mort, 1937.

McCurdy, James G. **Indian Days at Neah Bay** Gordon Newell, ed. from an unfinished manuscript by the late James G. McCurdy. Seattle: Superior Publishing Company, 1961.

McDonald, Lucile. "The *Clallam* Sinks." *Seattle Times* (January 6, 1963).

McDonald, Lucile. "Holmed Termed First Port Angeles Settler." *Seattle Times* (January 5, 1958):1.

McDonald, Lucile. **Search for the Northwest Passage**. Portland, Oregon: Binfords and Mort, 1958.

McDonald, Lucile. "Holmesound Cooperative Colony, Port Angeles." *Seattle Times (July 19, 1960)*.

McDonald, Lucile. **Swan Among the Indians: Life of James G. Swan, 1818-1900 Based upon Swan's Hitherto Unpublished Diaries**

and Journals. Portland, Oregon: Binfords and Mort, 1972.

McDonald, Lucile. "Victor Smith and Port Angeles, The Second National City and Customs Collector." *Seattle Times* (January 19, 1958 and July 2, 1961).

McDonald, Lucile. "Was He Port Angeles' First White Settler?" *Seattle Times* (December 29, 1957):5.

McDonald, Lucile. **Washington's Yesterdays (Before There was a Territory) 1775-1853**. Portland, Oregon: Binfords and Mort, 1953.

McKenney, Thomas L. **History of the Indian Tribes of North America with Biographical Sketches and Anecdotes of the Principal Chiefs Embellished with One Hundred and Twenty Portraits., from the Indian Gallery on the Department of War, at Washington**. Three Volumes. Philadelphia: D. Rice and A.N. Hart, 1855.

McLaughlin, Inez. **We Grew up Together**. n.p., 1959.

Meany, Edmond S. **History of the State of Washington**. New York: Macmillan Company, 1909.

Meany, Edmond S., ed. "Lincoln-time Letters." *Washington Historical Quarterly* 16:265-272.

Meany, Edmond S. **Origin of Washington Geographic Names**. Seattle: University of Washington Press, 1923.

Meany, Edmond S. **Vancouver's Discovery of Puget Sound: Portraits and Biographies of the Men Honored in the Naming of Geographic Features of Northwestern America**. Portland, Oregon: Binfords and Mort, 1942.

Middleton, Lynn. **Place Names of the Pacific Northwest Coast: Origins, Histories and Anecdotes in Bibliographic Form about the Coast of British Columbia, Washington and Oregon**. Victoria, British Columbia: Elldee Publishing Company, 1969.

Moore, Earl F. **Silent Arrows: Indian Lore and Artifact Hunting**. Klamath Falls, Oregon: Paul Tremaine Publishing, 1977.

Morgan, Murray. **The Last Wilderness**. Seattle: University of Washington Press, 1955.

Morse, Mary Gay. **Lore of the Olympic-Land**. n.p., 1924.

Newell, Gordon. **Pacific Steamboats**. New York: Bonanza Books, 1958.

New Columbia Encyclopedia. Fourth Edition. New York: Columbia University Press, 1975.

Oregon Historical Quarterly Index, 1940-1960. Portland, Oregon: Oregon Historical Society, 1967.

Pacific Northwest Quarterly Index. Volume 1, 1906 – Volume 53, 1962. Hamden, Connecticut: ShoeString Press, Inc., 1964.

Pethick, Derek. **First Approaches to the Northwest Coast**. Seattle: University of Washington Press, 1979.

Pethick, Derek. **The Nootka Connection: Europe and the Northwest Coast, 1790-1795**. Vancouver, British Columbia, Canada: Douglas and McIntyre Ltd., 1980.

Phelps, Mary Merwin. **Kate Chase, Dominant Daughter: The Life of a Brilliant Woman and her Famous Father**. New York: Thomas Y. Crowell Company, 1935.

Piatt, Donn. **Memories of the Men Who Saved the Union**. Second Edition. New York: Belford Clarke, 1887.

Phillips, James W. **Washington State Place Names**. Seattle: University of Washington Press, 1977.

Pollard, Lancaster. **A History of the State of Washington**. Four volumes. New York: American Historical Society, Inc., 1937.

Port Angeles Evening News. Centennial Edition. (June 16, 1962).

Port Angeles Evening News. "Washington's Territorial Centennial, 1853-1953." (November 28, 1953).

Priestly, Marilyn, compiler. **Comprehensive Guide to the Manuscripts Collection and to the Personal Papers in the University Archives**. Seattle: University of Washington Library, 1980.

Richards, Kent D., et al, ed. **Washington: Readings in the History of the Evergreen State**. Lawrence, Kansas: Coronado Press. n.d.

Richards, Kent D. **Isaac I. Stevens: Young Man in a Hurry**. Provo, Utah: Brigham Young University Press, 1979.

Ross, Ishbel. **Proud Kate, Portrait of an Ambitious Woman**. New York: Harper, 1953.

Rothschild, Alonzo. **Lincoln, Master of Men**. Boston: Houghton, 1906.

Ruby, Robert H. **Indians of the Pacific Northwest: A History**. "Civilization of the American Indian Series," Volume 158. Norman: University of Oklahoma Press, 1981.

Russell, Jervis, ed. **Jimmy Come Lately: History of Clallam County**. Port Orchard, Washington: Clallam County Historical Society, 1971.

Sandburg, Carl. **Abraham Lincoln: The War Years**. Four volumes. New York: Harcourt, Brace and Company. 1939.

Schafer, Joseph. **A History of the Pacific Northwest**. New York, Macmillan, 1935.

Schnuckers, Jacob William. **Life and Public Service of Salmon Portland Chase: to which is Added the Eulogy on Mr. Chase delivered by W.M. Enants, before the Alumni of Dartmouth College, June 24, 1874**. New York: Appleton, 1874.

Seaman, N.G. **Indian Relics of the Pacific Northwest**. Portland, Oregon: Binfords and Mort, 1961.

Shrader, Graham. **The Phantom War in the Northwest**. n.p., 1969.

Simpson, Peter and James Hemanson. **Port Townsend: Years that are Gone – an Illustrated History**. Port Townsend, Washington: Quimper Press, 1979.

Smith, LeRoy. **Pioneers of the Olympic Peninsula**. Forks, Washington: Olympic Graphic Arts, Inc., 1977.

Smith, Marian W., ed. **Indians of the Urban Northwest**. New York: Columbia University Press, 1949. (Columbia University Contributions to Anthropology, No. 36.)

Smith, Norman R. **Victory: The Story of Port Angeles by the Son of Victor Smith, Founder of the City**. n.p., 1950.

Snowden, Clinton A. **History of Washington: The Rise and Progress of an American State**. Four volumes. New York: Century History Company, 1909.

Sokoloff, Alice Hunt. **Kate Chase for the Defense**. New York: Dodd, Mead and Company, 1971.

Spencer, Lloyd and Lancaster Pollard. **A History of the State of Washington**. Four volumes. New York: American Historical Society, 1937.

Spier, Leslie. **Tribal Distribution in Washington**. Number Three of the General Series in Anthropology. Menasha, Wisconsin: George Banta Publishing Company, 1936.

Stevens, Hazard. **The Life of Isaac Ingalls Stevens by His Son**. Two volumes. Boston: Houghton, Mifflin and Company, 1900.

Stevens, Isaac Ingalls. **Speech of the Hon. Isaac I. Stevens, Delegate from Washington Territory, on the Washington and Oregon War Claims**. Fairfield, Washington: Ye Galleon Press, 1970.

Stevens, James. **Green Power, The Story of Public Law 273**. Seattle: Superior Publishing Company, 1958.

Stewart, Edgar I. **Washington: Northwest Frontier**. Four volumes. New York: Lewis Historical Publishing Company, Inc., 1957.

Stewart, Hilary. **Indian Artifacts of the Northwest Coast**. Seattle: University of Washington Press, 1973.

Swan, James G. **Almost Out of the World; Scenes from Washington Territory: The Strait of Juan de Fuca, 1859-61**. Tacoma: Washington State Historical Society, 1971.

Swan, James G. **The Indians of Cape Flattery, at the Entrance to the Strait of Juan de Fuca, Washington Territory**. Seattle: The Shorey Book Store, 1964.

Swan, James G. **The Northwest Coast; or, Three Years Residence in Washington Territory**. Seattle: University of Washington Press, 1972.

Swanton, John R. **Indian Tribes of Washington, Oregon and Idaho**. Fairfield, Washington: Ye Galleon Press, 1968.

Taylor, Eva Cook. **The Lure of Tubal-Cain**. Port Orchard, Washington: Publishers Printing, 1972.

Thomas, Benjamin. **Abraham Lincoln, a Biography**. New York: Alfred A. Knopf, 1976.

Thompson, Wilbur and Allen Beach. **Steamer to Tacoma**. Bainbridge Island, Washington: Driftwood Press, 1963.

Tyler, Robert L. **Rebels of the Woods: The I.W.W. in the Pacific Northwest**. Eugene, Oregon: University of Oregon Books, 1967.

Underhill, Ruth Murray. **Indians of the Pacific Northwest**. U.S. Office of Indian Affairs, 1944.

U.S. Congress. House. "Change of Location of Port of Entry for Puget Sound Collection District From Port Townsend to Port Angelos." 37th Cong., 2nd session, H. Rept. 119 to accompany S. 241. Washington: 1864.

Vancouver, George. **Voyage of Discovery to the North Pacific Ocean and Round the World**. Volume I, New York: Da Capo Press, 1967.

Wagner, Henry R. **Spanish Explorations in the Strait of Juan de Fuca**. Santa Anna, California: 1933.

"Washington, Centennial of the Territory," 1853-1953. An Exhibition in the Library of Congress, Washington, D.C..

Washington (State) Secretary of State, B. Reeves. **Historical Highlights**. Olympia: Washington (State) Secretary of State, 1941.

Washington Historical Society. **Building a State: Washington, 1889-1939**. Tacoma, Washington: Historical Society, 1940.

Washington Pioneer Project. **Told by the Pioneers: Tales of the Frontier Life as Told by Those Who Remember the Days of the Territory and Early Statehood of Washington**. Washington Pioneer Project, 1936.

Washington State Associations of County Commissioners and County Engineers. **The Book of the Counties., 1853-1953**. 1953.

Webber, Bert. **Retaliation: Japanese Attacks and Allied Countermeasures on the Pacific Coast in World War II**. Corvallis, Oregon: Oregon State University Press, 1975.

Weinstein, Robert A. **Tall Ships on Puget Sound: The Marine Photographs of Wilhelm Hester**. Seattle: University of Washington Press, 1978.

Welsh, William D. **A Brief History of Port Angeles**. Port Angeles: Crown Zellerbach Corporation, 1960.

White, Horace. **A Review of the Resources of Clallam County, Washington**. Port Angeles: Port Angeles Commercial Club, 1903.

Whitebrook, Robert Ballard. **Coastal Exploration of Washington**. Palo Alto, California: Pacific Books, Publishers, 1959.

Winthrop, Theodore. **Canoe and Saddle**. Nisqually Edition. Portland, Oregon: Binford and Mort. n.d.

Wiring, Dale R. **Builders, Brewers and Burghers: Germans of Washington State**. Tacoma: Washington State American Revolution Bicentennial Commission, 1977.

Wood, Robert L. **Across the Olympic Mountains: The Press Expedition, 1889-90**. Seattle: Mountaineers and the University of Washington Press, 1967.

Woodcock, George. **Peoples of the Coast: The Indians of the Pacific Northwest**. Bloomington, Indiana: Indiana University Press, 1977.

Wright, E.W., ed. **Lewis and Dryden's Marine History of the Pacific Northwest**. New York, Antiquarian Press, Ltd., 1961.

Manuscripts

Patricia Campbell Papers, University of Washington.

Alexander Sampson Papers, University of Washington.

Oral History Tapes

Wilda Smith MacDonald

Lucile McDonald

Samuel Howard Morse

Madge Nailor

Ivor Smith

Clay Wolverton

Newspapers
The Beacon (Port Angeles, Washington)
British Colonist (Victoria, B.C., Canada)
Clallam County Courier (Port Angeles, Washington)
The Commonwealth (Port Angeles, Washington)
The Daily Colonist (Victoria, British Columbia)
The Daily News (Port Angeles, Washington)
The Daily Tribune (Port Angeles, Washington)
The Democrat (Port Angeles, Washington)
The Democrat-Leader (Port Angeles, Washington)
Dungeness Beacon (Dungeness, Washington)
The Herald (Port Angeles, Washington)
The Leader (Port Angeles, Washington)
The Model Commonwealth (Port Angeles, Washington)
The North-West (Port Townsend, Washington)
The Olympic (Port Angeles, Washington)
The Olympic-Leader (Port Angeles, Washington)
The Olympic-Tribune (Port Angeles, Washington)
The Overland Press (Olympia, Washington)
Port Angeles Evening News (Port Angeles, Washington)
Port Angeles Times (Port Angeles, Washington)
Port Angeles Tribune (Port Angeles, Washington)
Port Crescent Leader (Port Crescent, Washington)
The Register (Port Townsend, Washington)
Seattle Times (Seattle, Washington)
The Simoon (Port Angeles, Washington)
The Times-Tribune (Port Angeles, Washington)
Washington-Democrat (Olympia, Washington)
Washington Standard (Olympia, Washington)

Index

Acknowledgments

Though it is difficult to list — or even remember — all those who have helped us during the past three years, the author and researcher wish to acknowledge the contributions of the following people:

Ginger Alexander and the entire staff of the Clallam County Museum for many of the illustrations found in this book.

Staff members of the North Olympic Library System for their seemingly endless patience over a period of time that surely must have seemed to them longer than three years.

For their invaluable assistance in studying the manuscript for errors and omissions — and there were a few — we are indebted to Sandy Keys, Hank Brown, Graham and Opal Ralston, Ann Gehrke, Ed Gaul, Ivor Smith, Don Smith, Esther Webster, Mrs. Ivy Bork, Don and Dua Feeley, Mr. and Mrs. Herb McGee, Gayle Whattam, and Bill Oliver.

Several Port Angeles residents graciously took time out of their schedules to locate and identify photographs and other documents. For their assistance with this essential task, we wish to thank Jim Phillips, Pete Capos, Tom Thompson, Tony Masi, Harvey Hussey, Laurie Bower, Mary Harper, Pat Neal, "Chuck" Beam, Jerry Lawrence, Merton Franklin, Dr. Harlan McNutt, Jack Thompson, Ev Tinkham, Em Lawrence, Bob Mc-Mahan, and staff members of the Port of Port Angeles.

We also would like to thank the author's former associate, Al Whattam, who for nearly a year and one-half, absorbed a heavier-than-normal workload so that a vast amount of daytime reading and writing could be accomplished.

A special "thank you" must go to the Wishiks, Tony and Cindy, who devoted countless hours to this lengthy project. Tony's fine editorial and layout work, combined with Cindy's graphic talents, produced what we think is an accurate and aesthetically pleasing finished product.

And to Bert Kellogg, we wish to express our profound appreciation for his outstanding contributions, not only to this book, but to the people of the North Olympic Peninsula. Mr. Kellogg's enormous collection of photographs — many of which he has generously donated to the North Olympic Library System — have preserved a vital slice of Clallam County's early days.

Finally, the author wishes to acknowledge the ongoing help and the constant, gentle encouragement of his wife, Ann, during the entire length of this project. Thank you.

Paul J. Martin is the owner of Peninsula Publishing Inc., and co-owner of Pen Print, Inc., in Port Angeles, Washington. Before moving to the State of Washington eleven years ago, he was an administrator in the Regional Medical Program at the University of Pittsburgh, and before that served as Executive Director of a Community Action Program in western Pennsylvania.

Paul holds a Bachelor's Degree in Business Administration and a Master's Degree in Industrial Relations from St. Francis College in Pennsylvania. He previously compiled and published the popular seven-book series of booklets entitled **The Early Days . . . IN PHOTOGRAPHS.**

Peggy M. Brady is Head of the Reference Department at the North Olympic Library System, Port Angeles, Washington. She was formerly a Reference Librarian at Dallas Public Library (Dallas, Texas) and at the University of Oregon Library (Eugene, Oregon). Born in Port Orchard, Washington, she spent most of her life in Hillsboro, Oregon. Peggy has degrees from Pacific University (Forest Grove, Oregon) and the University of British Columbia (Vancouver, British Columbia). Ms. Brady earlier was the compiler of "Business History Collection: A checklist" published by the Dallas Public Library in 1974.